Civil

The Last
Civil War Veterans

The Lives of the Final
Survivors, State by State

FRANK L. GRZYB

*Foreword by Brigadier General
Richard J. Valente USA (Ret.)*

McFarland & Company, Inc., Publishers
Jefferson, North Carolina

The author has made a concerted effort to obtain permission for use of all photographs and illustrations in this book. Any copyright holders who feel their work is not properly attributed may contact the author (via the publisher) so that corrections can be made in future editions.

Library of Congress Cataloguing-in-Publication Data

Names: Grzyb, Frank L., 1946– author.
Title: The last Civil War veterans : the lives of the final survivors, state by state / Frank L. Grzyb ; foreword by Brigadier General Richard J. Valente USA (Ret.).
Description: Jefferson, North Carolina : McFarland & Company, Inc., Publishers, 2016. | Includes bibliographical references and index.
Identifiers: LCCN 2016012526 | ISBN 9781476665221 (softcover : acid free paper) ∞
Subjects: LCSH: United States—History—Civil War, 1861–1865—Veterans—Biography. | Veterans—United States—Biography. | Veterans—Confederate States of America—Biography.
Classification: LCC E467 .G799 2016 | DDC 973.7086/97—dc23
LC record available at http://lccn.loc.gov/2016012526

British Library cataloguing data are available

ISBN (print) 978-1-4766-6522-1
ISBN (ebook) 978-1-4766-2488-4

Front cover: photograph of two Civil War veterans seated and shaking hands at the Gettysburg Celebration in Pennsylvania (Library of Congress); flag images © 2016 iStock/Christophe Boisson; back cover: Memorial to John H. Riley, II (courtesy Lloyd Lincoln Colvin and photographed by the author)

Printed in the United States of America

McFarland & Company, Inc., Publishers
Box 611, Jefferson, North Carolina 28640
www.mcfarlandpub.com

To
Tina Ann Jackman.
A loving, thoughtful, and compassionate soul
I am privileged to call my sister

and

Jay S. Hoar.
A renowned author, biographer and educator
whose extensive research and perseverance
on the subject of America's last Civil War veterans
helped lay the foundation for this work.

The power of noble deeds is to be preserved and passed on to the future.—Joshua Lawrence Chamberlain, Medal of Honor recipient

It really matters very little who died last, but for some reason we seem fascinated with knowing.—William Marvel

Table of Contents

Acronyms and Abbreviations

aka—Also known as
b.—Born
Bvt. Brig. Gen.—Brevet Brigadier General
CCC—Civilian Conservation Corps
CDV—Carte de Visite, a small albumen print mounted on cards
  2½ by 4 inches
Cpt.—Captain
CSA—Confederate States of America
CSS—Confederate Submersible Ship
d.—Died
D.C.—District of Columbia
Ft.—Fort
GAR—Grand Army of the Republic
MOH—Medal of Honor
NAACP—National Association for the Advancement of Colored
  People
PTSD—Post-Traumatic Stress Disorder
SUVCW—Sons of Union Veterans of the Civil War
UCV—Association of United Confederate Veterans
USCT—United States Colored Troops
USS—United States Ship
VRC—Veterans Reserve Corps (formerly the IC, or Invalid
  Corps)

Acknowledgments

Writing about history is never a singular effort. An author learns early in the craft that it takes a host of knowledgeable individuals to construct a satisfactory product, in this case a book about Civil War veterans. And with heartfelt gratitude I say without reservation that I have been afforded invaluable support throughout the entire research and writing process from a wide array of people from America to Australia. Included in this tally are the following: family descendants of Civil War veterans; research librarians; historians; a city mayor; a photographer; newspaper editors; a former college professor; and, yes, even everyday citizens whose contributions were as important as professionals plying their trade. In the final analysis, all have contributed immensely to the success of this endeavor.

The right thing to do would be to thank each and every one personally. Unfortunately that is not to be, as time and distance preclude me from doing so. The only alternative—as it is for most writers—is to show my gratitude by listing their names here. To be fair, I've chosen to acknowledge them in no particular order. They are: Sue Ellen Wright-Novak; Jim Flack; Ken Garthee; Petra Chesner Schlatter; Ralph Thomas Kam; Joel Reese; Darla Brock; Dick Johnson; Donna Wolf; Mack McCormick; Debbie Keitt; Mike Connor; Ann Poulos; Rich Aarstad; Sherry Pillow; John M. Grochowski; Jean Fisher; Rachel S. Adler; Lisa Marine; Robert "Bob" Pimentel; Nanette Napoleon; Angela Plagge; Jim Duran; and Eric Full, as well as Edward "Mack" Coffman; Anita Manning; Peggy Crook; Crawford Harris; Ron Han; Nancy Price Graff; Lena Taylor McKee; Merle Rudebusch; Terry Thompson; Mary Anne Denney; David Lee Colglazier; Stephen C. Nedell; Ann Chiampa; Rebecca "Becky" Evans; Linda Fay Maggee Murrhee; David D. Porter; Annemarie Paikai; Ben Saracco; Wendy Hall; Dennis Atkinson; Sheila Mullowney; Garry Victor Hill; and Margaret R. Sullivan.

A special note of gratitude is extended to the U.S. National Park Service for the republication of regimental histories that are listed within; also, to the friends and staff at the Alaska Veterans Museum, and the Grand Army of the Republic Civil War Museum & Library.

The editorial comments by Russell J. DeSimone, Fred Zillian, and Virginia "Ginny" Grzyb simply made this a much better offering than the rough draft they were initially provided. The tedious work they undertook on my behalf is deeply appreciated.

One of my greatest thrills was talking or corresponding with some of the veterans' descendants. The stories and photographs they provided transported me back in time to a period I so enjoy learning about. These descendants are Judy Miller, great-granddaughter of Daniel A. Clingaman of Co. D, 195th Regiment, Ohio Volunteer Infantry; Celia B. Milam, grandniece of Pleasant Riggs Crump of Co. A, 10th Regiment, Alabama Volunteer Infantry; Orin Hunkins, great-grandson of Hiram Alonzo Hunkins of Co. K, 48th Regiment, Wisconsin Volunteer Infantry; Ross Kennemore, from the family of John Greene Chisum of the 45th Regiment, Arkansas Cavalry; Sandra Williamson, great-grandniece of James Patterson Martin of Battery H, 1st Regiment, Wisconsin Heavy Artillery; Lloyd Lincoln Colvin great-grandson of John H. Riley II of Co. H, 2nd Regiment, Rhode Island Volunteer Infantry (and Lloyd's wife, Barbara); and Ron Colvin, Lloyd's nephew. As Lloyd reminded me so eloquently upon departure from his home, "I got to shake the hand that shook the hand that shook the hand of President Abraham Lincoln."

There is always that one individual who deserves special recognition. In this case it is Jay S. Hoar, professor emeritus, University of Maine, Farmington. Professor Hoar has quickly become my comrade-in-arms and Civil War guru. Without his vast subject-matter knowledge, expert guidance, and friendly advice this book might never have come to fruition. Though the professor and I have differences of opinion about some of my selections, he respected my right to scrutinize and question the existing evidence and in the end make my own decisions. For that I am eternally grateful.

Foreword
by Brigadier General
Richard J. Valente USA (Ret.)

Author and historian Frank Grzyb has already written several well-researched scholarly volumes focusing on America's Civil War. Each work, especially his history of the U.S. Army General Hospital at Portsmouth Grove, Rhode Island (an extensive medical complex located on the shores of Narragansett Bay in Rhode Island and nearly forgotten after the Civil War), required exhaustive time and effort to research and write. However, those efforts pale in comparison to his latest undertaking: to publish a volume that identifies and provides personal information and, in a majority of instances, photographic images of the last surviving Civil War veteran from each state and other locations. Frank is to be commended for his foresight and fortitude in launching and bringing to fruition such an endeavor, which fills a void in our understanding of what happened to many of these veterans after the conflict had ended. While well written and an interesting read, his latest work also provides a deeper look into a past that has, unfortunately and in many cases, been remanded to the dustbin of history.

Frank is to be thanked wholeheartedly for his dedication in making the memories of these honored veterans come alive again.

Retired after 35 years of military service, Gen. Valente has served since 2006 as Commander of the Providence Marine Corps of Artillery (the founder of today's 103d Field Artillery, Rhode Island National Guard) overseeing the historic 1842 Armory and Museum in Providence, Rhode Island.

Preface

This work pays tribute to the last surviving Civil War veteran from each state, including those who lived in the Border States and territories that eventually became part of the United States of America. As an added feature, the last Civil War veteran from the District of Columbia is also represented. Within these pages are relevant details about these veterans' prewar years, military experience, and postwar years. In the end, the reader will learn how each individual managed to survive, age, and outlive more than 3,000,000 of his fellow veterans.

Arguably the last surviving veterans fought in the most devastating war this nation has ever experienced. Some witnessed major historical events unfolding before their eyes. Several saw President Abraham Lincoln from a distance, while a few experienced the privilege of shaking his hand and briefly conversing with him. Many fought in major battles, others in only skirmishes. Some never experienced combat. In the end, all were joined by a universal bond: they served in the military at an extremely young age; they were incredibly naïve; and, above all, they were unwaveringly patriotic. When they returned home, they not only became members of an elite group—Civil War veterans fortunate to have survived the chaotic times and tumultuous ordeal—but also emissaries of peace, especially as the years progressed.

Though a majority of veterans enlisted in their home or neighboring states, after the war many migrated among states and territories. They were a transient group looking for a better way of life not only for themselves but also their families; their post–Civil War travels proved them to be consummate opportunists. Along the way, they were witnesses to a remarkable period of technological innovations and major events in our nation's history such as the introduction of gas-driven automobiles, passenger planes, the telephone, radio, and television as well as two devastating world wars, a major depression, numerous medical advances, and revolutionary social change. When the last reported surviving Civil War veteran gasped his final breath, the entire nation mourned the loss with heartfelt emotion. Americans had come to realize that with his passing an astonishing and tumultuous era had concluded.

Introduction

Founded on April 6, 1866, by Benjamin F. Stephenson in Decatur, Illinois, the Grand Army of the Republic (GAR) was composed of veterans of the Union army, navy, and the Revenue-Marine (an armed customs enforcement service). At its peak in 1890 the organization claimed 490,000 members. Twenty-three years later, on June 10, 1889, a similar fraternal organization, the Association of United Confederate Veterans (UCV), was organized in New Orleans, Louisiana. It consisted of nine previously formed but loosely knit veterans associations throughout the south. At its reunion in 1898, more than 1,555 Southern camps were represented. The primary mission of the GAR was to encourage social, literary, historical and benevolent activities while the UVC's main purpose was to provide for widows and orphans of former Confederate soldiers, preserve relics and mementos from the war, care for disabled veterans who served the Confederacy, maintain and protect Confederate service records, and organize reunions and fraternal gatherings for its members.

For years, both organizations packed a wallop in the political arena in their respective regions and on the national scale. The Union consisted of departments on the state level and posts in the field; the South had a general headquarters also with camps in the field. At their separate meeting halls GAR and UCV members relaxed—smoked, played checkers and card games—reminisced about the war, and offered camaraderie and support to their fellow veterans. As part of their patriotic duties they marched in parades and took part in various military and civic functions, thus paying homage to the memory of their fallen comrades.

For Civil War veterans, the years passed all too quickly. As members died, the roles of the GAR and the UCV diminished, first slowly then dreadfully fast. By the late 1940s and early 1950s only a few hundred were left. The vast majority were invalids requiring convalescent care, and when the time arrived both organizations held their final reunion. The eighty-third and last GAR encampment was held in Indianapolis, Indiana, the week of

August 28 through September 1, 1949. Only six aged veterans were able to attend: the current and last commander in chief of the GAR, Theodore Penland from Vancouver, Washington; Albert Woolson from Duluth, Minnesota; Robert Tolliver Barrett from Princeton, Kentucky; James A. Hard from Rochester, New York; Joseph Clovese from Pontiac, Michigan; and Charles L. Chappel from Long Beach, California. The sixty-first and final UCV reunion was held the week of May 30 through June 3, 1951. Three elderly men gathered at the Monticello Hotel in Norfolk, Virginia. They were John Salling of Slant, Virginia; William D. Townsend from Olla, Louisiana; and William Joshua Bush from Fitzgerald, Georgia. Those who attended their respective reunions were centenarians. (Years later, all three alleged Confederates had their veteran credentials reexamined by historians.)

In the May 30, 1949, issue of *Life* magazine, pictures of 68 surviving American Civil War veterans are displayed with name, age, city and state printed below each image.[1] The facial expressions of some of them appear determined, while others seem fatigued by age and the trauma of war that still lingered (see Appendix A, which lists the age of all the last state veterans). Once they were young … so very young. To make achieving this illustrious hallmark (the last men standing) possible, most, if not all, were in their early adolescence when they enlisted. Some had barely reached puberty.

Life published a two-page spread in a follow-up story four years later, titled "The Last Five Civil War Veterans."[2] The 1949 feature, along with the 1953 article that included brief excerpts and photographs, rekindled the interest and curiosity of many Americans who for the past several years had been paying homage to returning World War II and Korean War veterans. Until then, Civil War veterans who served in the military more than 90 years earlier had been relegated for the most part to the back burner. Had it not been for the stories published in *Life* and state and local newspapers and the diligence of a small contingent of veteran family members and other patriotic groups, the last veteran fanfares might have passed with little notice.

Six years elapsed before another memorable image of a Civil War veteran was published in the May 11, 1959, issue of *Life*. In it, a gentleman is shown lying in an elevated bed with a blanket snugly pulled up to his chest. A cigar can be seen dangling from his lips. The man's left arm overlaps his chest; the right arm rests comfortably by his side. No one knows for certain, but it appears he is contemplating the final days of his life. Draped in the background are two large flags, one Confederate and the other Union. Between both hangs the uniform of a Confederate officer. The celebrated photograph became a symbolic image of the last of a dying breed, a final glimpse at the last surviving veteran of America's Civil War. The gentleman depicted in the image is Walter Washington Williams of Houston, Texas. When the image was produced, Williams claimed to be 116 years old.[3]

By 1959 many believed that when Virginia's John B. Salling died the final chapter of the war had been written. But waiting in the wings after Salling's death on March 16, 1959, was Walter Washington Williams of Texas. Williams claimed that he was actually the last Civil War survivor, a claim many believed at the time, so much so that when he died on December 19, 1959, a national day of mourning was declared by President Dwight D. Eisenhower. Later, Williams was memorialized by the federal government with an inscription on the Soldiers and Sailors of the Confederacy Monument attesting that he was "the last surviving Confederate veteran."[4] The tribute was paid despite the fact that Williams' credentials had been debunked a few months prior to his death by Lowell K. Bridwell. Bridwell, a journalist and Associated Press correspondent, was unable to find a single thread of evidence to substantiate Williams' claim to his alleged veteran's status. Not long after that, another researcher found census records indicating that Williams was only five years old in 1860. Salling, from Scott County, Virginia, had died nine months earlier and was now reconsidered to be the last surviving Civil War veteran. However, like Williams, Salling's credentials were also debunked. In the 1860 U.S. Federal Census, Salling was recorded as being four years old and would have been no more than nine at the close of the war. Another document displayed his birth date as being two years earlier. Salling claimed that during the war he had worked for the Confederacy mining saltpeter, a necessary ingredient in the production of gunpowder. The two people Salling said helped him mine were no longer alive, thus making it nearly impossible to confirm his claim. Yet when Salling applied for his pension in 1933 using only notarized affidavits from local citizens attesting to his service, and despite the pension clerk's inability to locate any record of his Confederate service, the pension was granted.

In an article published in *Blue and Gray* magazine in the February 1991 issue that was titled "The Great Imposters," author and historian William Marvel found that "every one of the last dozen recognized Confederates was bogus."[5] Though his blunt assertion might be correct, his findings aroused new suspicions by historians about these seemingly unsubstantiated claims, especially those supported solely by questionable affidavits. In the end, Marvel proposed the name of the last Confederate veteran that could be certified using existing data (military service records, rosters, pension documents and a death certificate). That person, whose identity will be revealed later, eventually became accepted as the last surviving Confederate veteran by an overwhelming number of Civil War historians.

Over the ensuing years several authors have written about the seemingly endless list of Civil War veteran imposters. In his book *Last of the Blue and Gray* Richard A. Serrano provided additional insight into the most notable frauds. He also detailed the credentials of the man who deserved the laureate as America's last standing Civil War veteran.[6] Nearly all Civil War historians now concur with the selection. Ironically, the last veteran was a Union soldier who never experienced the horrors of combat.

In the 1949 *Life* article, six veterans of the 68 featured in the pictorial were eventually discredited or lacked sufficient evidence to certify their veteran's status. In the follow-up article of 1953, three of the five supposed veterans pictured were eventually challenged and their credentials either debunked or their military service left unsubstantiated. In Ohio, a neighbor who grew up near a purported veteran said she had a difficult time believing his claim of being a former Confederate soldier. Even a journalist wondered if the same individual was old enough to have served.[7] Yet there were considerably more believers than naysayers. People wanted to believe and thus found it difficult to comprehend that anyone had the audacity to misrepresent themselves in the diminishing ranks of Civil War veterans.

The list of imposters or unsubstantiated claimants is not limited. Men from both sides of the Mason-Dixon Line attempted to deceive federal, state and local officials. This alone presents a perplexing question: Why did so many take such elaborate pains to claim military service in the Civil War? The most obvious answer is easy: stolen honor. Many bogus veterans reveled in the attention and adulation bestowed upon them, something they did not experience as civilians. Not surprisingly, over time there were those who came to believe their own lies. Perhaps some, though knowing their charade, found it difficult if not impossible to admit to the spurious tales after years of lies. But the main reason for the deception was something more material: monetary gain. By obtaining a military pension through identity theft, lying about their age, or finding individuals (friends and neighbors) who were willing to falsify affidavits to buttress their claims, they were able to significantly improve their family's welfare.

The United States began granting veteran disability pensions to Union veterans in 1868 retroactive to the date of the veteran's discharge. Then, in the late nineteenth century, Congress liberalized the pension rules. Not surprisingly, a significant number of legislators were Civil War veterans and sympathized with their fellow comrades. The revised legislation allowed placing "upon the pension rolls all survivors of the war whose conditions of health are not practically perfect."[8] Thus, the legislation created an enormous conundrum for veterans' records verification, not to mention the ultimate financial impact upon the American taxpayer. It is not surprising that up until 1900 disability pensions were the federal government's highest expenditures.[9]

Years after the war, former Confederate states began paying pensions. Because these Southern veterans "aided or abetted the rebellion," they were not allowed to apply for a federal pension.[10] Each former Southern state financed the payments individually through state-sponsored initiatives. John Salling was one of those men who received a state pension until his death in 1959. He applied for his pension in 1933 largely on the basis of affidavits. At the time, the Great Depression had caused significant economic hardship upon those trying to support families. Jobs were scarce. Being granted a military pension meant having the means to put food on the table without having to stand in breadlines or using soup kitchens. For far too many, the temptation and ease of applying for a veteran's pension made the effort worthwhile.

Writing about the imposters or those whose claims have yet to be proven beyond a reasonable doubt at the expense of men who served honorably in both the Union and Confederate military seems contradictory to the main purpose of this study. Yet, to better appreciate the difficulties in assessing credentials and the trail of lies or inconclusive evidence, their identities need to be revealed, at least some of them. As for the outright imposters who have been unmasked, it might be too late to rectify the damage inflicted. A grave injustice had been perpetuated on the unsuspecting public and, worse, on the bona fide surviving veterans from the war who truly deserved the accolades and recognition. Though men were unveiled as outright frauds during or after their lifetimes, quasi-veterans were still afforded special consideration by high-ranking government officials, state and local dignitaries and the general population. Perhaps folks had a difficult time believing someone would perpetuate such a misguided sham regardless of what appeared to be mounting evidence against them.

In Slant, Virginia, the Virginia Division of the Daughters of the Confederacy erected a monument in Salling's honor. Inscribed on the headstone were the words *Virginia's Last Confederate Veteran* and his birth date, *May 15, 1846*.[11] Despite seemingly damaging evidence that has come to light over the past decades, an Internet post from the archives of the Library of Virginia reads, "Although the Confederate Pension Rolls and recently processed Confederate Pension Records neither confirm nor deny Salling's claim, in the eyes of the Commonwealth of Virginia, he was, in fact, who he said he was."[12] In the eyes of a majority of Civil War historians, however, the overwhelming evidence weighs heavily against Salling's selection as the last Confederate. The author concedes that Salling most likely mined saltpeter for the Confederacy and was paid accordingly for his labor by that government, but his service appears to be more in keeping with the definition of an independent government contractor, not as a soldier performing duties in a military capacity.

Numerous books, volumes of newspaper articles, and an abundance of Internet blurbs have been published listing names and relevant details about the last surviving Civil War veterans. In earlier works there were errors because the misrepresentations came at a time when no one suspected fraud to such a great extent. The first detailed pioneering work regarding the last Civil War veterans was undertaken by C. Stewart Peterson and self-published as *Last Civil War Veteran in Each State* (1951). The groundbreaking initiative was a valiant effort by the author, but it contained suspect material that proved to be erroneous as the years passed, thus losing some credibility in the process. More than a quarter of a century later, author and historian Jay S. Hoar published *New England's Last Civil War Veterans* (1976) followed by *The South's Last Boys in Gray*, vols. 1, 2, 3 (1986, 2010) and *The North's Last Boys in Blue*, vols. 1, 2, 3 (2006, 2008, 2010). Peterson's typed manuscript and Hoar's earlier publications, for the most part, came at a time when personal computers and the Internet were either nonexistent or in their infancy. Despite the obstacles, both men did a remarkable job researching, assembling names, stories, and pertinent data and thus laying the foundation for future Civil War historians. The challenge both faced was made murkier not only because of the imposters but also, more so, because of the paucity of Confederate records they had at their disposal (an abundance of regimental documents had been destroyed during the war). Had it not been for the imposters, the inability to verify service records and finding of key information from unexpected sources that seemed to materialize out of nowhere, a certifiable listing of the last Civil War veterans might have been completed decades ago. But in the end, Hoar's exhaustive research stands the test of time. If not for his labors much of the information we have about these veterans would have been lost forever. The reader will observe by the reference notations that the author—with a few exceptions—relied heavily on Hoar's findings and, to a much lesser extent, Peterson's work. In some cases, family lore seemed to be more conjecture than fact and, therefore, had to be discounted as authoritative source material.

It is also important to note that not all veterans joined the ranks of the GAR and the UVC. Some chose not to rekindle wartime memories; others preferred not to be bothered, whatever the reason. Why some veterans were reticent about joining a fraternal military organization can only be surmised. In his autobiography, *The Buffalo Harvest*, veteran Frank H. Mayer explained his feelings: "At the close of any war there are bound to be thousands of young men who had peacetime pursuits too dull for their adventure-stirred lives. Maybe that was truer after the Civil War than at any other time. I know how I felt. I was restive. I wanted out. Fortunately for us then we had what you don't have now: we had a frontier to conquer. It was a very good substitute for war."[13]

Making the identification process even more problematic was the fact that if a veteran did not draw a pension his chances of being recognized as one of the last was virtually impossible to determine. Because of this, some aged veterans might have fallen through the cracks.[14] Yet, according to Central Press correspondent Raymond Wilcove during the 1950s, "the last of the non-members died several years ago."[15] Unfortunately, the gentleman offered no evidence in the article to substantiate his assertion.

During the writing of this book, the author was faced with making some difficult decisions. Almost daily, the research and accompanying findings turned into a "lesson learned" experience. As new facts materialized, initial selections were either displaced or, in extreme cases, rightfully discredited. As one writer and historian forewarned early in the project, "The topic is a minefield in a morass." The warning proved prophetic on more than one occasion.

The reader is advised that not every veteran's story has an image. Although photographs exist for all but three state veterans (Maryland, Nevada, and New Jersey have yet to be found by the author), in some cases the reproduction quality is inadequate for publication.

In an effort not to be remiss, I acknowledge the dedicated work of Civil War nurses who, as volunteers or civilian contractors, performed their difficult assignments so admirably. Some historians have chosen to include these "angels of mercy" in their selection process and maybe they should be (in 1933 fifteen nurses were receiving federal pensions). Arguably the charitable and courageous work of these tireless women is worthy of recognition. Therefore, an appendix has been added that acknowledges the last ten surviving nurses of America's Civil War (Appendix B). But for this current work, the author's main premise was to include only those veterans who were drafted or who enlisted in the military.

Undoubtedly these findings will continue to be scrutinized by Civil War scholars, as well they should. If potential errors or omissions are found, they need to be verified and noted in subsequent works. Unfortunately, with the passage of time America may never possess a perfect and uncontestable accounting of the last Civil War veteran from each state.

Chapter 1

An Overview

When they enlisted, many of the last survivors of America's Civil War were young boys, so young that a significant number lied about their age to enlist in a regiment. Not all of them served full terms in the units they were mustered into. Boys from the North and the South had joined the ranks as replacements to fill the void created by those whose enlistments had expired or, worse, as replacements for someone killed or maimed in battle or felled by disease. How awkward these fledgling recruits must have felt standing in formation alongside combat-weary and battle-hardened veterans. Veterans in these units must have had a similar feeling gazing upon the new recruits. They surely were thinking, *They're nothing more than calves waiting for slaughter.*

Many of these fresh recruits eventually saw battle. Others did not. After the war some bragged that they never fired a shot at the enemy. For those who did "see the elephant"—as Civil War veterans came to call their first battlefield experience—their attitude changed overnight. The war they experienced was nothing compared to what they had initially envisioned. Adding to the misery were the diseases these country boys were susceptible to contracting, and usually did. Those who survived their first combat or illness were the lucky ones, and the few who made it unscathed to the end were the most fortunate.

As time passed after the Civil War, veterans from both sides of the conflict pined for the old days, not the war per se but the camaraderie they experienced while in the service. To keep friendships alive, they joined local or regional veterans' group with the main headquarters facility for gatherings. For the North it was the GAR and for the South it was the UCV. There they told stories, played cards, smoked tobacco, read books and newspapers, and lounged in an atmosphere free of distractions by the contemporary world. Some sought seclusion; others savored the limelight and wallowed in the admiration and attention they usually received because of their age and past military accomplishments. While they were able, these men were honored at civic and military affairs. Some travelled to final reunions both statewide and on a national scale. Those who earned the title through nothing more than longevity carried honorary titles like "Colonel" or "General," all given to them by family, neighbors, and friends. Others were affectionately called "Uncle," though perhaps there was never any bona fide family relationship.

During their twilight years most aged warriors remained at home or moved in with sons and daughters when they became too feeble to adequately take care of themselves. Some might have wondered if living so long was a blessing or a curse. Those requiring constant medical supervision were unable to pick up the pieces or became financially destitute with no one alive or willing to care for them and spent their final days between soldiers' homes and veterans hospitals. For the worst cases, there were state-operated insane asylums where a veteran's mental problems were hidden from the public eye.

For the last surviving veterans, the war had a profound impact upon their lives; it's to be hoped the impact was more positive than negative. These proud veterans were the final players in the most unsettling yet momentous event this country has ever experienced. They might not have realized it during their lifetimes, but their service to their country (Union or Confederate) gradually and steadfastly launched America into a new era.

It is with this in mind that the last Civil War veterans from each state and territory and the District of Columbia are discussed.

Chapter 2

The Union

Known as the land of opportunity, America became the destination for countless immigrants wishing to test their fate and begin anew. During the mid-nineteenth century, America's economy was flourishing in both the northern and southern states. Because of recent technological advances in the north and increasing agricultural output in the slave-driven south, the country experienced a 300 percent population explosion in just 50 years.[1] By 1860 America had become an economic giant among nations. The literacy rate (excluding slaves) was considered among the highest in the world at an estimated 90 percent.[2] But there existed a vast difference of opinion between the two geographical regions, especially when it came to slavery. Whereas northern manufacturers were fabricating products by water-powered machinery while employing inexpensive immigrant laborers, the southern cotton and rice planters relied heavily upon slaves to achieve their fortunes.

On March 4, 1861, when Abraham Lincoln was sworn in as president of the United States, his inauguration speech was geared toward saving the Union and appeasing citizens and legislators from the southern states. His remarks included the following refrain: "We are not enemies, but friends. We must not be enemies. Though passion may have strained, it must not break our bonds of affection."[3] In the south, for the most part, Lincoln's speech fell on deaf ears. Southern separatists were already whipping crowds into a frenzy. It was not long before the southern states seceded from the union and the first shots were fired on Fort Sumter. America now found itself fighting a new self-proclaimed nation: The Confederate States of America. The states that remained loyal to the union were California, Connecticut, Illinois, Indiana, Iowa, Kansas, Maine, Massachusetts, Michigan, Minnesota, Nevada, New Hampshire, New Jersey, New York, Ohio, Oregon, Pennsylvania, Rhode Island, West Virginia, Vermont, and Wisconsin. (Minnesota, Nevada, and West Virginia became states during the Civil War).

In the end, the Union won the ultimate victory, but it came with a hefty price both in manpower and money. What the North initially envisioned as a short-lived war of 90 days or less turned into years of carnage and suffering. When Union veterans returned home as victors, they were as fatigued and troubled as their former adversaries: Southern soldiers proved to be a formidable foe. However, there was a saving grace for the Union: the North's infrastructure remained untouched, as a majority of the fighting had taken place on Southern soil.

Attempting to readjust to civilian life, veterans from both sides did their best to rekindle family relationships while rebuilding their own lives. But the transformation from soldier to civilian did not come easily. There are numerous stories about returning veterans of the conflict arriving at their front doorsteps only to find the unexpected. For example, an Iowa veteran abruptly learned that his children had scattered and his wife was buried in a nearby grave. Apparently no one had written to inform him of her passing. "I had nothing to live for," he said, "and I wanted to lie down in the grave by her side."[4]

Besides the psychological issues, including a mental health disorder that today is called post-traumatic stress disorder (PTSD), there were other serious medical health issues and major dependency problems. In 1879, the U.S. surgeon general estimated that 45,000 veterans were addicted to morphine.[5] Many more experienced alcohol dependency.

Fortunately most Union veterans successfully melded back into society. Some achieved greatness like William McKinley from the 23rd Regiment, Ohio Volunteers, who became the 25th president of the United States. Others were far less successful but proved to be consummate patriarchs and patriotic citizens. Regardless of their eminence or future successes, all were grateful to have survived the terrible ordeal.

Before reading the following stories, there are a few items to keep in mind. The author chose to arrange his work by separate and distinct regions of the country: the Union; the District of Columbia; the Confederacy; the Border States; the Western Territories; and the Territories of Alaska and Hawaii. The reader will notice that within each section, the last surviving veteran is presented alphabetically under the state in which he died. This unique approach seems to make more sense than listing all fifty states and the District of Columbia in alphabetical order without regard to allegiances held during the war. Also, to better understand the veteran's service, regimental briefs are listed here and throughout the remaining sections as a prelude to the veteran's personal sketches. Each concise history highlights major events that took place during the regiment's existence described in accordance with the U.S. National Park Service records. They might seem mundane, but the briefs are essential to understanding exactly where and when each veteran fit into his unit's history. As the reader will see, because of their tender age many of the last surviving Civil War veterans joined their organization late in the war and, in a majority of cases, might not have been a member for the entire time the unit was activated. It is also important to remember that even though the veteran was listed in the regimental rolls, this alone does not constitute his active participation in a campaign or battle—he might have been ill and confined to a field or general hospital, on detached duty to another organization, or furloughed.

California

William Allen Magee
(b. August 19, 1846, d. January 23, 1953)
Squadron M, 12th Regiment, Ohio Volunteer Cavalry

Regimental Brief: Organized at Cleveland, Ohio, the cavalry unit was mustered into service on November 24, 1863. Initially the squadron defended against a Confederate invasion of Kentucky, taking part in the action for less than a month. After several confrontations with the enemy in Kentucky, the cavalry unit operated in Southwest Virginia until mid–October. Later the squadron fought in a number of battles against Confederate forces in Tennessee and North Carolina. On November 14, 1865, the unit was mustered out at Nashville, Tennessee.

Losses: 50 enlisted men killed and mortally wounded and 112 enlisted men dead from disease.[6]

Veteran's Brief: For an old soldier who served in two wars, a person would surmise that the deceased veteran from California left behind a substantial paper trail. Not so. Much of what we know about William "Billy" Allen Magee came from a series of descendant interviews conducted by author and historian Jay S. Hoar years later and a *Los Angeles Times* newspaper obituary of January 24, 1953.

On October 2, 1863, at the age of 17, William Allen Magee enlisted as a bugler in the 12th Ohio Cavalry,

William Allen Magee (from an original wire service photograph credited to Wide World Photos titled "Surviving Civil War Veterans," author's collection).

with whom he fought in a number of skirmishes and battles.[7] The Civil War was not the last conflict in which he participated. He also served in the Spanish American War before retiring as a master sergeant, having served for over 32 years. Unlike the veterans who qualified for a Civil War pension, Magee received a Regular Retired Army pension instead for his postwar service.[8]

After all of his years travelling while serving in the military, Magee found the West and California to his liking and that is where he chose to retire. But there was another reason for his selection. Some of his daughters and his grandchildren were already living in the state. Arguably, with ideal weather and a loving family to look after him, Magee's life was prolonged far beyond that of the average Civil War veteran.

The day before his 106th birthday, Magee was interviewed by a newspaper reporter. Maintaining his remarkable gift for jest right up until the end, he told the reporter that "Buffalo Bill Cody was the best-looking man I ever saw, and I'm in second place right behind him."[9] The next day at his birthday celebration, Magee gave some advice—perhaps to the same reporter—about consuming alcoholic beverages: "Haven't had a drink of liquor myself for the past 50 years. And when I did drink, it was pure corn whiskey that the mountaineers made. It was good for a man. Today the young men mix their drinks. That is what shortens their lives."[10]

Until the end, Magee was said to be "spry, alert, and able to read newspapers without the aid of eyeglasses." But without warning, he suffered a stroke in Van Nuys, California, at the home of his daughter, where he resided for a while. He was rushed by ambulance to Wadsworth General Hospital at the Veterans Affairs Center at Sawtelle (a district in the west side of Los Angeles). He died there at the age of 106 without regaining consciousness. William Allen Magee left three daughters, seven grandchildren and seventeen great-grandchildren. The burial took place at the Los Angeles National Cemetery not far from his daughter's home.[11]

Connecticut

Charles Douglass
(b. May 23, 1847, d. January 29, 1950)
Co. C, 15th Regiment, Connecticut Volunteer Infantry

Regimental Brief: Organized at New Haven, Connecticut, on August 25, 1862, the regiment was sent to Washington, D.C., where it remained until mid–September 1862. The regiment crossed the Potomac and then in

December took part in the Battle of Fredericksburg, which proved a Union disaster, followed a month later by another travesty, General Burnside's infamous "Mud March." For the next year-and-a-half, the regiment took part in a number of battles in places like Chickahominy, Virginia, and New Bern, North Carolina, both well-known names in Civil War history. The regiment was mustered out on June 27, 1865, and officially discharged at New Haven, Connecticut, on July 12, 1865.

Losses: 4 officers and 34 enlisted men killed and mortally wounded and 5 officers and 142 enlisted men dead from disease.[12]

Veteran's Brief: Charles Douglass was a lifelong resident of New Haven, Connecticut. At the age of 17, he enlisted on August 6, 1862, as a drummer in the 4th Regiment, Connecticut Volunteer Infantry, a unit his father was serving in at the time. But before seeing action, the young boy was taken ill. As the recovery process seemed slow, he was sent home on a surgeon certificate. After recovering, he reenlisted in the 15th Regiment, Connecticut Volunteer Infantry, also as a drummer. Douglass was assigned as an orderly to Col. Charles L. Upham and fought alongside him at Fredericksburg. Though Douglass survived the Confederate onslaught, he was not as fortunate when advancing on a Confederate position months later in Kinston, North Carolina. After heavy fighting, Douglass was captured by the enemy and sent to Richmond's Libby Prison. (The prison usually housed officers, but in some cases the Confederates also incarcerated Union enlistees.) His capture was late in the war and his stay in Richmond did not last long. While imprisoned, he contracted typhoid fever and was not expected to live. In an unusual show of compassion, prison authorities allowed his release so he could die at home.[13] He beat the odds and survived. On June 15, 1865, Douglass was discharged from the army.[14] After the war, he married Ellen Carroll, in February 1873. They had a son, Frank, in December, but the child lived only until August 1875.[15]

Douglass first became a mechanic and then a stationer selling various writing supplies and paper goods. Making a living in the latter profession must have been ideal, as he remained in the business for thirty-five years. During that time he became active in the Grand Army of the Republic. In 1937 he was elected the GAR Commander for the Department of Connecticut. In 1943 he was named to the post again, one that he held for the remainder of his years. At the age of 97, though his health was failing, he still marched in Memorial Day parades in New Haven. It was one of the last times he was able to participate in such events. The aged veteran died less than three years later at the age of 102. His wife Ellen died in 1907.[16] Today, Charles Douglass rests in peace at New Haven's Evergreen Cemetery, New Haven, Connecticut.[17]

Illinois

Lewis Fablinger
(b. October 11, 1846, d. March 14, 1950)

Co. H, 21st Regiment, Illinois Volunteer Infantry,
Co. C, 140th Regiment, Illinois Volunteer Infantry, and
Co. F, 96th Regiment, Illinois Volunteer Infantry

Regimental Brief for the 21st Regiment, Illinois Infantry: The regiment was organized at Mattoon, Illinois, and mustered in on June 28, 1861. The infantry unit's first duty station was in Ironton, Missouri, where it remained until January 1862. By March the regiment had moved to Arkansas. From there the regiment was ordered to Missouri and then to Mississippi, where it remained until August. The soldiers were subsequently ordered to pursue General Bragg and his army into Tennessee and Kentucky. On October 8, the regiment fought at the Battle of Perryville. Two months later, it saw action at the Battle of Stones River. In early 1863 and for the next six months the men performed reconnaissance. The balance of 1863 was considerably more hectic. The regiment participated in several campaigns and fought at the Battle of Chickamauga (Georgia) on September 19 and 20. In late September and most of October, the infantry unit took part in the Siege of Chattanooga. In May of the following year, the regiment participated in the Atlanta Campaign, which lasted until September 1864. During this period, the soldiers fought in a number of skirmishes and battles. By October, the regiment was in full pursuit of General Hood in Alabama. For two days in mid–December, it fought at the Battle of Nashville. Again the regiment was in pursuit of Hood to the Tennessee River. By March 1865, the soldiers were ordered to Huntsville, Alabama, where they awaited further orders. In mid–April they were sent to Tennessee and remained there until June. They were then moved to Louisiana and finally Texas before mustering out at San Antonio, Texas, on December 16, 1865.

Losses: 6 officers and 124 enlisted men killed and mortally wounded and 2 officers and 140 enlisted men dead from disease.[18]

Regimental Brief for the 140th Regiment, Illinois Infantry: Organized at Camp Butler, Illinois, the regiment was mustered into service for 100 days on June 18, 1864. Ordered to Tennessee, the men guarded railroad lines for two months. The infantry unit was able to repulse Nathan Bedford Forrest's attack on Memphis in late August, after which it was ordered to Camp Fry, Chicago, Illinois. The regiment mustered out on October 29, 1864.

Losses: 5 enlisted men killed and mortally wounded and 24 enlisted men dead from disease.[19]

Regimental Brief for the 96th Regiment, Illinois Infantry: The regiment was organized at Rockford, Illinois, and mustered in September 6, 1862. Until the end of November the regiment operated in Ohio and Kentucky. From there it moved to Nashville, Tennessee. Soon after, the 96th helped to repulse the Confederates at the Battle of Ft. Donelson (February 4, 1863). For the next seven months, the regiment saw action in a number of battles throughout the Tennessee area. In early September, it moved into Georgia and took part in the Battle of Chickamauga (September 19 and 20). The unit fought at Lookout Mountain and remained there until December 1, 1863, before moving back to Tennessee at the end of February 1864. The 96th then moved to Georgia, where it fought during the Atlanta Campaign (May 1 through September 8). In June 1864, the regiment operated near Marietta and against Confederate forces at Kennesaw Mountain (June 10–July 2). From July 11 through August 25, 1864, the 96th participated in the Siege of Atlanta. After a few months of skirmishing, it took part in the Nashville Campaign (November through December 1864). During that period the unit fought at the Battle of Franklin (November 30) and the Battle of Nashville (December 15 and 16). At the end of the month, it was in full pursuit of General Hood's army. The unit was subsequently ordered to Huntsville, Alabama, where it performed duty until late March 1865. Eventually the regiment moved back to Nashville, where it remained until June. The 96th was mustered out on June 10, 1865.

Losses: 5 officers and 111 enlisted men killed and mortally wounded and an officer and 124 enlisted men dead from disease.[20]

Veteran's Brief: Lewis Fablinger was born in Frederick, Maryland. At the age of two, his parents moved to the small village of Elizabeth, in Jo Daviess County, Illinois. Over a decade later, when the Civil War commenced, he attempted to enlist but was rejected because of his age. However, his second attempt at joining the army a few years later met with success, as he was seventeen.[21] Before the war was over, Pvt. Fablinger had served with three different Illinois infantry regiments: the 21st, 140th and 96th.

After the war, Fablinger entered a normal school (an institution that trained high school graduates to become teachers) and received his diploma in June 1872 (the school was located in Galena, Illinois, home of Ulysses S. Grant and several other Civil War generals). He first taught in Illinois before moving to California, where he continued in the profession. There is also evidence that he once sold fire insurance policies.[22] Fablinger married Austa Weir on May 4, 1876, in Elizabeth, Illinois. They had four children.[23]

Upon retirement, Fablinger began raising ginseng plants, first as a hobby and later as a business as he watched his leisure pursuit become a profitable endeavor.[24] In 1889 his government pension application was approved. Some sixty years later, on October 11, 1949, Fablinger celebrated his 103rd birthday with a small group of family and friends. The low-key affair was held at the home of his daughter, Sadie Rogers, with whom he had been living for several years. At the time, he was commander of the GAR for the State of Illinois—a ceremonial honor bestowed upon him as the last Civil War veteran alive from the state.[25] If he told any wartime stories during his long life, they may have been lost to posterity. Five months after his birthday party, he passed away in a veterans hospital in Hines, Illinois.[26] His wife, Austa, had predeceased him in death by nine years.[27] Fablinger had been in poor health for a number of years and during the final months of his life he labored through blindness and near deafness while also being confined to a wheelchair during his waking hours.[28] Lewis Fablinger was laid to rest in Elizabeth City Cemetery, Elizabeth, Illinois.[29]

Indiana

John Christian Adams
(b. August 17, 1847, d. February 17, 1949)
Co. C, 17th Regiment, West Virginia Volunteer Infantry

Regimental Brief: The regiment was organized at Wheeling, West Virginia, on September 26, 1864. A day later, it was ordered to Clarksburg, West Virginia, where the men guarded railroad lines and performed garrison duty. The regiment mustered out on June 30, 1865.

Losses: 1 killed and 24 dead from disease.[30]

Veteran's Brief: John Christian Adams was born in northwestern Virginia in a section of the state that held heavy Union sentiment. On June 20, 1863, West Virginia broke away from Virginia and became a new state. Less than a year-and-a-half later Adams mustered into the 17th Regiment, West Virginia Infantry, as a drummer. He was only 17 years old. Though the regiment never fought in any major battles, it did participate in skirmishes against Con-

John Christian Adams as commander in chief of the Grand Army of the Republic (*Journal of the Eighty-First Encampment of the Grand Army of the Republic, Cleveland, Ohio, 1947*).

federates scattered throughout the state. In the ten months the regiment existed, Adams most likely took part in several of these skirmishes.[31]

Eleven years after the war Adams married Anna Eliza Masters. They had four children: Ella, Edward, Anna, and Caroline. During the 1880s, the family moved to Grant County, Indiana. There he worked for U.S. Glass Company as a manager of the shipping department.[32]

Adams was a member of the GAR for several years and from 1946 through 1948 served as the GAR department commander for the State of Indiana. At the 82nd National Encampment in Grand Rapids, Michigan, Adams was elected national assistant adjutant general and assistant quartermaster general, positions he held until his death. He was 101 years old. At his funeral, according to one source, "the tiny town of Jonesboro [Indiana] was filled with dignitaries from all over the state." He rests in Riverside Cemetery, Gas City, Indiana.[33]

On May 21, 2006, the Indiana Chapter of the Sons of Union Veterans planned to rededicate Adams' grave by placing a bronze plaque at the site. Unknown to just about everyone, a descendant of Adams was living in Greentown. Barbara J. Middleton had heard about the rededication ceremonies on a local radio station and used the Internet to introduce herself to the proper official and advise that person she was the grandniece of Adams. She had attended his funeral in 1949 when she was 15 years old. Naturally the Sons of Union Veterans and the rededication committee were overjoyed to hear from her. Middleton was invited to the ceremonies as a special guest of honor. When the ceremony concluded, Middleton told those around her that "it was a really neat presentation."[34]

Iowa

James Patterson Martin
(b. November 10, 1847, d. September 20, 1949)
Battery H, 1st Regiment, Wisconsin Heavy Artillery

Regimental Brief: Batteries E through M were organized between September and October 1864. These batteries were ordered to Washington, D.C., where the men defended the capital until June of 1865. Batteries "E" through "M" were mustered out on June 26, 1865.

Losses for the entire regiment: 4 enlisted men killed and mortally wounded and 2 officers and 77 enlisted men dead from disease.[35]

Veteran's Brief: Born in Aberdeenshire, Scotland, James Patterson Martin came to America with his entire family when he was only five years old, arriving after a seven-week voyage in a sailing vessel.[36] At the age of 16, he enlisted in the 1st Regiment, Wisconsin Heavy Artillery, receiving permission to join from his parents because he was underage. At the time, he was living in Mineral Point, Wisconsin. Four of his brothers also served in the Union army: William, the oldest brother, was placed in charge of an African American unit; Samuel, the third oldest, died of measles (it remains unclear whether he died while serving his country). On the night of President Lincoln's assassination, James and his brother John were assigned to Ft. Lyon just outside of Washington, D.C., to perform garrison duty. According to family records, John later attended the Lincoln conspirators' trial.[37]

At the close of the war, after fighting in a number of minor skirmishes, Martin, along with a friend, journeyed to Kansas. Here Martin filed a land claim and soon met his future bride, Mary Elizabeth Brady. The union produced several children. Eventually, the Martin family returned to Wisconsin by covered wagon.[38] For reasons yet to be identified, the family moved to an area near Sutherland, Iowa.[39]

Martin worked at many trades and professions: farmer, businessman, stonemason, carpenter and blacksmith. He also served as a constable and a school director.[40] Always a patriot, he often traveled to state and national encampments as a member of the GAR. In 1938 as an aged veteran he attended the commemoration of the fiftieth anniversary of the Battle of Gettysburg in what must have been the thrill of a lifetime.[41]

At the age of 94, James P. Martin was able to drive a car, and at 97 he could still work in his garden. But during his final

James P. Martin. Civil War Veteran

Union soldier James Patterson Martin proudly posed for this CDV (courtesy Sandra Williamson, descendant of James Patterson Martin).

James Patterson Martin as he appeared later in life (courtesy Sandra Williamson, descendant of James Patterson Martin).

years his eyes failed and he could no longer read a newspaper or hear his favorite radio programs. However, he still possessed a good appetite up until the time he became critically ill a few months before his passing. Martin's wife, Mary Elizabeth Brady, had died in 1916. Twenty years later, because of his age he moved in with his daughter, Elise Hill.[42]

Many of Martin's memories faded with age but on occasion he remembered carrying the news of President Lincoln's assassination to Ft. Lyon, Virginia. In 1947, he was named state commander of the GAR, Department of Iowa—a mostly ceremonial position with little responsibility because of his age. Yet, only a few years earlier he was seen on numerous occasions "driving his car here and there at his will, even when well past 90."[43] Known by many in the small community, he was said to possess a "friendly, pleasing personality."[44] As his days became numbered, however, he was unable to recognize many of his old acquaintances. Martin died in Sutherland with his doctor and daughter Elise by his bedside. He was 101. A monument acknowledging his credentials as the last surviving Civil War veteran from the State of Iowa was erected in the town.[45] He is buried in Waterman Cemetery in the town where he spent his final years.[46]

Kansas

Charles W. Bailey
(b. February 10, 1848, d. January 29, 1951)
Co. E, 41st Regiment, Wisconsin Volunteer Infantry;
Co. G & C, 47th Regiment, Wisconsin Volunteer Infantry;
Co. K, 5th Regiment, Wisconsin Volunteer Infantry.

Regimental Brief for the 41st Regiment, Wisconsin Infantry: The regiment was mustered in for 100 days on June 8, 1864, at Milwaukee, Wisconsin. From June 15 through 19 the unit moved to Memphis, Tennessee. In the vicinity of Memphis, the men performed garrison, railroad guard, and picket duty until September. It was during this period that the regiment repulsed Gen. Nathan Bedford Forrest's attack on Memphis. The regiment was mustered out on September 24, 1864.

A debonair Charles W. Bailey (courtesy Peggy Crook).

Losses: 18 dead from disease.

Regimental Brief for the 47th Regiment, Wisconsin Infantry: The regiment was organized at Madison, Wisconsin, and mustered into service on February 27, 1865. The men guarded railroad lines at Tullahoma and in the district of Middle Tennessee. On September 4, 1865, the regiment mustered out.

Losses: 39 dead from disease.[47]

Regimental Brief for the 5th Regiment, Wisconsin Infantry: The regiment was organized at Madison, Wisconsin, and mustered in on July 12, 1861. Only two weeks passed before the regiment was ordered to Washington, D.C. There the men helped construct Fort Marcy on the northern bank of the Potomac. In late March the regiment was ordered to Fortress Monroe in Virginia, where the soldiers performed general reconnaissance until early April. From April until early May the regiment participated in the Siege of Yorktown. From mid–April to early May it fought in the Battle of Williamsburg. From there the soldiers moved toward Richmond, encamping at several locations until moving back to Alexandria in mid–August. In September, the regiment participated in the Maryland Campaign before fighting in the Battle of Antietam on September 16 and 17. During mid to late October it attempted to intercept General Stuart's cavalry. In December, the regiment fought in the Battle of Fredericksburg and reluctantly participated in the infamous "Mud March" a month later. It subsequently participated in two major actions in 1863: the Battle of Chancellorsville (April 27 through May 6) and the Battle of Gettysburg (July 1 through 3). In 1864 the men of the 5th Wisconsin Infantry were present at the following engagements—Battle of the Wilderness (May 5 through 7); Spotsylvania (May 8 through 12); Spotsylvania Court House (May 12 through 21); Cold Harbor (June 1 through 12); Siege of Petersburg (until July 9); and Weldon Railroad (June 22 and 23)—before moving back to Washington in July. After a few additional battles, the weary soldiers were assigned provost duty at Winchester and Cedar Creek, Virginia. By October, the regiment was back at Petersburg, where they participated in the Siege of Petersburg from early December 1864 until early April 1865. Before the conflict ended, the regiment also participated in the Appomattox Campaign (March 28 through April 9) and the assault and fall of Petersburg (April 2). For a week the regiment was in hot pursuit of General Robert E. Lee's devastated army. On the 9th, men from the regiment witnessed General Lee's surrender at Appomattox Court House. The regiment mustered out on July 11, 1865.

Losses: 15 officers and 180 enlisted men killed and mortally wounded and 2 officers and 132 enlisted men dead from disease.[48]

Veteran's Brief: Born in a cabin on an Indian reservation near Watertown, Wisconsin, Charles W. Bailey enlisted at the age of 15, either with his parents consent or by lying about his age. He served in three Wisconsin infantry regiments during the war: the 47th Regiment, Wisconsin Infantry, during the last few months of the war and earlier, and for a considerably longer period with the 5th Regiment, Wisconsin Infantry.

On August 21, 1864, the 41st Regiment, Wisconsin Volunteer Infantry, repulsed the attack of Gen. Nathan Bedford Forrest at Memphis, Tennessee. During the battle, Pvt. Bailey was wounded twice. In the turmoil Bailey lost his canteen, a regrettable occurrence for a foot soldier.[49] No doubt it was replaced shortly thereafter. When interviewed years later by the *Topeka Daily Capital*, Bailey provided only vague generalities about with whom and where he fought during the war. Arguably his age contributed heavily to his memory lapse.

After returning home from the battlefields, Bailey worked as a cowboy before finding his way to Humboldt, Kansas, where he worked as a farmer and later herded wild Texas longhorns. In 1877, he met and married Mary Etta Stark, a schoolteacher. As Bailey put it, "One day in Fort Dodge I saw a girl and that busted up my cattle driving … [and] you'll have to guess the rest."[50] During the next decade, Bailey found his true calling. He and his wife enrolled at Baker University. Bailey graduated in 1887 and became an ordained Methodist minister.

Mary and the Reverend Bailey were blessed with nine children; eight of the nine attended Baker University, two of whom also became ministers. During his own ministry, Bailey held several pastorates before retiring at the ripe old age of 90. On November 15, 1945, after 66 years of marriage, Mary died. The Reverend Bailey survived another six years before passing away at the age of 102, weeks shy of his 103rd birthday. He had taken ill just before his 100th birthday and never managed to fully recover. The Rev. Charles W. Bailey is buried in Oakwood Cemetery in Baldwin City, Kansas.[51]

In a letter to author Jay S. Hoar dated January 31, 1978, Herbert A. Bailey, the Reverend Bailey's son, who was then 88 years old, paid tribute to his deceased dad: "My father was 'one in a million,' a perfect example of a man that a son would like to emulate. He was the most selfless person I have ever known; a kind, honest, helpful, considerate human being, gifted with a warm personality. He had a strong physique, was absolutely fearless, contagiously friendly, devoted to his family, and a true patriot."[52]

Maine

Zachary Taylor McLaughlin
(b. November 18, 1848, d. November 7, 1947)
Co. F, 12th Regiment, Maine Volunteer Infantry

Regimental Brief: Organized at Portland, Maine, the regiment was mustered in on November 16, 1861. Its first duty station was in Mississippi, where it remained until October 1862. The regiment eventually moved to the Louisiana swamps and operated there until March 1863. From March to August it participated in a number of assaults against the enemy in that area. From mid–August until October, the unit moved to Mississippi then back to Louisiana, where it remained until the veterans were furloughed in April 1864 (those with less service time remained with the regiment in Louisiana). The furloughs were necessary because of the large number of deaths from disease. On June 16, the veterans returned from furlough. In mid–July the regiment received orders to move to Virginia until month's end. On July 31, it was transferred to Washington, D.C., then to Maryland, where it participated in the Battle of Cedar Creek (October 19). Veterans left the front in mid–November and mustered out on December 7, 1864. The remaining soldiers were consolidated into a battalion of four companies and ordered to Savannah, Georgia. Six new companies were formed in February and March 1865 and assigned as Companies E through K. They were mustered out in February and March 1866. The balance of the regiment was mustered out on April 18, 1866.

Losses: 3 officers and 49 enlisted men killed and mortally wounded and 2 officers and 237 enlisted men dead from disease.[53]

Veteran's Brief: In many ways, Zachary Taylor McLaughlin was a lucky man. At the age of sixteen, and by stretching the truth about his age, he enlisted as a private in the 12th Regiment, Maine Volunteer Infantry, on February 9, 1865, at Augusta, Maine. Why was he fortunate? He became a member of

Zachary Taylor McLaughlin relaxing outside his home (courtesy Phillips Historical Society, Phillips, Maine).

a newly formed company in a regiment that never faced the wrath of being indoctrinated by battle-hardened soldiers. Above all, he was blessed that the war ended only a few months after his enlistment. Reminiscing years later, McLaughlin remembered listening to President Lincoln giving a short speech before the regiment departed for Savannah, Georgia. Later McLaughlin wrote that the "speech was a good one an' he lookt jest as his portraits did at that time—kinder old an' a bit sad."[54]

Despite his short enlistment, McLaughlin suffered from dysentery and spent several weeks in a field hospital before fully recovering. The young soldier was administered a folk remedy for a cure: a liquefied concoction of cherry tree bark probably laced with alcohol. He survived the ordeal, but no one will ever know for certain if the potion had an effect on resolving his illness.[55]

Returning home after the war (sometime after August 14) and still 16 years of age, he wanted to see more of America. For the next few years he worked as a stonemason in Tennessee and then in an Ohio sawmill. Returning to Maine, he obtained employment as a guide in the Rangeley Lakes region for three summers and as a lumberman during the winter months. After his marriage to Electa Record, he kept a similar work pattern in place: woodsman in the winter and gardener in the summer. He and his wife had six children. Like his Vermont counterpart, Gilbert Charles Lucier, he, too, became a road commissioner.[56]

In 1926 McLaughlin's beloved wife died. Those who knew him said that after Electa's passing, he turned a bit "crotchety." His lone respite seemed to be fishing local streams, a sport he enjoyed into his eighties. From 1936 until the time of his death at the age of 98, he lived with a member of his family. Zachary Taylor's remains lie in Evergreen Cemetery in Phillips, Maine.[57]

Massachusetts

George Riley
(b. November 5, 1849, d. October 10, 1947)
U.S. Navy

Naval Service Brief: Details remain sketchy.

Veteran's Brief: Selecting George Riley, a naval veteran from Massachusetts, as the last Civil War veteran to die in the state was not an easy decision. His selection does not preclude a bit of apprehension. As Jay S. Hoar explained in his book *New England's Last Civil War Veterans*, "a certain mystery surrounds the Civil War service rendered by *this* George Riley."[58] Making matters difficult was discerning which of the five George Rileys from Massachusetts served the longest. Hoar chose the most logical method, a process of elimination. He discounted a few by examining their ages at enlistment and how old they were while serving. What made Hoar's investigation even more difficult was that there were five George Rileys from the commonwealth who had served in the navy.[59] The person Hoar finally settled on was estimated to be 13 years old. Hoar believed that the Riley who deserved the honor was a second- or first-class boy serving onboard a Union vessel during the summer of 1863.

George Riley as he appeared in the Boston Police Department's annual yearbook in 1901 (courtesy Boston Police Department Records Center and Archives).

Although the Navy Department and the National Archives cannot substantiate his wartime service, George Riley had long been accepted as a Civil War veteran by the Commonwealth of Massachusetts. How the commonwealth determined his military status remains uncertain.[60]

On July 1, 1895, George Riley became a member of the Boston Police Department and worked for a number of years in the Jamaica Plain section. In 1920 he was reassigned to the downtown area of the city. One of his varied duties was to inspect for potential fire hazards in theaters (these duties were later transferred to the city fire marshal). A person can almost imagine what a patrolman encounters while walking a beat during a regular shift in a major section of a city. Over the years of wearing down the leather of the soles of his shoes while walking his beat, George Riley most certainly encountered a number of unusual events that required his intervention. But one in particular stands out and is worth retelling. The affair was reported in the January 10, 1907, edition of the *Boston Daily Globe* (later retold on an Internet BlogSpot). Subscribers of the newspaper who read the tongue-in-check account must have laughed; we hope Riley also chuckled, though we will never know for certain.

The story concerns two police officers, two guns and one rather large, rabid tiger cat that purportedly weighed more than 20 pounds. The account stated that the animal had "been prowling about the neighborhood and acting like a wild cat. It had no fear of attacking man, woman or child, and … a number of children had been bitten and scratched by it." A day earlier the cat had entered the residence of a Mr. Roger E. Tileston, who was also attacked by the animal while attempting to drive it out of the house and off his property. After receiving an official complaint from Mr. Tileston, two patrolmen were swiftly dispatched to the scene. Officer Jack McAdams, "one of the biggest men in the department," and Officer George Riley (described by the newspaper as being "not more than 5 feet 4½ inches in height") showed up at the domicile. After some quick detective work, they found the feline menace under Mr. Tileston's porch and decided to wait it out; but the cat never budged from its hiding place. Using Yankee ingenuity, the officers asked Mr. Tileston to boil some hot water and place it in a container. After handing it to the officers, they poured it over the cracks of the floorboards on the porch. Almost instantaneously, the cat sprang out of its hiding spot. Seeing the cat scamper for open ground, Officer McAdams emptied his revolver but hit nothing but air. Officer Riley then nudged Officer McAdams to the side and fired five rounds of ammunition. But "when the smoke cleared away, kitty was still there glaring at the marksmen."

Frustrated, the officers sent for reinforcements. Officer Nathan Haskell Dole soon arrived and gave his loaded revolver to one of the officers, whose name remains unknown. But before the officer could take aim, a local neighbor threw a brick and knocked the beast senseless. The cat, now dazed and lying on its back, "received the contents of the third revolver before it gave up its life." In the end, 15 rounds were fired at the intended target; yet in the end, all it took to subdue the rabid feline and solve the case was a solitary brick.[61] The incident, although amusing, was not indicative of the difficult police work performed by the men of the Boston Police Department in the early twentieth century. Arguably the occurrence was an anomaly and a break from the grueling work of a police officer in the big city.

Accounts from the period state that Riley loved his job as a patrolman. He was also well respected by the citizens of Boston and the police force, so much so that he was permitted to work past the normal retirement age. On June 22, 1929, he officially retired, just short of his eightieth birthday.[62]

Ironically, this man who performed fire inspections died in a Boston fire. Riley was living with his daughter in a Back Bay apartment when a careless smoker set the building ablaze. His daughter was at work at the time. Riley died from leg burns and carbon monoxide asphyxia. The oldest retiree of the Boston Police Department lived to be 97. He is buried at Holy Cross Cemetery in Malden.[63]

For those who feel that the meager evidence presented above does not justify George Riley's selection as the last Civil War veteran from the Com-

Charles Benjamin Burt, the second to the last Civil War veteran from Massachusetts (courtesy Jay S. Hoar, *New England's Last Civil War Veterans***).**

monwealth of Massachusetts, the next in line for the honor is Charles Benjamin Burt from Springfield, Massachusetts. Born August 1, 1848, he died three months before George Riley lost his life in the fire. Burt's death was officially recorded as June 28, 1947.

On July 11, 1864, after working over a year at the U.S. Armory in Springfield, Burt convinced a local recruiter from Co. H, 8th Regiment, Massachusetts Volunteer Infantry, that he was eighteen when in truth he was only sixteen. A redhead and noticeably tall (six feet at enlistment, eventually topping off at 6'4"), Pvt. Burt probably had little difficulty defending his white lie because of his stature; he towered over all the other enlistees. As far as can be ascertained, Burt's entire military career was spent performing guard duty in Washington, D.C. He never experienced combat.[64]

Michigan

Joseph Clovese
(b. January 30, 1844, d. July 13, 1951)

*Co. G, 9th Regiment, Louisiana Infantry (African Descent).
The Union regiment's name was changed to the
63rd Regiment, U.S. Colored Troops (USCT)*

Regimental Brief: The black regiment was organized on March 11, 1864. The unit's primary responsibility was to perform post and garrison duty in Mississippi and later in Louisiana. The men were involved in several skirmishes during their enlistment. On January 9, 1866, the regiment was mustered out. No records were found to document any regimental losses; but considering the history of substandard rations and inadequate medical support received from Union supply trains to black units in the field, the losses might have been substantial and perhaps even higher than comparable white units.[65]

Veteran's Brief: Affectionately called "Uncle Joe" by many of his friends and neighbors, Joseph Clovese (aka Clovrse and Cloviece) was born into slavery on a southern plantation in St. Bernard Parish, Louisiana. Considered a favorite houseboy of his master, the youngster was granted special privileges, including a "good" education, a rarity for slaves.[66] Yet he, like so many other slaves, yearned to be free. When fighting broke out during the Siege of Vicksburg, Clovese, now in his teens, ran away from his master and joined the Union army as a lowly private. Because of his age he was assigned as a musician. "In the army I played the drum and [it] sure made a racket too. A drum is proud and it said everything I felt," he professed years later.[67] But drummers, as important as they were on Civil War battlefields for loudly tapping out rhythmic commands conveyed by a commanding officer during the heat of battle, did not kill the enemy. It was not long before he was handed a rifle and made an infantryman.[68]

After the war, Clovese worked on steamboats on the Mississippi River before stringing telegraph wires between New Orleans, Louisiana, and Biloxi, Mississippi.[69] On April 22, 1911, he applied for a government pension, an application that was swiftly approved.

At the age of 104, the aged veteran moved to Pontiac, Michigan, to be closer to his family. By now illness had incapacitated him and he had to use a wheelchair. When the community realized that he was the last Civil War veteran from the state, the citizens embraced him with large birthday celebrations during the last years of his life.[70] At the age of 107, Clovese was transported to the Dearborn Veterans Hospital at Dearborn, Michigan, where his body simply gave out.

Joseph Clovese was more than just the last surviving Civil War veteran from the State of Michigan; he was also the last black veteran to have served in the Union army during the war. His remains rest in Perry Mount Park Cemetery in a veteran's plot at Pontiac, Michigan.[71] Clovese's celebration of life took place five months later when over 300 friends packed the Newman A.M.E. Church at Dearborn to hear the Rev. J.A. Parker declare something that may have already been obvious to those in attendance: "Uncle Joe, [was] born to glory [and] had four great loves: his country, his God, his church, [and] his home."[72]

The few photographs of Joseph Clovese that exist today tell a great deal about the man many people surely admired. Those who paid their final respects at the

A cheery-eyed Joseph Clovese (from an original wire service photograph credited to Wide World Photos titled "Surviving Civil War Veterans," May 17, 1951, author's collection).

funeral and later at the remembrance celebration could never forget Uncle Joe's engaging smile and stately manner. In the end, his passing proved a devastating loss not only for the State of Michigan but also the country he cherished.

Minnesota

The story about this veteran unfolds in a later chapter for reasons that will become obvious.

New Hampshire

James Marion Lurvey
(b. December 2, 1847, d. April 7, 1950)

Co. A, 40th Regiment, Massachusetts Volunteer Infantry,
and Battery H, 4th Regiment, Massachusetts Heavy Artillery

Regimental Brief for the 40th Regiment, Massachusetts Infantry: Organized at Lynnfield, Massachusetts, in August 1862, its first duty station was Washington, D.C., where it remained until April 1863. In April the regiment was ordered to Virginia, where it took part in the Siege of Suffolk. From early May until mid–July, it participated in a number of raids and expeditions. On July 10, the regiment moved back to Washington. From mid–August until mid–November the unit operated in South Carolina, taking part in siege operations on Folly and Morris islands against Confederate forces at Ft. Wagner and Ft. Gregg and again at Ft. Sumter in Charleston Harbor, where it remained until mid–January 1865. In early February the regiment moved south into Florida, where it fought in a number of lesser known battles. In late April, the men proceeded north to Virginia, where they fought at Drewry's Bluff (May 14 through 16) and Cold Harbor (June 1 through 12). In mid–June 1864, the regiment became a part of siege operations against Petersburg and Richmond that lasted until early April 1865. On April 3, the regiment became one of the occupying forces in Richmond. The unit was mustered out on June 16, 1865, and discharged at Readville, Massachusetts (now called Hyde Park), on June 30, 1865.

Losses: 5 officers and 67 enlisted men killed and mortally wounded and 125 enlisted men dead from disease.[73]

Regimental Brief for the 4th Regiment, Massachusetts Heavy Artillery: Organized in August 1864, the unit was mustered on November 12,

Left: James Marion Lurvey as a young drummer (courtesy Londonderry Historical Society, Londonderry, New Hampshire). *Right:* A 1949 photograph of James
Marion Lurvey at the age of 102 (courtesy Londonderry Historical Society, Londonderry, New Hampshire).

1864, for a one-year period of service by consolidating the 17th through the
28th unattached heavy artillery units from Massachusetts. It officially
became a regiment on November 12, 1864. Until June 1865, the men performed garrison duty on the south side of the Potomac, near Washington,
D.C. On June 17, 1865, the regiment was mustered out.

Losses: 2 officers and 23 enlisted men dead from disease.[74]

Veteran's Brief: James Marion Lurvey was like so many others: still a
boy when he enlisted as a musician (a drummer) five months shy of his
15th birthday. He was mustered into the 40th Regiment, Massachusetts
Infantry, on August 23, 1862.

Lurvey was born in Palmyra, Maine, but his family moved to Lowell,
Massachusetts, when he was 10 years old. Lowell was a northern mill town
located not far from the Maine-New Hampshire border. Most likely the
Lurveys moved there looking for work.[75]

While serving with the 40th in the Military District of Washington,
Lurvey frequently became ill (years later, after looking at Lurvey's wartime
image, his granddaughter described his build as "slight" and his appearance
as "childlike").[76] During the late spring of 1863, he found himself in a Washington, D.C., hospital because of an illness, perhaps diarrhea or dysentery
Decades later, he suffered from bouts of chronic diarrhea as noted in the

1890 census records (see Appendix C to learn about the special 1890 U.S. Census and Veterans Schedule). After his recovery, Lurvey was sent back to the field. But on his way to join his unit at Gettysburg, Pennsylvania, his regiment clashed with the Army of Northern Virginia. Because of his age and frailness, Lurvey was assigned to the Medical Corps, where he worked in a field surgical tent during and after the battle. This is what he remembered: "I was to stand by and carry out the soldiers' arms and legs as the doctors amputated them. I guess that was the day I grew up and left boyhood forever, and I wasn't yet sixteen."[77]

Lurvey's health continued to deteriorate after Gettysburg. Eventually he was discharged at Portsmouth, New Hampshire, on October 3, 1863. Less than a year later (August 25, 1864), he reenlisted in the 4th Regiment, Massachusetts Heavy Artillery, again as a drummer. Much to his relief, during the brief time he was with the regiment he saw no action.[78]

After the war, Lurvey joined the Merchant Marines and traveled the world. After eight years at sea, he returned to New Hampshire and became a carpenter and later a poultry farmer. On June 13, 1874, he married Sarah M. McConnell, a schoolteacher from Canaan, New Hampshire. The union brought forth four daughters and lasted seventy-four years.[79] But Lurvey had a dark side that countered his mild demeanor and weak constitution. According to newspaper clippings from an August 1902 Manchester, New Hampshire, newspaper, a robber stole an American Express Company package containing approximately $2,700 (the exact amount was $2,711). The account went on to state that while wearing a mask and brandishing a revolver the thief threw red pepper into the eyes of James H. McDermott, acting station agent, to disarm him before making off with the heist. At the time, Lurvey was serving as a postmaster in the fourth-class post office in Goff's Falls (now part of Manchester), where the robbery took place. As an alibi, Lurvey told friends that his newfound wealth was from a blacksmithing business he had recently sold in Providence, Rhode Island. On October 24, 1903, a Nashua, New Hampshire, jury thought otherwise. Lurvey, now 55 years old, was found guilty of the crime and sentenced to New Hampshire's state prison "for not less than six nor more than 10 years."[80] The harsh sentence was imposed despite much sympathy and a request for leniency by the GAR. There was considerable damaging evidence that made it particularly difficult for the defense, however. While in Providence, Lurvey was "unusually well supplied and free with money immediately following the robbery."[81] Further, Lurvey, seeking an alibi, gave $200 to a Providence woman, asking that she testify on his behalf "that they were at her house in Providence on Aug. 27, 1902 [the date of the robbery], when, as a matter of fact, she testified, he was not there on that day."[82] The case was all but sealed after the handkerchief worn by the thief (when and where it was found is unclear) during the robbery bore the same laundry mark found on clothes worn by the defendant.[83]

According to the *Portsmouth Herald* (Portsmouth, NH) of February 14, 1907, Lurvey was pardoned by the governor after serving a little more than three of his six to ten year sentence. His release was granted because of declining health. For the most part, the next 35-plus years of Lurvey's life remained undocumented.

Years later, when asked how he managed to live so long, he deduced that it was from eating "bountiful breakfasts, drinking 'fortified' morning coffee (with brandy, of course) and good genes from the Lurvey side of the family." A true New Englander, he loved to eat lobster and proudly proclaimed that if he could he'd eat it every day of his life. Even at the age of 102, he could still tell a ribald joke, as writer and historian Jay S. Hoar revealed in one of his books: "There's the one about the Police Officer Moriarty," Lurvey said. "He was walking along the street when a woman asked him if he had the time. Moriarty replied.... But on second thought, you'd better not quote me on that one."[84]

Recent postings on the Internet by the Gettysburg National Military Park (U.S. National Park Service) acknowledged James Marion Lurvey as the "most likely ... sole survivor of Meade's army" and "the last living link to the Battle of Gettysburg." Though Lurvey attended the commemoration of the fiftieth anniversary of the Battle of Gettysburg, he decided against attending the seventy-fifth. He had been offended by the consumption of alcoholic beverages at the prior event held twenty-five years before.[85]

Upon his death at the age of 102 no mention was made of James Marion Lurvey's criminal past. His funeral was held at his home in Goff Falls, New Hampshire. The soldier born in Maine who served in a Massachusetts regiment and lived a large part of his life in New Hampshire died while a patient at a veterans hospital near the New Hampshire border. The old soldier's remains are buried at Pleasant View Cemetery in Londonderry.[86] He is interred next to his wife and two of his daughters, Lula and Gladys.

New Jersey

George Ashby
(b. January 25, 1844, d. April 26, 1946)
*Co. H, 22nd Regiment, U.S. Colored Troops (USCT),
and Co. H, 45th Regiment, U.S. Colored Troops*

OUR COLORED TROOPS AT WORK—THE FIRST LOUISIANA NATIVE GUARDS DISEMBARKING AT FORT MACOMB, LOUISIANA—SKETCHED BY OUR SPECIAL ARTIST.
[SEE PAGE 145.]

The First Louisiana Native Guards in which George Ashby was a soldier (NPS.gov, *Harpers Weekly* 7 [February 28, 1863], 133).

Regimental Brief: This black regiment was organized at Philadelphia, Pennsylvania, in January 1864. The regiment's first assignment was at Yorktown, Virginia, where it remained until May 1864. From early May until mid–June, the soldiers took part in General Butler's operations south of the James River and against Petersburg and Richmond. Shortly thereafter the soldiers guarded supply transport wharves along the James River, where they also constructed battle fortifications. From mid–June of 1864 until early April of 1865, the regiment participated in the siege against Petersburg and Richmond. During that period, the regiment fought in the Battle of Chaffin's Farm, New Market Heights (September 29 and 30) and Fair Oaks (October 27 and 28). On April 3, 1865, the soldiers helped occupy the former Confederate capital of Richmond. Later they were moved to Washington, D.C., where they were given the honor of participating in the obsequies of Abraham Lincoln and afterward the hunt for the assassins. The soldiers were then ordered to Texas until October 1865. The regiment mustered out on October 16, 1865.

Losses: 2 officers and 70 enlisted men killed and mortally wounded and an officer and 144 enlisted men dead from disease.[87]

Veteran's Brief: In August 1864, George Ashby, a 20-year-old free black man originally from Virginia, was living in the hamlet of Crosswicks about twelve miles from Allentown, New Jersey, when he decided to enlist in the Union army as a private. Patriotism aside, the enlistment bonus of $100 probably played a large part in his decision, as he was a simple farmer and the money was probably considered a godsend. The 22nd Regiment, U.S. Colored Troops, consisted of approximately 90 percent New Jersey men, most of whom mustered in the beginning of 1864 and had already experienced combat in the Petersburg and Richmond area when Ashby arrived for duty. For the next eight months, Ashby took part in the Siege of Petersburg and the Siege of Richmond, which encompassed several major battles in late 1864 and early 1865.[88]

Shortly after the fighting in Virginia ended, veterans from the regiment were discharged, but not before taking part in President Lincoln's funeral procession and the hunt for his assassin. The remaining men with time left on their enlistment, which included Ashby, were transferred to Co. H, 45th Regiment, U.S. Colored Troops. The regiment, now part of the XXV Corps, was dispatched to the Texas border "as a show of force to intimidate Emperor Maximilian from encroaching onto American territory." While in Brownsville, Texas, Ashby was promoted to first sergeant for his gallantry in action.[89] In November 1865 the unit was mustered out. Ashby returned to New Jersey, where he married Phoebe Cole and along with her raised nine children.

When interviewed years later, Ashby was keen to talk about World War II. "Fighting's different nowadays, but, if I were younger, I certainly would enlist all over again," he said. He also predicted an all-out victory by the Allies but only after a difficult struggle.[90]

Up until the end, George Ashby was said to be "sharp witted" and in full possession of his faculties. He died at the age of 102 and is buried in the Hamilton Street Cemetery in Allentown, New Jersey.[91]

George Ashby left a fitting legacy. Harold J. Ashby, George's grandson, became a graduate of Rutgers University and Rutgers School of Law and eventually went on to become a deputy state attorney general and chairman of the state parole board. At the time, both offices were the highest that an African American had presided over in the State of New Jersey.[92]

New York

The story about this veteran unfolds in a later chapter for reasons that will eventually become obvious.

Ohio

Daniel A. Clingaman
(b. September 25, 1846, d. February 18, 1951)
Co. D, 195th Regiment, Ohio Volunteer Infantry

Regimental Brief: Organized at Camp Chase, Ohio, the regiment was mustered into service between March 14 and March 20, 1865. The regiment first moved to Harpers Ferry, West Virginia, before heading to Winchester, Virginia. On April 28, it was ordered to Alexandria, Virginia, where it performed provost duty for several months after the war had ended. The unit was mustered out on December 18, 1865.

Losses: 32 enlisted men dead from disease.[93]

Veteran's Brief: According to Judy Miller, Daniel A. Clingaman's great-granddaughter, Daniel and his elder brother Andrew happened to be in Wauseon, Ohio, on the day when men were drafted into the Union army. While watching the proceedings unfold, Andrew looked at his brother and said, "I wonder who the next one will be?" Paradoxically the name pulled from the lottery was none other than his own (Andrew Jackson Clingaman). Jack, as he was called, said to Daniel, "I don't want to be drafted, let's volunteer." On the next day they enlisted in the 195th Regiment, Ohio Volunteer Infantry. Unlike his brother, Daniel was paid $300 by serving as a substitute for a resident in Defiance, Ohio. He gave the money to his mother, who in turn loaned it to a needy family from Bryan, Ohio.[94]

During their brief tours, the brothers experienced some skirmishing but nothing greater, as the war was rapidly winding down. (A third brother, John, had enlisted earlier with the 10th Regiment, Ohio Volunteer Cavalry.) The regiment's nemesis was not combat but disease, which took a substantial toll on their ranks.[95]

When the unit mustered out in December 1865, Daniel Clingaman became a blacksmith in the small town of Tedrow (also called Spring Hill),

A proud Daniel A. Clingaman holds his great-granddaughter Judy Miller (courtesy Judy Miller).

Ohio, before he decided to take up farming as a livelihood. The money he earned at enlistment for serving as a substitute was never repaid. The family from Bryan was too destitute to make restitution to his mother.[96]

On December 22, 1874, Clingaman married Louisa Ellen Minnich. They had two children: a son, Peter, and a daughter, Jessie. Several years later, Clingaman bought land north of Wauseon, Ohio, where he built a Victorian home for his family.[97]

Still spry in 1938, Clingaman, along with his daughter, Jessie, attended the commemoration of the seventy-fifth anniversary of the Battle of Gettysburg. According to his great-granddaughter, the New York Central Railroad made an exclusive stop in Wauseon to pick them up on the way to Pennsylvania.

At the age of 103, and now needing assistance, Clingaman moved in with his daughter and son-in-law. A year later he passed away. Daniel A. Clingaman's remains rest in Wauseon Union Cemetery, Wauseon, Ohio.[98]

Oregon

James W. Smith
(b. July 8, 1842, d. March 22, 1951)
Olney's Detachment of the Oregon Cavalry

Regimental Brief: No official records exist for this detachment. What is known is that this forty-man cavalry troop was organized in July 1864 and was responsible for patrolling and providing security at strategic locations along the Columbia River Gorge.[99] The cavalry unit, however, lasted but three months before being disbanded because of questionable activities by the men.[100]

Veteran's Brief: For years, the State of Oregon recognized Theodore A. Penland as their last Civil War veteran. A true gentleman, Penland held an enviable and unblemished record of service to his state and community. During the postwar years,

A detail image of James W. Smith taken near his homestead (courtesy Oregon Historical Society, Portland [OrHi 23687]).

he joined a number of civil and veterans organizations and his contributions to each group were considered exemplary. Adding to his list of illustrious achievements, Penland served as the last commander in chief of the Grand Army of the Republic (1948–1949). But only after another veteran passed away with greater longevity than Penland did the state realize their mistake. Fortunately for James W. Smith, a former private in the Union army, he died before learning that he was to be celebrated as Oregon's last Civil War veteran.[101] Why fortunate? There is every reason to believe that Smith might have preferred to hide under a rock than accept the honor. In many ways, it was better that he died before the reputation of his detachment caught up to him nearly a century after the war ended.

Smith served in the Union army for only 90 days. The detachment in which he was assigned developed quite a reputation, all the reasons considered unfavorable. For nearly the entire tour of duty, Smith's detachment plundered local civilians living along the Columbia River Gorge. Their scams entailed some fairly deceitful, dishonorable, and unlawful maneuvers, none of which had anything to do with the military or the war. For instance, men of the detachment sold their coats and other military supplies in one town, while claiming in another that Indians had seized the items in battle. Days later, the detachment placed requisitions for new coats and supplies through the military supply system. They did this not once but on numerous occasions. The detachment also had the reputation of operating a "protection racket," making money the old fashion way: stealing from friends and neighbors. The detachment came to be called "Olney's Forty Thieves" by regular army soldiers familiar with their unscrupulous activities. It was not long before military authorities caught on to their antics and disbanded the entire unit. James W. Smith returned to Lebanon, the town in which he was born and where it is said he lived a life outside the limelight. For many years, he prospected for gold and bragged that at the age of 90 he was still earning a living.[102]

Though a veteran, he never applied for a pension nor did he ever apply for membership in the GAR. Up until his death at the age of 108 he was still spry. According to the *Lebanon Express* in a front-page article published five days after the veteran's passing, he went deer hunting, tended a small garden near his one-room cabin, and did his own housecleaning chores up until the age of 105.[103] Not surprisingly, his obituaries in the *Albany Democrat-Herald*, the *Lebanon Express*, and the *Portland Oregonian* never mentioned his detachment's less-than-glorious exploits. How deeply James W. Smith was involved in the detachment shenanigans no one will ever know. Certainly there is guilt by association that continues to tarnish the legacy of all the detachment's members. Although it does not justify any of the men's questionable actions during their abbreviated service, the period through which they lived was a difficult one. Certainly "mistakes were made." In a guest editorial published in the *Portland Oregonian* the contributor suggested the best way for James W. Smith to be remembered: "It seems to us that Uncle Jimmy's fame should rest primarily on his personification of Oregon's early struggles. The attributes of the sturdy pioneers—fortitude, a willingness to work hard, common sense—all were his. He exerted them not only in his home state but all over the west…. He retained them to the last."[104]

Pennsylvania

Charles H. Duckworth
(b. December 6, 1846, d. April 10, 1949)

*Co. I, 18th Regiment, Pennsylvania Cavalry (163rd Volunteers),
and Co. F, 3rd Regiment, Pennsylvania Provisional Cavalry*

Regimental Brief for the 18th Regiment, Pennsylvania Cavalry:
Organized at Pittsburg and Harrisburg, Pennsylvania, between October

Pennsylvania veterans marching during the 49th National Encampment of the Grand Army of the Republic, September 30 and October 1, 1915, held at Washington, D.C. (Library of Congress).

and December of 1862, the regiment was first assigned in-state duty before being ordered to Washington, D.C., where it remained until June 1863. After fighting a few skirmishes in Virginia, the regiment returned to Pennsylvania and fought in the Battle of Gettysburg (July 1 through 3). From July 1863 until year's end the regiment had a number of clashes in places like Williamsport and Hunterstown, Pennsylvania, and Rapidan, James City, and Culpeper, Virginia. In early 1864 the regiment prepared fortifications near Richmond. From May 5 through May 7 it fought in the Wilderness, and from June into August it participated in the Siege of Petersburg. The skirmishing continued for the regiment while in Virginia through September before it participated in the Battle of Cedar Creek in mid–October. For the next several months and into May of 1865, it remained in or near Winchester, Virginia, and was then ordered to Cumberland, Maryland. In June the cavalry unit was consolidated with the 22nd Pennsylvania Cavalry to form the 3rd Provisional Cavalry.

Losses: 5 officers and 55 enlisted men killed and mortally wounded and 2 officers and 232 enlisted men dead from disease.[105]

Regimental Brief for the 3rd Regiment, Pennsylvania Provisional Cavalry: The 3rd was organized at Cumberland, Maryland, on June 24, 1865, by consolidation of the 18th and the 22nd Pennsylvania Cavalry. It saw duty at Clarksburg, West Virginia, until October 1865. The regiment was mustered out on October 31, 1865.

Veteran's Brief: Though he lived a long life, Charles H. Duckworth left only a scant paper trail to depict his legacy. One of the few documents found is a record from the Commonwealth of Pennsylvania, Department of Military Affairs, that lists his final place of interment. This single record incorrectly lists Duckworth's middle initial as "I." It does, however, acknowledge him as the "Last Penna" [Pennsylvania] survivor of the Civil War.[106]

Charles H. Duckworth (left) standing next to store proprietor Edward "Ned" Duckworth. Ned was killed in Italy during World War II (courtesy *Lansdale* [PA] *Advance of Bucks County*).

What we do know is that Duckworth already had three brothers in the service before he enlisted at sixteen, lying about his age. His decision was prompted by a call for 10,000 able-bodied men to reinforce defensive lines in the vicinity of the nation's capital. Though it was just before Gettysburg, he never saw action there. He served as a private in both Co. I, 18th Regiment, Pennsylvania Cavalry (163rd Volunteers), and Co. F, 3rd Regiment, Pennsylvania Provisional Cavalry. While with the 18th, he must have experienced considerable combat as delineated in the regimental histories for units in which he served. Luckily he was never wounded in action.[107] There was a fortunate event Duckworth liked to reminisce about in his later years. He was one of the few surviving veterans who had seen Lincoln in Washington, D.C. His mounted regiment was passing the Capitol when he got a glimpse of the president.[108]

By the time Duckworth turned eighteen, he had been promoted to sergeant. On October 31, 1865, he was discharged from the army at Cumberland, Maryland.[109] Four years later he married Mary K. Pownail, a marriage that produced seven children. For years, the Duckworths lived in Bucks County, Pennsylvania, where Charles supported his family by working as a cabinetmaker and carpenter for over fifty years.[110] Even at the age of ninety-nine he was capable of walking unassisted in the downtown area of Newtown, Pennsylvania, where he lived for a number of years, stopping frequently to chat or buy chewing tobacco.[111]

When he died at his final residence in Newtown, he was 102 years old. He had outlived his wife by 17 years and all three of his older brothers by at least fifty years. Duckworth was the last commander of the Cpt. H. Clay Beatty GAR Post No. 73 in Bristol, Pennsylvania. His remains lie in Newtown Cemetery, Newtown, Pennsylvania, along with those of his wife and two of his daughters: Emma P., born in 1875, and Eleanor F., born in 1887. Neither ever married.[112]

Rhode Island

John Henry Riley II
(b. June 9, 1841, d. May 7, 1943)
Co. H, 2nd Regiment, Rhode Island Volunteer Infantry

Regimental Brief: After being organized at Providence, Rhode Island, in June 1861 the regiment proceeded to Camp Sprague in Washington, D.C., where it remained until July 16, 1861, before proceeding to Manassas, Virginia, and fighting in the Battle of Bull Run (July 21). After the Union defeat, the regiment headed back to Washington and remained there until March 1862. In late March, it took part in the Peninsula Campaign, fighting at the Battle of Williamsburg (May 5), the Battle of Fair Oaks (May 31 through June 1), the Seven Days Battle around Richmond (June 25 through July 1), and Malvern Hill (July 1). After the battles the regiment moved toward Harrison's Landing, where it remained until mid–August. For the next several months the soldiers performed reconnaissance duty while moving throughout Virginia. Then, in December, the regiment fought in the Battle of Fredericksburg (December 12 through 15) while also taking part in the infamous "Mud March" a month later. For the next few months, it participated in two major battles: Chancellorsville (April 27 through May 6) and Gettysburg (July 1 through 3). In 1864, it fought in more major battles: the Wilderness (May 5 through 7); Spotsylvania (May 8 through 12); and Cold Harbor (June 1 through 12). Around the middle of June, battle-weary veterans whose enlistments were ready to expire were mustered out. From mid–June to early July, the regiment was at Petersburg. On the 9th of July it was ordered to Washington, D.C., to repulse General Early's attack on the city (July 11 and 12), eventually returned to Petersburg in early December and participated in that siege until April 1865. From March 28 through

Left: **Twenty-two-year-old John Henry Riley as a Union soldier (courtesy Jay S. Hoar; from the collection of granddaughter Gladys L. Parker).**

   Right: **A spry and confident John Henry Riley II sits outside his home (courtesy Lloyd L. Colvin).**

April 9 the soldiers took part in the Appomattox Campaign and witnessed the fall of Petersburg. From April 3 through 9 the regiment continued to pursue General Lee's army. In late May and into early June, it marched to Washington. On July 13, 1865, it mustered out.

Losses: 9 officers and 111 enlisted men killed and mortally wounded and 2 officers and 74 enlisted men dead from disease.[113]

Veteran's Brief: When asked the secret to his longevity, John Henry Riley II told his listeners, "Go ahead. Do what you want. But never cross the line of moderation."[114] Riley certainly lived life to the fullest; as to moderation, he probably told a white lie. He loved a good time, "had a rugged constitution," and enjoyed his ale, especially with friends who always seemed to appear like clockwork when Riley's pension check arrived by mail. They all departed to visit Jackson Tavern, in Jackson, Rhode Island (an unincorporated town where Riley had built the tavern for another individual). As the story goes, the "boys" travelled to the tavern each day to play cards, smoke, and drink until Riley's funds were depleted—usually within three days. The fun was over, until Riley's next pension check arrived.

According to his great-grandson, Lloyd Lincoln Colvin, his great-grandfather's demeanor appeared gruff, at least on the surface. Though some were taken aback by the "Old Gent" (that's what many called him) and his brusque personality, others knew it was just his way. Colvin remembers that as Riley aged his clothing appeared disheveled and loose fitting. "As a youngster, I used to sit on his lap after dinner and listen to his stories," Colvin said. "I talked to him a great deal and took a keen interest in everything he had to say about the war." Colvin especially relished stories about how his great-grandfather saw President Lincoln while Riley was stationed in Washington, D.C., and that on one occasion Riley even got to shake his hand when Lincoln paid a visit to his regiment in camp.

Those who knew Riley said he possessed a remarkable memory throughout his entire life. Colvin remembers that his great-grandfather didn't take kindly to General Sickles' advance toward a wheat field (aka the Wheatfield) at the Battle of Gettysburg—an unauthorized maneuver that jeopardized the safety of the troops. "He wasn't very happy about that," Colvin reiterated. Riley also told his great-grandson that he witnessed Pickett's Charge but only from a distance, as Riley's regiment was not directly engaged that day. They were, though, as written in the state's adjutant general's report, "constantly moving under a storm of shells to different parts of the field, in support of points hard pressed."[115]

John Riley II was born in Dover, New Jersey, to parents who emigrated from Ireland. His father had worked the iron mines for a number of years. Riley was only a year old when the family moved to Johnston, Rhode Island.

In his youth, he worked in Morgan Mill in Johnston being paid 75 cents a week. Though he never received much of a formal education (two years of schooling at best), he did learn to read, write, and, as Riley himself said, "reckon."

Riley enlisted on February 28, 1863, and experienced quite a bit of fighting in a regiment that had already seen its fair share of combat. He wanted to fight not because he was patriotic, which he was, or a Lincoln Republican—which he was, a staunch one at that—but because he wanted to avenge the death of his father, John, mortally wounded at First Bull Run and who died four days later in a Richmond prison pen. For the rest of his life, Riley never forgot standing on a sidewalk in Providence watching his father leave for war. Adding to his ill feelings was the fact that his brother was seriously wounded at Manassas.

After his regiment took part in the Grand Parade in Washington, D.C., Riley was discharged from the service on July 13, 1865. He moved to Scituate, Rhode Island, and worked as a millwright in local mills around Pawtucket Valley, where his skills at the trade seemed to be in constant demand. He also worked as a carpenter, mechanic, farmer, steam stationary engineer, and even stagecoach driver.

Working in a mill a few months after his discharge, Riley met Anna Marie Mason, who was originally from Newport, Rhode Island, but living in Arctic (now part of West Warwick, Rhode Island). Their affection for one another was immediate. When his mother found out that her good Irish Catholic son intended to marry a Protestant, she immediately and vehemently protested. Riley was determined to marry Anna Marie and told his mother that nothing could stop him. Thinking it a grave sin and a serious stain upon the family name, his mother, in a state of rage, threatened to have him killed if he went through with the engagement and wedding. She even went so far as to tell another of her sons to kill him. "I can't do that," the brother protested, obviously upset at his mother's insane proposal. The marriage did take place, however, and eventually produced eleven children. But the animosity continued unabated within the family for years.

Riley was 80 years old when he decided to retire. After Anna Marie passed away during the influenza pandemic of 1918, he moved to a two-room summer house owned by one of his four sons (the chief of police of Scituate). Though he entertained his friends in the smaller house, Riley ate his meals and slept at his son and daughter-in-law's home next door. He knew not to be an unnecessary burden on the family, maintaining his own sense of independence.

Once a member of the GAR, he had let his membership lapse fifty years earlier. But at the age of 100, he was convinced, perhaps by outside influences, to renew his association with the veterans group. In his final year, Riley told a newspaper reporter that he was "at peace with the Lord and ready when the time came." During the last six months of his life, his health deteriorated badly. His Irish pride never wavered, however. On his deathbed, although gasping for every breath, he whispered in his great-grandson's ear, "I was the last of 24,000 Rhode Islanders … mostly Irish." When he died at the home of his son, John H. Riley III, the aged veteran was a month shy of his 102nd birthday.

Riley's funeral was attended by an estimated 500 people. The coffin in which the body was placed was lifted onto a caisson and drawn to the funeral service and then the cemetery by a team of horses. Colvin attended his great-grandfather's funeral and distinctly remembers the funeral escort included six Spanish American War veterans, a fife and drum, and a bagpiper. John Henry Riley II lies at rest in Manchester Cemetery in Coventry, Rhode Island. But the story of John Henry Riley II does not end here.

In 2009, Lloyd Lincoln Colvin erected a lasting tribute to his beloved great-grandfather in Hope, Rhode Island. Along with family members, friends and neighbors, Colvin erected a black India granite memorial in his side yard that was placed in the center of a position aptly named Lincoln Circle. Etched by laser at the top of the stone is an image of Riley, enhanced at the lower level by laser-etched artwork of major battles in which he fought

A monument to John Henry Riley II, erected on the property of his great-grandson Lloyd L. Colvin (photograph by author).

and including battle descriptors. It might be the only such memorial erected on private property for any of the states' last surviving veterans. On July 11, 2009, honored guests and state dignitaries joined together to help consecrate the monument.[116]

Before we leave Rhode Island, there are two other veterans from the state worth mentioning. When Edward F. Gillett of Providence died on February 2, 1943, a Rhode Island newspaper erroneously reported that he was the last Civil War veteran from the state (he actually was third from the last). Gillett had served with the 22nd Regiment, Michigan Volunteer Infantry. Two months later, on May 1, 1943, Joseph Thomas Ray died at the age of 96. Had he lived another seven days, he would have unseated John H. Riley II as the last Civil War veteran from the state. Born a slave in Virginia, Ray escaped bondage and managed to find his way to Newport, Rhode Island, most assuredly via the Underground Railroad. In the spring of 1865, at the age of 18 and living in Bristol (across Narragansett Bay from Aquidneck Island), Ray and a companion trekked to Providence to enlist in the 14th Regiment, Rhode Island Heavy Artillery (Colored). But enlistments were closed for that regiment; therefore, Ray joined the 118th Regiment, United States Colored Troops, staying with them for over a year in the vicinity of Brownsville, Texas.

The second to the last Civil War veteran from Rhode Island was African American Joseph Thomas Ray of Newport, Rhode Island (courtesy *Newport Daily News*).

Joseph Thomas Ray was the last survivor of Newport's Lawton-Warren Post No. 5, of the GAR. When he died the post ceased to exist. His funeral took place at Newport's Mt. Zion African Methodist Church. Ray's earthly remains were laid to rest in the family plot at Newport's city cemetery.

Vermont

Gilbert Charles Lucier
(b. April 8, 1847, d. September 22, 1944)
Co. F, 1st Regiment, Vermont Heavy Artillery (originally mustered in as the 11th Vermont Infantry). Subsequently transferred to

the Veterans Reserve Corps (VRC). The VRC was organized to free up able-bodied soldiers for the field by giving light duty assignments to partially disabled soldiers.

Regimental Brief: The regiment was formed at Brattleboro, Vermont, and mustered in on September 1, 1862. Its first duty was defending Washington, D.C., from September of 1862 to May of 1864. Each company was sent to defend different areas. Company F was ordered to Ft. Bunker Hill until mid–November 1862, then to Ft. Slocum until March 1864 and later to Ft. Thayer until May 1864. On May 12, 1864, the companies were ordered to rejoin the regiment in the field. Three days later, the regiment became part of the 6th Army Corps at Spotsylvania Court House, Virginia. The regiment moved toward Petersburg and fought at the Battle of Cold Harbor (June 1 through 12). To repulse General Early's suspected attack on Washington, the regiment was ordered back to the city. In the ensuing months, the soldiers fought at the Battle of Opequan (September 19) and the Battle of Cedar Creek (October 19). In mid–December it was ordered back to Petersburg, where it took part in the siege until the beginning of April 1865. The soldiers also took part in the pursuit of General Lee's army. Veterans whose enlistments were near expiration were mustered out on June 24, 1865. The remaining veterans and recruits consolidated into a battalion of four companies and were sent to Ft. Foote, Maryland, until August. These men were mustered out on August 25, 1865.

Losses: 10 officers and 154 enlisted men killed and mortally wounded and 2 officers and 410 enlisted men dead from disease.[117]

Veteran's Brief: The contemporary town of Jay, Vermont, a community along the Canadian border where Gilbert Charles Lucier spent most of his life, is a far cry from the one of yesteryear. According to Nancy Price Graff, a freelance writer, "The Jay he [Lucier] lived in had one intersection, a school, small farms, thick stands of trees, and mud deep enough to swallow a horse."[118] Today the town features waterslides in the summer and snow skiing in the winter along with other seasonal attractions to draw year-round tourists.

Gilbert Charles Lucier while still a young man (courtesy Vermont Historical Society, South Barre).

Lucier enlisted as a private on November 9, 1863. When he joined the unit, many of the men he served with in it were already seasoned veterans. Soon he, too, became one. Lucier saw action at the Battle of the Wilderness, the Battle of Spotsylvania, and the Battle of Cold Harbor. At Cold Harbor on June 1, 1864, Lucier was hit in the left leg by a minié ball. His wound became septic. As if that was not bad enough, he contracted typhoid fever. It was his last stint with the 1st Regiment, Vermont Heavy Artillery. He was transported to a Union general hospital in his home state at Montpelier, Vermont, where his chances for recovery were deemed better. After recuperating from his wounds—though never fully—he was officially transferred to the VRC on November 25, 1864.

According to the *Newport Daily Express* and noted in Graff's article, as a member of the VRC Lucier was sent to St. Albans, Vermont, to squelch any further Confederate attacks upon the town. As unbelievable as it seems, on October 19, 1864, twenty-five Confederates crossed the Canadian border and after arriving at St. Albans, robbed several banks and businesses. Though managing to escape unscathed over the border, the Confederates were eventually apprehended by Canadian authorities. The Canadian government returned $88,000 recovered from the men but never extradited the Confederates on the grounds that they were in the military. The raid went down in history as the northernmost land battle of the Civil War. Ironically, on the same day of the Confederate raid at St. Albans while Lucier was recuperating in a Vermont hospital, his former Vermont regiment turned back the Confederates at the Battle of Cedar Creek in Virginia. There the regiment earned its greatest triumph of the war.[119]

On September 1, 1865, months after the war officially ended, Lucier was discharged. He returned home to Jay. His wound had healed, but the resultant limp remained for the rest of his life. Lucier married Lucy Ann King of Berkshire, Vermont, and fathered five children, of which only two survived to adulthood.[120] According to Graff, "He could read and write, and owned his home and farm. But he had pretty much seen all of the world he was ever going to see."[121] Perhaps that is all he wanted—to be back home and out of harm's way. In her article, Graff recounts an episode taken from Lucier's short biography. A great-grandnephew drove Lucier to the commemoration of the seventy-fifth anniversary of the Battle of Gettysburg. The nephew wandered off for a short while from the tent they were assigned to. When he returned, Lucier asked where he had been. The nephew replied, "I've been across the road talking with Confederate veterans." Lucier, none too happy, responded, "Start packing. We're going home."[122]

During the post–Civil War years, Lucier enjoyed telling folks about meeting President Lincoln, thereby joining the ranks of fellow veterans like

Michael Bon Doll of Nebraska, John Riley II of Rhode Island, and James Albert Hall of New York, who were fortunate to have a similar and unique experience.[123] During his long life Lucier was elected to the Vermont legislature (1891 and 1920) and was Jay's road commissioner for two decades.[124]

Gilbert Charles Lucier, a staunch Republican and Lincoln man, died at Orleans County Memorial Hospital at the age of 97. The blue house in Jay where he lived is still standing but the entire contents were sold at auction, much to the chagrin of at least one of Lucier's descendants.[125]

Wisconsin

Lansing Alphonse Wilcox
(b. March 3, 1846, d. September 29, 1951)

Co. F, 4th Regiment, Wisconsin Volunteer Cavalry
(originally mustered in as the 4th Regiment, Wisconsin Infantry)

Regimental Brief: Organized at Racine, Wisconsin, on July 2, 1861, the cavalry first guarded railroad lines near Baltimore, Maryland, while spending most of its time there until February of 1862. From mid–February through mid–April the cavalry was stationed in Mississippi before proceeding to New Orleans, Louisiana, at the end of the month. After occupying New Orleans for three months, the regiment fought at the Battle of Baton Rouge on August 5, 1862. It spent over a year operating throughout Louisiana at places with names Northerners had never heard before: Carrollton, Camp Parapet, Opelousas, Chicot, Bayou Boeuf, Port Hudson, Clinton, Donaldsville, and Black Bayou. Much of the area was swampland wrought with disease that took a heavy toll on the soldiers. The regiment moved to Baton Rouge at the end of July and operated there until September 1863. On August 22, 1863, the designation of the regiment was changed to the 4th Wisconsin Cavalry. Continuing to skirmish, scout, picket and operate against guerrillas and take part in several expeditions, the regiment remained in Louisiana for the remainder of the war with the exception of a few expeditions into Mississippi, Alabama,

A detail of Lansing A. Wilcox (courtesy Wisconsin Historical Society, Madison).

and Georgia. After returning to Baton Rouge, in May 1866, the cavalry was ordered to perform guard duty and patrol along the Rio Grande from Brownsville to Laredo, Texas. The soldiers were mustered out at Brownsville on May 28, 1866, before moving to Madison, Wisconsin, where they were discharged on June 19, 1866.

Losses: 11 officers and 106 enlisted men killed and mortally wounded and 3 officers and 311 enlisted men dead from disease.[126]

Veteran's Brief: Enlisting as a private at the age of 17 on February 17, 1864, at Chippewa Falls, Lansing A. Wilcox spent the next year and two months performing scout and picket duty throughout Louisiana. When the war ended, the regiment was ordered to Texas, where the men patrolled along the Rio Grande until mustering out in late May of 1866. After the war ended, Wilcox returned to Wisconsin, but soon moved to Kansas. For whatever reason, he went back to Wisconsin after only a few years. In 1873 he married Matilda Amelia Ginnold. After eight years of marriage the couple separated and eventually divorced.[127]

In 1881, Wilcox moved to Cadott, Wisconsin, where he worked several occupations over the years: sawmill operator, schoolteacher, and village assessor. A year later, he applied for his government pension. In 1888, he met and married Mary Ann Kaiser. This union lasted for over thirty-eight years.[128] Approximately twenty years later, while still living in Cadott, he became the village postmaster, a position he held for a decade.[129]

In 1928, Wilcox moved to Tacoma, Washington. Exactly why he decided to move to Tacoma remains a mystery. Not long after his arrival there, he transferred his GAR membership to the State of Washington. Soon he was named GAR department commander of Washington and Alaska. Apparently things did not work out as planned, as he moved back to Wisconsin in 1938. Five years later at the 1943 National GAR Encampment held in Milwaukee, he was elected national senior vice commander in chief.[130]

Wilcox married two more times, first to Mary F. Sutherland. After her death, he married Marie Buttke four years later on December 2, 1942. Marie happened to be thirty-four years his junior. On farm land near Cadott, he and his fourth wife built a small house where they raised chickens and cultivated a garden.[131]

In 1949, Wilcox traveled to the last GAR National Encampment, in Indianapolis, and experienced his first plane ride. Shortly after the encampment, his age caught up with him. He became ill and was admitted for the fifth and final time to the Grand Army Home at King, Wisconsin. While there, he celebrated his 105th birthday with his wife, along with members of the Sons of Union Veterans of the Civil War and staff from the Grand Army Home. A God-fearing man, on his previous birthdays and if his health permitted, Wilcox donated $25 to each church in Cadott. He had now reached the point where he was unable to do so, physically and perhaps financially.[132] Near the end, although he could still recognize names and faces, he could no longer sit upright in a wheelchair.[133] His days were numbered. The headline in the October 4, 1951, edition of the *Thorp Courier* noted his passing accordingly: "Lansing A. Wilcox, Wisconsin's last surviving veteran of the Civil war, is dead."[134] His remains rest at Brooklawn Cemetery in Cadott, Wisconsin.

Before closing this chapter, it is worth mentioning a brief comment Wilcox made to a reporter during his twilight years: "What a wonderful thing [it is] to be an American citizen."[135] Certainly scores of Civil War veterans felt the same way.

Chapter 3

The District of Columbia

Prior to the outbreak of the Civil War, the nation's capital was a small city with approximately 2,000 inhabitants. During the summer months, the population became even less dense as residents fled the area seeking relief from the high temperatures, unbearable humidity, and disease-infested waters. President Abraham Lincoln and his family also found the conditions unbearable. On June 13, 1862, the Lincolns moved from the White House to a Gothic Revival cottage situated on a hill three miles north of the city. The house was built on the site of the Washington Soldiers' Home, where cool winds brought soothing relief to the Lincolns for the next three summers.

In the mid-nineteenth century, Washington, D.C., did not appear an advantageous place to either live or raise a family. But when the first soldiers arrived to defend the capital, the troop and logistics buildup transformed the slowly developing capital area into a sprawling urban region. Virtually overnight, Washington became the hub of the Union military war effort. Arguably the defensive posture taken to protect the nation's capital against possible Confederate attacks and the enormous continuous outlay of funds to insure its safety sparked the city's phenomenal growth that continues unabated to this day.

Though some veterans were born in Washington, D.C., and remained there long after the conflict, scores of former soldiers and sailors settled within the city limits as the years went by. They came from small towns and diverse walks of life; many were farmers, carpenters, and general laborers. Washington afforded them work opportunities and leisure pursuits they never could have envisioned while living in their home states. The migration was reminiscent of the pre–World War I song, penned just before America's entry into World War I, "How Ya Gonna Keep 'Em Down on the Farm? (After They've Seen Paree)." But the last surviving veteran from the District of Columbia, who happened to be a Confederate, moved to the nation's capital for an entirely different reason.

The District of Columbia

James Albert Spicer
(b. May 15, 1844, d. February 9, 1948)
Company K, 7th Regiment Virginia Cavalry

Regimental Brief: The 7th Regiment Virginia Cavalry was organized in May 1861, at Manassas Junction, Virginia, made up of men from Giles, Madison, Rappahannock, Culpeper, Greene, and Albemarle counties. The 7th saw action at First Manassas. In April 1862, the troop had 700 effectives and later was active in the various campaigns of the Army of Northern Virginia. It participated in Longstreet's Suffolk Expedition, was prominent in the capture of Plymouth, then fought at Drewry's Bluff and Cold Harbor. It continued the fight in the Petersburg trenches south of the James River and around Appomattox. The unit sustained 47 casualties at First Manassas, 77 at Williamsburg, 111 at Frayser's Farm, 59 at Second Manassas, and 4 at Fredericksburg. Of the 335 engaged at Gettysburg about 40 percent were disabled. The 7th lost 39 men at Drewry's Bluff, and many were captured at Five Forks and Sayler's Creek. Only 20 officers and men were present at the surrender.[1]

Veteran's Brief: Inside the pages of the *Orange County Historical Society Newsletter* of December 2006 is a hazy photograph of an aged and bearded James Albert Spicer holding the reins of his horse. With hat in hand, Spicer's right arm is raised in salute to those standing curbside as he and his "spirited horse" pass in review. The year is 1930 and the Confederate veteran is riding in his hometown parade. Spicer looks every bit as majestic as he likely appeared while riding in his heyday with the 7th Virginia Cavalry.[2]

The brief narrative of Spicer's life that follows has been extracted from an article in the aforementioned newsletter that was written by Frank S. Walker, Jr., and titled "James Albert Spicer and His Mill by the Rapidan." Other than this story and an obituary in the city's newspaper, there is little else to go on. But the article contains enough

James Albert Spicer posing with unidentified family members (from "Spicer Descendants" as posted on the Internet).

pertinent details to understand the man and his wit and appreciate his life and labors.[3]

Prior to the war, Spicer was the owner of a grist mill located in Orange County, Virginia. In fact, the operation carried his family's surname: Spicer Mill or Spicer's Mill (no one today is certain whether it should be possessive). Spicer, having worked the mill since his youth, inherited the business from his father, Samuel. When the war commenced, the Confederate government considered Spicer "an essential civilian worker." However, his service exemption lasted only until the Confederacy began showing signs of unraveling. The need for additional able-bodied men appeared apparent and Spicer was ready to join his brother, Walker, who was already serving the cause.

In August 1864, Spicer enlisted as a private in the 43rd Battalion, Virginia Cavalry (Mosby's Rangers). By late October, the Confederate army was assigned to the trenches of Petersburg.[4] In late autumn, he was transferred to Co., K, 7th Virginia Cavalry, a unit that was populated with a large contingent of men from the Culpeper area. By April the Union army had breached the softened Confederate lines. Spicer was captured and sent to Point Lookout, Maryland, as a prisoner of war. In late June, he took the Oath of Allegiance to the United States of America and was released.[5] After

One of the last reunion photographs of Colonel John Singleton Mosby's Rangers (Library of Congress).

returning home, he married Virginia Battle on August 22, 1875. Many years later, and now a widower in his eighties, he moved in with a neighbor, Fred Higgins and family. How long Spicer remained there is unknown, but he eventually moved in with his daughter, whose residence happened to be Washington, D.C.[6]

During the later years, Washington reporters beat a path to Spicer's home looking for good Civil War stories to write, especially those from a former Confederate soldier. Spicer accommodated their requests. Amusing himself, he told some whoppers so unbelievable that any credible reporter who took the time to investigate his tales could have easily seen through his farce. The aged veteran spoke of enlisting at the age of sixteen (he was sixteen a year before the war commenced), engagements he never fought in like Pickett's Charge (the battle took place a year before he enlisted), and his long stay in a Union prisoner of war camp (he was a prisoner for less than three months). For Spicer, it was sheer comic relief. For some gullible reporters, it was words that filled a page and helped meet a deadline.[7]

Spicer died only months shy of his 104th birthday at his daughter's home in Washington. It was a Monday night, February 9, 1948. Upon his death, he was correctly recognized as the last surviving member of Mosby's Rangers but erroneously reported in the obituary section of the *Washington Post* as the last Confederate veteran from Virginia (Martin Luther Peters, who died on October 28, 1951, held that distinction). James Albert Spicer's funeral was held at Walker's United Methodist Church in Madison County, Virginia, and the burial took place in the adjacent churchyard.[8] According to writer Frank S. Walker, Jr., Spicer's descendants have long since departed the area of Virginia where Spicer lived.

Approximately three-and-a-half years earlier, the remains of John Montgomery Kline were laid to rest. He was the last Union soldier from the District of Columbia. On February 10, 1864, he enlisted in the battle-hardened 49th Regiment, Pennsylvania Infantry, as a replacement. Though Kline came into the war near the end, he saw considerable action during his enlistment. He was discharged at Harrisburg, Pennsylvania, a month-and-a-half after General Lee's surrender. Apparently he found army life to his satisfaction, as he reenlisted on September 29, 1866, for a three-year stint.[9]

Almost three months to the day after his discharge, Kline married Orilla Hipsher from Story County, Iowa. He married for a second time two years later to a lady named Catherine Alice Parkinson in Washington, D.C. Before his life was over, he married a third time, to a lady named Margaret (maiden name unknown) also in Washington, D.C. It remains uncertain why Kline married three times. What is known is that he fathered four children, three boys and a girl. To support his family, he worked as a carpenter before finishing his career as a clerk for the U.S. Treasury Department.[10]

John M. Kline died a widower at the U.S. Soldiers Home Hospital in Washington, D.C. He was 97 years old. His remains lie at Rock Creek Cemetery in the nation's capital directly across from the soldiers home that was used by President Lincoln and his family as a summer retreat.

Chapter 4

The Confederacy

A split between the northern and southern states had been brewing for years. Using European immigrants as an inexpensive labor force, northern states were able to significantly expand their efforts at industrialization; but because of an agricultural economy Southern states were highly dependent upon slave labor. The cultivation of rice, cotton, sugar, and tobacco had been the South's livelihood for years, and slaves were needed in abundance to make the system profitable. During the antebellum period the federal government received its income from tariffs. It was a blessing for the northern states, as high tariffs helped protect an industrialized nation. But for the southern states it was a completely different scenario. High tariffs raised the cost of imports on which the South was exceedingly dependent. As well, southern planters feared a loss of political power in Washington if slavery was not allowed to expand into America's territorial acquisitions.

There was also the issue of "states rights." A preponderance of Southerners believed that each state had the right to nullify any federal law that the government enacted. Northerners thought otherwise. Then more trouble began brewing. First, the new Republican Party established a platform aimed at preventing the spread of slavery beyond its then-current boundaries. Second, radical Republicans, many of whom were staunch abolitionists, wanted slavery to end outright. The die was cast in 1860 when former Whig Party member and now Republican Abraham Lincoln won the election for president of the United States. After years of debate, the southern states finally acted on their threat: they seceded from the union. A provisional secessionist government was formed called the Confederate States of America (CSA). This new nation consisted of eleven states that seceded from the Union: Alabama, Arkansas, Florida, Georgia, Louisiana, Mississippi, North Carolina, South Carolina, Tennessee, Texas, and Virginia. Legislatures in the Confederacy established a constitutional government similar to that of the United States of America. The men also elected their first and what proved to be last president: Jefferson Davis. The capital of the newly formed nation was located in Montgomery, Mississippi; but when the Commonwealth of Virginia seceded from the Union after the battle of Ft. Sumter, the capital was moved to Richmond, Virginia.

In 1861, the CSA—also called the "Confederacy" or simply the "South"—had a population of approximately 9 million; of that, over 40 percent were slaves. With regard to manufacturing and existing workforce capabilities, the South fell far short of the North. Whereas the North boasted 101,000 factories, the South could claim only 18,000. Further, the South's labor force was sadly outnumbered. Financially the Union entered the war with $234 million in bank deposits and specie, while the Confederacy could claim only $74 million. The impending conflict was expected to be a four-legged war; the North had nearly three times the number of horses to move soldiers, supplies, and armament than the South. By sheer numbers, the Confederacy seemed doomed from its inception. Yet, amazingly, though Union soldiers and sailors outnumbered Confederate forces by over 2 to 1, the South was victorious in most of the key battles from July of 1861 through the first half of 1863.[1]

It is doubtful that anyone will ever know the exact number of casualties suffered by both sides in the war, but estimates published by the U.S. National Park Service list 642,000 for the North and 483,000 for the South. (By comparing census records before, during and after the war, a recent study places the number substantially higher.) On the surface it appears that the North should have soundly defeated the South—and much earlier than it did. But proportionately, when comparing losses to the entire population for both sides, the South suffered the greater blow. The high number of casualties proved devastating, one from which the South never recovered. In the end, it was not the lack of heart or determination of the Southern soldier that lost the war—far from it—it was the lack of manpower, financial resources, and logistics support that caused the South's ultimate demise.

After the surrender of General Robert E. Lee to General Ulysses S. Grant at Appomattox Courthouse, Lee told his troops, "Boys, I have done the best I could for you. Go home now, and if you make as good citizens as you have soldiers, you will do well." And they did "do well."[2] But their struggle to forge ahead in life did not come without suffering. The carnage inflicted upon Southern soil by "invading Northerners," as Southerners chose to call them, took decades to overcome. When the veterans returned home they found homes ransacked or destroyed, farmland laid waste and their hopes and dreams in ruins. A century later, some of the last surviving veterans from the former Confederacy still held grudges against their wartime adversaries, including the government they fought against and of which they were now, as paroled Confederate soldiers, *reconstituted* U.S. citizens.

When the Confederate veterans returned home after the war, most took up where they had left off. Before the war, 69 percent were farmers and 9 percent laborers. Slightly more than 2 percent were professionals. The numbers likely remained the same after the conflict. Many of the veterans remained in the states where they were born and served as Confederates. But others took more drastic measures. Unwilling to rejoin the union, an estimated 10,000-plus Confederate veterans along with their families migrated to the Portuguese-speaking city of Sao Paulo, Brazil. Though a large percentage returned to the U.S., several hundred took up permanent residence, where they were known as *Confederados*, and remained there until their deaths. Today, descendants of these veterans are scattered throughout Brazil (see Appendix D).[3]

At the close of hostilities, Confederate records were either woefully incomplete or destroyed by Union soldiers as well as by defeated Confederates on the run. Some archived records that did survive were ultimately lost to fires. After the war many veterans who depended on such records found it difficult to substantiate their wartime service, especially when applying for a state pension (they were disqualified from applying for a federal pension for obvious reasons). Therefore, legislators from the former Confederate states took the initiative to rectify the so-called inequality. The earliest to enact state pension laws were Alabama and North Carolina. Both granted disability pensions in 1867 to those who suffered the loss of a limb during the war (North Carolina expanded its criteria to include blindness). Georgia began offering pensions in 1870 to Southern veterans with artificial limbs. All the other former Confederate states followed suit. As time passed, eligibility requirements became more liberal. Pensions were now granted to indigents as well as the disabled. Louisiana and Kentucky eventually approved the granting of pensions to widows of Confederate veterans.[4] Today, several historians have found pensioners from both sides of the conflict with unproven credentials that were highly suspect especially when comparing census birth records. Much of the pension fraud can be attributed to the relaxation of the pension laws over the years that made it relatively easy for anyone to circumvent the system. Also, as the years passed and with a multitude of applications, the work of pension clerks became mind-boggling. The clerks had neither the time nor the help to fully determine the accuracy of each and every claim placed upon them.[5]

The last Civil War survivors from both sides of the conflict were, on average, young boys when they served. They had to be to survive so long into the twentieth century. As with those who served in the Union army, many Southern boys lied about their age to gain enlistment. Many served as home guards or with state militia units where rosters were filled predominately with aged professionals, discharged veterans and a modicum of underage boys.

Presented below are the stories of the last surviving Confederate veterans who died in the former Confederate states. As stated earlier, incomplete Confederate military records, or the lack thereof, are not in the historian's best interest. Not all the veterans discussed below have solid credentials to authenticate their inclusion in this listing. However, the states in which they served validated their status by one means or another; and unless proven otherwise over time, they deserve the honor and recognition so bestowed.

Alabama

The story about this veteran unfolds in a later chapter for reasons that will eventually prove obvious.

Arkansas

John Greene Chisum (aka Chism)
(b. February 19, 1848, d. June 11, 1951)
Maj. Gen. Sterling Price's Arkansas Mounted Infantry
(aka 45th Regiment, Arkansas Cavalry)

Regimental Brief: The 45th Regiment, Arkansas Cavalry, fought from 1864 to 1865. Though authorized by the State Military Board as an infantry regiment, the unit was mounted for Maj. Gen. Sterling Price's Missouri Expedition, thus becoming a mounted infantry regiment—when a numerical designation was added to the regiment's name it was referred to as the 45th Regiment, Arkansas Cavalry. After the regiment was organized in 1864, the men were placed under the command of Maj. Gen. Sterling Price. His mission was to recapture the city of St. Louis for the Confederacy, thereby solidifying control of the State of Missouri. On September 19, 1864, after entering Missouri from northern Arkansas, Price ordered a frontal attack on the Union force heavily fortified behind earthen works. The attack proved disastrous, as his men suffered over 1,000 casualties. Seeing that his plan to capture St. Louis had to be abandoned because the Union had placed 4,500 cavalry and 8,000 infantry in well-fortified positions, Price marched westerly along the Missouri River destroying railroad bridges and track along the route. Though reinforced at Boonville, Price's new recruits were not only unarmed but also undisciplined. As he marched forward, Union generals were setting a trap by slowing his advance with diversionary tactics to his rear while employing flanking maneuvers as he slowly advanced. In the presence of a large Union support force, Price was now outmanned more than two to one. Though his cavalry put up a valiant fight, he was quickly trapped. He did what he thought was best and decided to attack near the town of Westport. In the early morning hours of October 23 the Battle of Westport (also referred to in subsequent years as the "Gettysburg of the West") commenced. The fierce struggle lasted for several hours and both sides experienced heavy casualties. After being brutally pressed on three sides, Price realized his charges were to no avail and he ordered a retreat. Had it not been for Confederate Gen. Joseph Shelby's skilled defensive maneuvers during the evacuation of the battlefield, Price and his men might have faced total annihilation. After fighting several skirmishes to evade capture, Price's remaining force made it through Indian Territory and eventually to Texas, where they found refuge. When the damage was assessed, the Missouri Expedition never came close to achieving its objective. In the end, Price lost approximately 4,000 men. Adding to the humiliation, though casualties were high desertion played a large part in the staggering defeat. After the 45th Regiment, Arkansas Cavalry, surrendered soon after the war the defeated Confederates were paroled on June 5, 1865.[6]

Veteran's Brief: The gentleman highlighted next is not the soldier who took part in the Missouri Expedition described above, but relaying his story is essential in setting the stage.

For years, William Murphy Loudermilk had been accepted as Arkansas' last Civil War veteran. But in 1991, author William Marvel debunked the gentleman's claim of military service by analyzing several U.S. Federal Census records. Loudermilk said he was 16 years old during the Atlanta Campaign (1864), but census records revealed he was only 13 when the war ended.[7] Contrary to Marvel's assessment, author and historian Jay S. Hoar believed Loudermilk to be authentic and so did scores of Arkansas residents over the years. Hoar wrote, "As late as 1948, Old Reb Loudermilk, then 101 years [or close to it], made a 1,000-mile pilgrimage to Murphy [a small town in North Carolina where Loudermilk was born] in an all-out effort to find a person or comrade who had known him, anyone who could testify to his age or that he had soldiered with in the C.S.A."[8] Unfortunately for Loudermilk, all of the men had predeceased him.

Why would an aged man approximately a century old make such a journey with virtually little to gain except to retain his honor? Further, Loudermilk claimed that he entered the Confederate service as a private serving as a water boy, which is certainly plausible for someone as young as he was, before being promoted to bugler—a natural progression—and then in 1864 a sharpshooter, which the Confederacy needed badly, as replacements were difficult to find, thus making age—young or old—a nonfactor.[9] As Loudermilk told it, he never received anything in writing that denoted his mustering out of the Confederate army. He, along with others, was simply told, "It's all over. You may go home." The statement seems a plausible response made by a superior to enlistees who held allegiance to a country that no longer existed.[10]

Recently, Australian author and American Civil War buff Garry Victor Hill investigated Loudermilk's case. Unlike William Marvel, who debunked Loudermilk's service outright, Hill found it "highly probable" that Loudermilk was, in fact, a bona fide Confederate veteran. But Hill still felt reluctant to fully certify the claimant. Using the phrase "almost verifiable," he determined that there were additional areas that required scrutiny. During his investigation Hill learned that attempting to certify Loudermilk as a Civil War veteran was fraught with problems. He determined just as others had in the past that there were local citizens who supported Loudermilk's alleged service, while others "laughed at his Confederate claims and baited him over it."[11]

The jury is still deliberating over Loudermilk's credentials. In lieu of the uncertainty as to Loudermilk's military status, the author has selected the next in line as the last Civil War veteran from South Carolina: John Green Chisum.

Veteran's Brief: Like Loudermilk, Chisum's military service record has never been recovered. But unlike Loudermilk, numerous affidavits were provided attesting to his service as a Confederate soldier when he applied in 1931 to the State of Arkansas for a veteran's pension. Also, unlike Loudermilk, there were no naysayers in Poke County, Arkansas, as Chisum had always been accepted as a former Confederate soldier.

Born in Ben Hur, Arkansas, Chisum joined the Confederate army at the age of sixteen. One can imagine the carnage he witnessed as a young soldier during the Missouri Expedition and subsequent failed raid. Few tales of his wartime experiences survived, but his fourth son, Bill, remembers his telling about what happened to Chisum's father and two of his buddies when they tried to elude capture by Union troops. According to Bill's account, "[T]hey had to swim the Mississippi with their overcoats on, breaking the ice as they went. But they made it and relived it over many times."[12]

Chisum was a farmer for most of his long life right up until the end. He never smoked or drank and, being a proud man, never took handouts.[13] His first marriage, to Nancy Morris, took place in Searcy County, Arkansas, on November 22, 1881. They had ten children before Nancy died on September 4, 1907. Thirteen months later, Chisum married again, on October 17, 1908. His bride's name was Sarah "Sallie" Elizabeth Goswick. Chisum's second marriage produced seven more children, adding to the already over-crowded clan.[14]

Over the ensuing years, Chisum attended numerous United Confederate Veteran reunions, including the largest combined reunion at Gettysburg when he was 90 years old. (Nineteen of the fifty-one Arkansas veterans attending the Diamond Reunion were Union veterans now living within the former Confederate state.)[15] Chisum was said to be in "good shape" up until his 100th birthday; but soon afterward he suffered a debilitating stroke that left him housebound. The Grim Reaper finally arrived, as he always does, and John Greene Chisum was led to his final muster. The 10-year-old Confederate died peacefully in his cabin at Camp Victor. His home had been a former Civilian Conservation Corps (CCC) building that was eventually abandoned and reclaimed for a permanent residence by Chisum.[16] The veteran's remains were interred at Boyd Cemetery, close to Sand Gap, near Hector and Ben Hur, Arkansas. His second wife, Sallie, outlived him by three years.[17]

Before we leave the State of Arkansas, the reader might be interested to learn that a Union veteran is buried at Fayetteville National Cemetery, having died on February 24, 1949, after living in the state for several years. His name is John W. Malott and he served as a private with Co. K, 53rd Regiment, Indiana Infantry. He was 103 years old at his passing and the last Union veteran to succumb in Arkansas. Malott predeceased Chisum by some twenty-seven months.

Florida

George Washington Keith
(b. January 17, 1852, d. November 7, 1951)
A soldier in the West Florida Home Guard
Company in the Homes County area.

Regimental Brief: There were at least five militia units (and possibly many more, though undocumented) that resided in the State of Florida: Norwood's Company, Florida Home Guards; Tampa City Guards, Florida; the West Florida Home Guards; the Coffee County Home Guards; and Wauchula Militia, Florida (misidentified on Internet sites as the Wauchilla Militia, Florida). The home guards (also called militia) were organized to provide an armed civilian defense against local insurrection and halt any incursion by Union forces.[18] The West Florida Home Guard Company operated in and around Florida's panhandle.

Veteran's Brief: Not until the 1980s did historians began to question William Allen Lundy's veteran's status and his right to be called the last Civil War survivor living in the state of Florida. Lundy had claimed a birth date of January 18, 1848, when census records showed that his actual birth was listed as May 1860. His age at death when compared to a handful of surviving veterans also led some to believe that his longevity was too good to be true. Adding to his lack of credibility, between 1870 and 1930 Lundy gave census marshals varying ages that placed his birth year as early as 1853 and in another instance as late as 1860. Upon further investigation nothing could be found to substantiate his service as part of the Coffee County Home Guards (not surprising, as most home guard unit rosters were incomplete or lost years ago). Today, most historians concur that Lundy's claim of veteran status is hard to defend. Though some see him as an outright fraud, the author believes that in Lundy's case the jury might still be out. But until additional credible evidence surfaces—if it ever does—Lundy's claim to the title must be withheld. The next in line for the honor is George Washington Keith.

Nearly all that is known about George Washington Keith has been

obtained through the investigative skills of Jay S. Hoar through a series of interviews conducted with surviving family members. His findings were eventually published in his book *The South's Last Boys in Gray* (vol. 3).

In January 1864 George Washington Keith was nearing his 12th birthday. Itching to become part of the state's war effort, and perhaps what he envisioned as an exciting adventure, he was wise enough to know that his age precluded him from joining any Florida regiment. So what did he do? He did what many a Southern boy did at the time. He lied about his age and

George Washington Keith (left) standing next to his brother William Thomas (courtesy Jay S. Hoar, *The South's Last Boys in Gray*).

declared himself fifteen.[19] Whether the recruiting officer knew of his deception little matters. Many able-bodied men in 1864 were already off to war, and finding troops for the militia regardless of their age (preteens or aged men) proved a formidable task. It is highly likely that the recruiting officer decided not to quiz young Keith about his youthful appearance, as his choices were extremely limited, which usually resulted in a take-what-you-can-find approach to manning the guard.

For the next fifteen months, young Keith learned the ways of the military by taking part in monotonous drills of arms and marching. There is no indication that he ever took part in any kind of action against bands of marauders or to curtail a civil disturbance. Though his name has never been found on a Florida state home guard roster, this in itself does not jeopardize his ancestors' claims about his service to the Confederacy. The few home guard rosters that have survived (regardless of state) are notoriously deficient, to say the least. As the war was nearing an end, record keeping became nothing short of abysmal.

After the war Keith married Carolyne Register, on April 10, 1873. The marriage lasted fifty-nine years and produced nine children. In his hometown of Graceville, Keith served as a policeman and constable and later as a deputy sheriff just across the border in Geneva County, Alabama, performing these duties for twelve years.[20] He was deeply involved with his region's United Confederate Veterans organization and attended several reunions, including the 27th National UCV Convention in Washington, D.C. In the Western Maryland Historical Library in Hagerstown, Maryland, an application filled out by Keith can be found in the library's collection. Its exact purpose is uncertain, but it appears to declare his intent to attend a reunion in Sharpsburg, Maryland, on the anniversary of the Battle of Antietam. The application was completed and mailed to the Washington County Historical Society in Hagerstown. The last question on the form asked if he had a recent photograph of himself, "especially in uniform." His reply was a simple, "Do not have one." Perhaps the hallmark of his battlefield visits came when he accompanied forty-five of his Florida UCV comrades to the commemoration of the seventy-fifth anniversary of the Battle of Gettysburg in 1938.[21]

Only a few misfortunes managed to slow Keith down. In his mid-to-late nineties, he suffered two serious accidents: a fall off the roof of his house while shingling it and being backed over by a ton-and-a-half truck at a construction site. Realizing that his days were numbered, he told a newspaper reporter, "I'd have lived to be 100 if that damned truck hadn't run over me!"[22] He missed it by less than three months. George Washington Keith rests in peace at the Antioch Freewill Baptist Church Cemetery about a mile over the Alabama border in Lauderdale County just north of Graceville.[23]

Georgia

William Jasper Brown (b. February 26, 1846, d. March 2, 1949)
Co. D, 22nd Georgia Artillery

Regimental Brief: No official records exist for this regiment.

Veteran's Brief: Before discussing the selection of William Jasper Brown as Georgia's last Civil War veteran, we need to look more deeply at the credentials of another Georgia resident. As with William Loudermilk from Arkansas, William Jordan Bush's assertions that he was a veteran came under more detailed scrutiny long after his death. When a historian reviewed U.S. Federal Census records, he found several age discrepancies relating to this man. He noted that in one census, Bush was listed as being five years younger than what he claimed, while in another it was only a year. Additionally, during the U.S. Federal Census of 1910, when given the opportunity Bush never declared himself a veteran. Known locally as a die-hard Confederate, even though given the opportunity to declare his military service he never claimed such status.

The census discrepancies are only one issue; there are plenty more. Yet regardless of the seemingly damaging evidence, the State of Georgia held steadfast to the accuracy of Bush's credentials and the documents he presented when applying for a pension. Others have also stood behind him right up until the present. Traditional beliefs tend to die hard. The author and a number of historians think otherwise, as there are more holes in Bush's story than there are in a pound of Swiss cheese.

According to Bush's second wife, Effie, she married William in 1922 as a widow with two small children. After she and William married, he told her that an older brother was already serv-

While lying in bed, William Jasper Brown poses for the camera on December 31, 1948 (photograph by Francis Miller/*Life* Picture Collection/Getty Images #50775095).

ing in the Confederate army when he himself lied about his age to enlist in Cpt. Tom Wilcox's Co. B, 14th Regiment, Georgia Infantry. He also told her that a fire destroyed his military records sometime in the late 1880s.[24] Was it a convenient excuse or an unfortunate incident? Investigators may never know for certain.

Affectionately called "The General," Bush spent most of his life in Fitzgerald, Georgia, where he gained local celebrity status by way of his claim to be a Civil War veteran and his longevity. No one doubted that he relished the spotlight. Known as a colorful figure—to some, perhaps more comical than colorful—he would go into a tirade, swinging his cane and cursing the "damn Yankees" in the middle of telling war stories, though his show of hatred was more bravado than reality. As for war stories, he was known to tell some whoppers. Many of them were so unbelievable that they were easily discredited and others were so incredibly contradictory they tended to devalue his credentials even further.

For years, historians knew there were several soldiers from the State of Georgia that served under the name Bush during the war; to be exact, there were five, two of whom carried the same middle initial. When investigators looked to ascertain William J. Bush's Confederate service in historical records, it became virtually impossible to differentiate who was who.

"From birth to death there are factual contradictions and vagaries open to differing plausible interpretations," wrote a researcher after meticulously investigating Bush's claim.[25] Though he felt Bush's service was, in the end, verifiable, his eventual decision shed a positive light based upon findings that still appear inconclusive. Whereas one author and historian debunks Bush's veteran status, another with similar credentials determines Bush's military service to be credible. It is difficult to ascertain who is right, as both offer substantial evidence to prove their case. This author believes there are still too many issues and unanswered questions. Therefore, selecting Bush as Georgia's last Civil War veteran must be deferred until such time as a majority of the discrepancies can be satisfactorily resolved.

It is time to turn the page and look at the next veteran in line for the honor. His name is William Jasper Brown. In Statesboro, Georgia, a group of patriotic citizens had gathered at the Methodist church for a Memorial Day program in 1937, waiting in anticipation for their guest of honor to arrive. He was late and nobody was sure if he would attend. In his early nineties, frail, and having to travel some twenty miles from Metter, Georgia, getting to the church was a tall order for the aged veteran. After waiting an appropriate amount of time, the speaker for the evening commenced delivering his opening address when suddenly the doors swung open and William Jasper Brown appeared in the entryway. The speaker stepped back from the podium. In the back of the church, those who had been awaiting Brown's arrival escorted the aged veteran down the aisle to a front-row seat designated for the distinguished guest. As the small entourage slowly walked down the aisle, the audience stood in reverence. Leading the way carrying a Confederate flag was a member of a local chapter of the Sons of Confederate Veterans. After the opening remarks, brief business meeting, music, and final address, the program adjourned. There is no indication that Brown gave a speech, but it is likely he exchanged pleasantries after the ceremony. For those in attendance, Brown's presence was enough.[26]

Born in Metter, Georgia, not far from Savannah, the tall, blue-eyed veteran never resided elsewhere. For nearly his entire life, William Jasper Brown was a simple farmer who also enjoyed fishing in a creek near his farm. Because his farm was small, it is fair to say, he was dirt-impoverished and struggled to make ends meet. Married to Matilda Williams, they had one daughter. On the farm he grew corn, cotton, and vegetables and raised cows and hogs, mostly for his own family needs. In a testimonial letter written years after Brown's passing, he was called "independent, honest, [and an] upright gentleman."[27] Like several of his comrades, he enjoyed an occasion sip of hard liquor. An old acquaintance once called Brown "quite the character."[28] She remembers that he convinced a family to move an abandoned and disabled automobile from the shade to a favorite place of his in the sun. During afternoons that followed, he would sit in the stationary car, take in the rays and sip a tad of whiskey—all without fear of being pulled over by a policeman.[29]

Though on rare occasions he talked about his exploits during the war, only minute details were revealed. He enlisted at Whitmarsh Island as a private in 1864 and remained with his regiment until the end of the war. Upon reflection, Brown remembered marching hundreds of miles along the coast of the Carolinas and Virginia. No mention was made if he saw combat.[30]

In the last thirteen years of his life, Brown was blind, "helpless and bedridden." For the last decade or so, he was nursed by a Mrs. J.M. Rooks. For nourishment she fed him soup with a spoon. Her pleas for a wheelchair that Brown so desperately needed were finally answered by a group of local Marines. When given the gift, he was barely able to lift his head, but he managed to whisper to Mrs. Rooks, "Tell them I thank them." When one of the men asked if he needed anything, he replied, "Give me a drink." As Mrs. Rooks noted later, "He didn't mean water." The Marines departed and returned not long after with two bottles of wine. The day was also his 103rd birthday and a good occasion for a minor celebration. Lifting his head for the first time that day, Brown saluted his guests and smiled. Before departing, the Marines could see that he was destitute. Mrs. Rooks told them that Brown would eventually be buried in a pauper's grave because neither he nor his caregiver could afford anything better. Deciding to rectify the indignity, the men eventually organized a fundraiser in Savannah.[31]

Five days after the Marine visit, Brown passed away at the age of 103. Resting on the bed's headboard was a Confederate flag presented to him months before by local legislators and an unnamed civic leader. Not only were the necessary expenses raised for his funeral, but the residual funds were given to Mrs. Rooks for her fine care of Brown. In an exemplary and compassionate gesture, Brown's $500 casket was paid in full by one of the Marines who had visited him less than a week earlier. The Marine requested to remain anonymous.[32]

William Jasper Brown rests at Lake Church Cemetery off Highway 46 East not far from his former residence in Metter. News reports stated that some 500 citizens of Georgia attended the funeral. On December 14, 2003, the Dixie Guards, Sons of Confederate Veterans, Camp #1942, rededicated Brown's final resting place. A new headstone now lies at his grave site.[33]

Louisiana

Burrell Maricle
(b. July 11, 1843, d. May 25, 1949)
Co. I, 6th Regiment, Louisiana Cavalry

Regimental Brief: The 6th Regiment, Louisiana Cavalry, was assembled near Minden, Louisiana, in January 1864. The unit was assigned to the Trans-Mississippi Department and saw light action in Louisiana. Later it operated a courier line between Camden, Arkansas, and Alexandria, Louisiana. In March 1865, the regiment was patrolling along the west bank of the Mississippi River before it disbanded.[34]

Veteran's Brief: In the late 1940s, folks in Louisiana could easily name the last surviving Civil War veteran from their state; that is, until that individual's past pension records came under more detailed scrutiny. Nearly all of the investigation centered on the gentleman's plight in obtaining a pension. The individual in question, William Daniel Townsend, initially had been turned down by a pension review board. The board's initial denial in granting a pension appeared well-founded. The commissioners were under the suspicion that the claimant had fraudulently used a deceased veteran's service records from the 27th Regiment, Louisiana Infantry, who just so happened to have Townsend's first and last name. This William Townsend, who happened to be the oldest veteran living in Louisiana at the time, was 48 in 1910 and apparently died not long afterward. In addition, there was a two-year discrepancy in birth years between the two. Townsend countered that it was a simple mistake on his behalf. Then he gave the commission names of five Confederates who could substantiate his service. The commission could not locate any of the men. Townsend was rejected a second time. Finally, he found an individual who would vouch for his service in the regiment.[35] With patience wearing thin, the pension board relented and granted him a small pension. Who really knows whether William Daniel Townsend was who he said he was? The jury is still deliberating and may be for years.

Townsend had been dead for a number of years before his service to the Confederacy came under question. After the pension disclosure and birth year discrepancy, authors, historians, and veteran groups searched again for another viable candidate deserving of the honor. An expert on the subject, author Jay S. Hoar, identified Robert Pendleton Wilson as the next likely individual. However, in his book *The South's Last Boys in Gray*, Hoar used the phrase "reputedly joined" while attempting to substantiate his selection of Wilson's claim to have served in J.E.B. Stuart's cavalry. Apparently the claim was based upon the word of a single individual: Wilson's great-granddaughter.[36] The descendant said that Wilson, a slave from Richmond, Virginia, accompanied his owner, a captain in the Confederate army, on the battlefield.[37] Though he could have fought for the Confederacy, Wilson's veteran status must be held in abeyance until additional evidence surfaces to enhance the dearth and singularity of the evidence at hand.

Next in line for the honor appeared to be Stephen Dupuis, a courier in the Louisiana Signal Corps. However, he moved to Texas in 1940 and was no longer considered a legal resident of the state. The baton was now passed to a gentleman named Burrell Maricle, and choosing him as the last Civil War veteran from Louisiana not only seems appropriate but, more importantly, certifiable. Born in West Point, Louisiana (now known by the peculiar name Occupy), Burrell Maricle served as a private in the 6th Louisiana Cavalry. Only scant information remains about his military service: he was captured and imprisoned by Northern soldiers before being released on parole in Alexandria, Louisiana, on June 9. 1865.[38]

Burrell was an extremely proud and hardworking gentleman. Nicknamed "Uncle Burr," he was well known in the Bethel community and the west Rapides Parish area. A farmer by occupation, he raised "corn, sweet potatoes, cane and peas."[39] He even had a "smokehouse to cure hams and bacon." In the fields, he had an apple and peach orchard and a sprinkling of fig and pecan trees.[40]

In 1869, Maricle married Rebecca Ray of Calcasieu, Louisiana. They had seven children, six boys and a girl. He loved children so much that he and his wife became foster parents for two other boys and helped raise them to manhood.[41] For a number of years the family lived in Rapides, Louisiana. After Rebecca's death on June 20, 1889, at the age of 43, Maricle married Nancy Sweat. The union produced no children. She died on January 22, 1925.[42]

According to a great-granddaughter, Maricle was a deeply religious man. He served as a deacon for fifty-seven years at Occupy #1 Baptist Church. According to his oldest daughter, Lizzie Johnson, when her father retired at night, "We could hear him talk to the Lord out loud."[43]

Maricle enjoyed making his own coffee, as most Civil War veterans were accustomed to having had the kitchen camp experience numerous times during the war. He would buy the raw green coffee beans and parch them and grind them on a hand mill before brewing the grounds and drinking it black. Coffee continued to be his daily breakfast and dinner drink for decades.

Burrell Maricle died a few months shy of his 106th birthday. He had been in ill health for about a year. At least three of the seven children survived him. He is buried at Occupy #1 Cemetery, in Glenmora, Louisiana.[44]

Mississippi

Thomas Wiley Guinn
(b. January 27, 1849, d. April 7, 1951)
Mississippi Home Guards

Regimental Brief: The State of Mississippi mustered at least two home guard units during the war: Barnes' Company, Mississippi Home Guards and Watts' Company, Mississippi Home Guards. Neither left a record of its service. What is known is that both companies consisted of local citizens anxious to protect against any Union military intervention in their state. Amateur historian Jim Taylor listed the ages and occupations of several Southerners he found who were members of Barnes' Company on his Internet home page. Most were middle-aged men with varying occupations such as civil officers: a minister, physician, discharged veterans, a probate judge and a tanner exempt from military service. Of the 42 enlistees Taylor was able to identify, eight were in their fifties and six were in their sixties.[45]

Veteran's Brief: Born in Butler, Alabama, Thomas Wiley Guinn's family moved to Mississippi while he was still a young boy.[46] In 1865, Guinn enlisted in the Mississippi Home Guards. Young Thomas (16 at the time) might have felt a need to enlist after his brothers Frank and David had served (David had been wounded in an earlier engagement). But by the time Guinn was properly trained to patrol the region, the war had ended.[47]

After the conflict, Guinn married Mary Sykes in July 1869 and later, after her passing, Ann Hays Wheeler, in June 1882. He had two daughters.[48] To support his family, he worked for the railroad as a common laborer. When his job with the railroad ended, he cut cedar shakes used for roofing houses. For decades afterward, he worked on the farm hoeing cotton and corn, until the age of 83.[49]

Those who knew Guinn, described him as a devote Christian and a Methodist by denomination. Throughout his adult life he enjoyed music— singing, playing the piano, even teaching music to students.[50] When interviewed by Bill Lewis a *Hattiesburg American* newspaper reporter in 1951 for a feature story about the centurion's upcoming birthday, Guinn looked up from his chair and responded thusly when asked what he wanted to drink: "I'll have coffee. I drink coffee whenever I can get it, and I hardly ever fail to get it!"[51]

A year before he died, Guinn was able to get up and walk around and "went outside whenever he wished."[52] However, in the fall of 1951, his health began to deteriorate. By winter, he remained indoors and spent most of his waking hours confined to a rocking chair trying to stay warm near the fire.[53] He died months later in the spring of 1951 at the age of 102. Thomas Wiley Guinn is buried in New Augusta Baptist Cemetery in New Augusta, Mississippi.[54]

North Carolina

Alfred Blackburn
(b. April 26, 1842, d. December 15, 1951)

Manservant to his father, John Augustus Blackburn
of the 21st Regiment, North Carolina Infantry, Co. F

Regimental Brief: Formerly known as the 11th North Carolina Volunteers, the 21st consisted of twelve companies that were organized at Danville, Virginia, in June 1861. Men of the regiment were recruited from the North Carolina counties of Davidson, Surry, Forsyth, Stokes, Rockingham, and Guilford. After taking part in the Battle of First Manassas (also known as First Bull Run) and General Jackson's valley operations, the 21st participated in the Seven Days' Battle. Later the regiment was engaged at the Battle of Drewry's Bluff (also called the Battle of Ft. Darling) and the Battle of Cold Harbor. The unit marched with General Jubal Early to the Shenandoah Valley, where it saw action around Appomattox. It sustained 80 casualties at First Winchester, 13 at Cross Keys and Port Republic, 45 during the Seven Days' Battle, 51 at Groveton, 18 at Sharpsburg, and 24 at Fredericksburg. It lost 78 men at Chancellorsville, 28 percent of the 436 engaged at Gettysburg, and 52 at Plymouth. In April 1865 the regiment surrendered with what little remained of the hard-fighting unit: 6 officers and 117 men, of which only 40 were armed.[55]

Alfred "Teen" Blackburn as he appeared in a January 25, 1949, photograph. Blackburn was one of the last surviving ex-slaves (courtesy Iredell County Public Library Photo Collection, Statesville, North Carolina; from a photograph by Max Tharpe).

Veteran's Brief: Alfred was the son of Fannie Blackburn, a Cherokee Indian (possibly half black), and John Augustus Blackburn, a white plantation owner.[56] Because of the color of his skin, Alfred, a former slave, never was able to receive a full pension for his service in the Confederate army. In the 1940s, he was categorized as a "Class B" veteran and received a monthly pension allowance of $26.26 as compared to a "Class A" veteran (a white soldier) who received $72.00.[57]

At the age of 19, Alfred set off to war. While shells exploded and bullets whizzed by, he faithfully performed his arduous duties as the manservant of John

Columbia asks why a black veteran amputee has been denied his constitutional rights (from an illustration by Thomas Nast for *Harper's Weekly*, August 5, 1865).

Augustus Blackburn, who happened to be his white father and master. His typical duties included "tending horses, cooking meals, acting as a bodyguard, and helping generally." As a bodyguard, he shined. At First Manassas (First Bull Run to a Yankee), he saved his father's life by taking up a sword against a Union soldier. According to Alfred, his father never thanked him for saving his life but "just turned around and walked off."[58] Such were the sad times.

After the war, Alfred, also called Uncle Teen, became a farmer and a contract mail carrier for the federal government for over forty years. During that time he married Lucy Carson of Hamptonville, North Carolina, and reared seven children, three daughters and four sons. He also had a tobacco farm. With the money he earned, he was able to finance formal educations for all of his children, an amazing accomplishment for a man of color in an era rife with racial discrimination. At the time of his death at his home in Hamptonville, Alfred Blackburn was 109 years and 7 months old. He had been married for seventy years.[59] Shortly after his death, the United States government allotted $100 to his surviving family for burial expenses for time spent as a Confederate prisoner at the hands of the Union army.[60] Alfred Blackburn's remains lie at Pleasant Hill Baptist Church Cemetery, two miles south of Fairmont, North Carolina.[61]

South Carolina

Vernon Emerson Lifrage
(b. April 22, 1848, d. August 4, 1950)

*South Carolina State Reserves (most likely Lifrage served
with the 4th Regiment, South Carolina State Troop Junior Reserves)*

Regimental Brief: By the end of summer 1864, South Carolina was running out of able-bodied men to fill its depleted ranks. It was decided that all males between the ages of 16 and 60 were liable for service. In addition, each state militia unit was to contribute one company of men so that four new regiments could be formed. These units were called Regiments of Junior Reserves, Regiments of South Carolina State Troops, or Regiments of South Carolina Militia. They were mainly deployed within the state. By the first part of April 1865, the regiments had disbanded, but the 16 and 17 year-olds were sent to Spartanburg, where they were trained for future service. By April 8, 1865, the reserves were either furloughed or disbanded. Records of their Confederate service are nearly nonexistent. The scant data that does exist is found in pension records, contemporary newspapers, or county histories.[62]

Veteran's Brief: Before he died, Vernon Emerson Lifrage knew that he was one of the last of two Civil War veterans living in the State of South Carolina. In the end, Lifrage died first, leaving the honor and the title of the last Civil War veteran from South Carolina to Arnold Murray. But long after Murray's death, a problem arose. Early census records uncovered by author and historian William Marvel nearly forty years after Murray's death showed that he was not older than ten when the war ended.[63] Murray had claimed that he was 18 years old in 1864 at the time of his enlistment in the Confederate

Vernon Emerson Lifrage at his 102nd birthday celebration. Insert: Lifrage at 99 years old with his daughter, Essie Davis (courtesy Jay S. Hoar, *The South's Last Boys in Gray*; Lifrage's photograph was originally in the possession of descendant Maude Davis, now deceased).

army. He said he served as a trainee before being assigned to harbor defenses.[64] When Murray died in 1952, he was given a state funeral attended by thousands that included the presence of many state and local dignitaries. Fifty years after his death, the South Carolina Department of the Sons of Confederate Veterans rededicated his grave site—Murray's tombstone states that he was *The Last Confederate Soldier from S.C.* It is difficult to dispute someone who has been placed on such a high pedestal, especially long after his death.

Over the past several years, author and historian Garry Victor Hill has performed extensive research about Civil War veterans whose claims have come under additional scrutiny. Arnold Murray was one of those investigated. On March 29, 2015, Hill was asked by the author to elaborate on his findings. This is what he said:

> While evidence still remains inconclusive for full verification for Arnold Murray's claims to Civil War service, enough evidence exists to lift him above the status of debunked. The census documents of 1870, 1880 and 1900 that supposedly disprove him on age are too full of errors, ambiguities, omissions, contradictions and dubious statements to prove or disprove anything. Newspaper accounts of his enlistment give three different dates (1864, 1865 and in his words. "late in the war." Similar confusion exists over his enlistment age, 14, 18, or when he was "a youngster." He had the two photographs; one from the Civil War is in this article [which is in a Department of South Carolina, Sons of Confederate Veterans, Web site blog]. The second photograph came on the market last year and comes from a 1913 Confederate reunion. It shows Murray in a group photograph and that he kept his Confederate uniform as the family claimed. His name is handwritten with the others on the back of the pho-

tograph. The face matches that in the 1949 "Life" magazine article. He knew the
names of his immediate commanding officers and where and when his unit trained.
He made the 1930 affirmation. In the censuses of 1910, 1920, 1930, and 1940, he gave
ages consistent with Civil War service; Life magazine's stated age did the same and
matched the later censuses.... [But t]he enlistment documents for an A.B. Murray are
ambiguous. Parts of this document match what Arnold Murray said he did in the
war, but other parts do not. This Arnold B. Murray enlisted in the cavalry in September 1863 joined the unit Arnold claimed to be in early 1864 and by May 1864 he was
in the fighting in Virginia, where he was soon wounded and shipped back to South
Carolina before returning to Richmond. His name on Confederate military documents concerning his transfer and war record is usually given as A.B. Murray due to
lack of space. On two documents with more space he is written in as Arnold Murray
and Charleston is written in as his location.[65]

There is more. In the 1950s, the United Daughters of the Confederacy refused
to recognize Murray as the last Civil War survivor from the State of South
Carolina. Their reason was simple: there was a lack of sufficient evidence
to verify his claim.[66]

Considering the above, it appears certain irregularities and questions
about Arnold Murray's service still remain unanswered. Until such time as
more convincing and certifiable evidence is presented, this author believes
Vernon Emerson Lifrage deserves to hold the title. Selecting Lifrage over
Murray as the last certifiable Civil War veteran from South Carolina—thus
overriding descendants, historians, and fraternal military organizations—
has not been an easy decision. It is hoped that in the coming months more
authoritative information will be found to resolve this issue (Murray or
Lifrage) once and for all. In the meantime, it is time to salute the service
of Vernon Emerson Lifrage.

Born on his grandfather's plantation in Williamsburg County, South
Carolina, Lifrage came from privileged stock. When he went off to war, a
body servant named Simon Williams was at his side. In the closing days of
the Confederacy, Lifrage fought in what was called Potter's Raid.[67]

In late summer of 1865, Lifrage, along with sixteen other horsemen
led by a former Confederate captain, James W. Edwards, banded together
against what was referred to as "marauding bands of Negroes, mulattoes
and renegade whites" who had pillaged several plantations in the area. The
ad hoc cavalry group caught up with the outlaws and "practically extermi-
nated the entire troop." While returning home and fearing grave conse-
quences from federal troops by taking the law into their own hands, each
swore an oath of secrecy before disbanding.[68]

Lifrage married his first cousin in February 1877. Her name was Chris-
tianna "Kitty" Montgomery. The union lasted more than sixty years and
produced eight children, five girls and three boys. To support his large clan,
Lifrage farmed the land, planting tobacco, corn, and cotton. Although he
was a tobacco farmer, he never smoked. In fact, he never drank or cursed.[69]

At the Blue and Gray Reunion at Gettysburg in 1938, Lifrage attended the event with his 19-year-old granddaughter, Maude Davis. She remembers that he told her to "'behave like a Southern lady,'" which of course she did.[70]

As the years passed, the proud Confederate veteran was showing his age and he spent the last three months of his life bedridden.[71] He died a widower in Williamsburg at the age of 102. Vernon Emerson Lifrage is buried at the Union Presbyterian Church Cemetery in Salters, South Carolina.[72]

Tennessee

William Nelson Morgan
(b. October 15, 1844, d. October 17, 1948)
Co. C, 7th Regiment, Tennessee Mounted Infantry (USA)

Regimental Brief: The regiment was organized at Athens and Nashville, Tennessee, in August 1864. It served at Nashville and Athens until March of 1865. While operating in Athens on January 38, 1865, the regiment saw its first action. On March 1 it was stationed in Philadelphia before departing for Athens (March 2 through 4). After the war, until July 1865, the regiment performed guard duty east of Athens. The unit was mustered out on July 27, 1865.

Veteran's Brief: At least one historian identified James Russell Davis, a Confederate, as the last Civil War veteran from the State of Tennessee. The author thinks otherwise. Davis's boasts seemed farfetched and most likely were more vivid imagination than fact. In the end, he was no different from many other so-called veterans from down South who were unable to furnish proof of military service. The denial of his Confederate pension application came at a time when state pension clerks were overwhelmed with applica-

William Nelson Morgan sites his muzzle loader as veterans of World Wars I and II look on (courtesy *Jackson* [TN] *Sun,* June 1, 1948, edition).

tions and tended to be liberal in their assessment. Further, Davis provided no affidavits from fellow veterans to support his claim, nor is there any evidence that he at least tried to obtain such documents. These facts alone provide solid evidence that he was not who he claimed to be.

The most likely candidate for the last Civil War veteran living in the State of Tennessee appears to be William Nelson Morgan. Morgan had been bestowed the honor by author C. Stewart Peterson as early as 1951.[73] Morgan (known as "Uncle Bill" to his friends and neighbors) was born in Knox County, Tennessee. While a youngster, he left Knox County for Rhea County. It is said he traveled on foot most of the way with his brother on his back."[74]

Years later, after a discussion with a cousin who was a recruiter for the Northern army, Morgan decided to join the Union ranks after being told "he would be fighting for a just cause and that his soul would be saved if he died on the battlefield" (Morgan survived the war and it's to be hoped his soul was among those finding salvation). He entered the war as a farmer and returned to that occupation after the conflict. During his military service, it can be assumed he saw little if any combat.[75]

On August 1, 1869, Morgan married Amanda P. Byerly, who died in 1919. On April 11, 1930, he married Zilpha E. Mansfield. Between both marriages he fathered twelve children, eight boys and four girls.[76]

Uncle Bill died at Dayton, Tennessee, at the age of 104 and is buried in the same town in Buttram Cemetery. According to a newspaper account at the time of his death, Morgan farmed his land until he was 102 years old (two years before his death). He left many grandchildren, great-grandchildren and great-great-grandchildren. Fourteen of his descendants fought in World War II, one being killed in action.[77]

If the reader is curious, the last certifiable Confederate veteran from Tennessee happened to be James Lemuel Barry. He served with Co. F, 4th Regiment, Tennessee Cavalry (CSA). James Lemuel Barry passed away on April 15, 1947, a year-and-a-half earlier than his Union counterpart, William Nelson Morgan.[78]

William Nelson Morgan at 103 years old (courtesy Crawford Harris, Nelson's great-grandson).

Texas

Joseph Haden Whitsett
(b. September 18, 1847, d. August 15, 1951)
Co. C, Shelby's Escort Company of Shelby's Missouri Cavalry

Regimental Brief: The 12th Cavalry Regiment, formerly the Jackson County Cavalry, was organized during the summer of 1863. The unit was assigned to General Shelby's Brigade, Trans-Mississippi Department, and became known as Shelby's Escort Company. The cavalrymen skirmished in Missouri and Arkansas. Later the unit became part of General Sterling Price's operations in Missouri.

Losses: 2 casualties at Marks' Mills and 35 during Price's Expedition. The regiment surrendered on June 2, 1865.[79]

Veteran's Brief: He was thought to be the third to the last Civil War veteran living in the State of Texas but after Joseph Haden Whitsett's passing, the first and second survivors (Walter W. Williams of Franklin and Thomas Evans Riddle of Austin) proved to be frauds. Thus, Whitsett's surviving family inherited the honor in his name. Stolen glory had again taken its ugly toll on yet another deserving Civil War veteran from the Confederacy.

Joseph Haden Whitsett was born in Kentucky but lived there only until

Left: Joseph Haden Whitsett as a younger man (public domain).
Above: Joseph Haden Whitsett (courtesy Hayden Whitsett, a descendant).

the age of six. His father, a doctor, moved to Texas, where he purchased land east of Bonham. It was on this land that young "Hade," as he was referred to by family and friends, learned to hunt game, even bagging a buffalo on one occasion. It is apparent that he came from an affluent family, as the father was a doctor, owned a plantation, and had slaves. Though Whitsett attended a rural school, outdoors was the place he preferred. As he said, "I much preferred to stay out and do the things I liked to do."[80]

As a teenager, Whitsett spent hours in the slave quarters learning to dance and listening to amusing tales while losing track of time, and it was not uncommon for a family member to go bring him home. Living on a plantation gave the young boy many opportunities. He became an excellent horseback rider and swimmer. To his credit, he saved several folks from drowning, the circumstances of which may be lost to posterity.[81]

Whitsett was underage when he joined Co. C., Shelby's Escort Company of Shelby's Missouri Cavalry, on May 6, 1864. After the war, he seemed happy to say, "I never fired a shot." But this fact should not be construed as cowardice on his part, as is evidenced when he heard a man in his cavalry unit cursing Texas and Texans and boasting that they did not want to fight. Not taking kindly to the remark, Whitsett challenged him to a duel. The outcome of the sword fight is unknown, but evidence suggests that the duel was probably cut short by a superior officer before anyone was seriously injured. Whitsett, however, did suffer a cut on his lip during the confrontation, which he proudly displayed for the rest of his life.[82]

After the war, Whitsett returned to college for a single semester. Apparently college life was not his forte, as he began hauling freight between Jefferson and Bonham, Texas, before the Pacific Railroad was constructed. During one of the trips, he won a jug of liquor for his dancing prowess.[83] He married Betty Stone on March 18, 1873, a union that lasted fifty-eight years. From 1900 until her death in 1931 their homestead was in Bonham. Earlier, he had operated a general mercantile store in Dodd City. It remains unclear whether the Whitsetts ever had children, but Betty and Joseph did take in a young boy who lived with them for awhile. Sadly he died while still a young man.[84]

Always a proud Confederate veteran, Whitsett attended numerous functions over the years, including the Blue and Gray Reunion at Gettysburg in 1938. But after suffering a debilitating hip injury, his travelling days were numbered.[85] During an interview in 1949, Whitsett was asked by a newspaper reporter if he could record his "Rebel yell." "Can't do the Rebel yell," he said. "I tried to learn it. Tried a thousand times when I was with Gen. Joe Shelby. But I didn't seem to have the right kind of voice."[86]

In the end, Joseph Haden Whitsett was blind and deaf and living with a niece. When he died a month shy of his 104th birthday, all business establishments in Bonham closed for the services. His earthly remains are buried at Willow Wild Cemetery, Bonham Texas.[87]

Virginia

Martin Luther Peters
(b. August 5, 1849, d. October 28, 1951)
26th Battalion, Virginia Infantry (Edgar's)

Regimental Brief: 26th Infantry Battalion was organized in May 1862 with men of the 59th Regiment Virginia Infantry who escaped capture at the Battle of Roanoke Island. It contained seven companies but was increased to nine in June 1863. The unit was assigned to Echols' and Patton's Brigade, and saw action in Tennessee, western Virginia, and the Shenandoah Valley. During April 1865 it disbanded. The field officers were Lieutenant Colonel George M. Edgar and Major Richard Woodram.[88]

Veteran's Brief: Prior to the war, Martin Luther Peters was a mail courier. At the age of 14, he was drafted into the Confederate army. He was living on his father's farm in Benhams, Virginia (a southwestern town near the Kentucky and North Carolina borders), when an "enrolling officer came around and took the young boys and old men."[89] During the war, he experienced only a single battle (Saltville). But one engagement was enough to quench his thirst for more combat. Years later he reminisced by writing down some of his thoughts during and after the Battle of Saltville: "I saw some of the awfulest [sic] things that day I ever saw in my life." Then he added some gruesome details: "When the Yankee dead were buried in shallow t[r]enches the next day, I went along and saw their hands sticking out."[90]

Martin Luther Peters (courtesy Jay S. Hoar, *The South's Last Boys in Gray*; Luther's photograph was originally in the possession of descendant Pauline V. Peters, now deceased).

After returning home, Peters married Dollie Whitaker. The marriage produced four children. To provide for his family he farmed the land in Benhams before moving to Bristol, Virginia. When he was 40 years old, he opened a fruit stand and a grocery store in Bristol. Woeful times lay ahead, as he lost Dollie and a son during the 1918 influenza pandemic. Four years later he married for a second time, a woman named Earlie Bowman. After retiring from his business at the age of 85, he applied for and received a veteran's pension. Years after the war, on the advice of his father—also a Confederate veteran, he declined to join the United Confederate Veterans organization. "Don't fool with those reunions, son. The war's over," his father said. "Let's smooth things over and drop it."[91] But like many a proud Confederate veteran, Peters did not always practice what he preached. He is quoted as having said the following: "The Yankees didn't whip us Rebels; they just subjugated us, just starved us out."[92]

When asked the secret of his longevity, he said it was due to the fact "he honored his father and mother." Prior to his passing at the age of 102, Martin Luther Peters had been ill for only five weeks. Years later, a surviving grandchild, Pauline V. Peters, described him as a "considerate and intelligent old gentleman."[93]

Chapter 5

The Border States

Shortly after the first shots of the Civil War were fired, slave states that did not secede from the Union became known as Border States. For four states in particular—Arkansas, North Carolina, Tennessee, and Virginia— the neutrality lasted but a short while. Each state seceded from the Union after the Confederates captured Ft. Sumter in Charleston Harbor, South Carolina. Four other Border States—Delaware, Kentucky, Maryland, and Missouri—chose to remain with the Union, though each had its fair share of Southern sympathizers throughout the conflict. Ironically, the states that remained loyal to the Union had failed to support Abraham Lincoln in the 1860 presidential election.

Before the war, northerners migrated south looking to set up a homestead and till the soil, while southerners rode north on wagons and railcars seeking work opportunities. During the initial frontier days, the area was a region of peaceful coexistence despite numerous differences in ethnic backgrounds, religious affiliations, and political beliefs. In the end, however, peace became nothing but an illusion. According to author Amy Murrell Taylor, "the Border States were both compromising in peacetime and antagonistic in war." Strong feelings began to surface as pro-slavery vigilantes and antislavery abolitionists stirred up the feelings of the populace and in the end "each state encompassed deep and enduring internal divisions." Guerrilla warfare between both factions quickly unfolded and became increasingly prevalent as the days passed. As the 1860s approached, as Taylor explained, "politicians saw among their constituents nothing less than the divided nation on a smaller scale."[1]

Early in the war, with feelings running deep and at a fever pitch, people living in the northwestern part of Virginia separated from their home state while professing their allegiance to the Union. On June 20, 1863, with the war raging and just weeks before the Battle of Gettysburg, West Virginia, was granted statehood. (West Virginia's last Civil War veteran is listed at the end of this section, as it had been a Border State prior to achieving statehood.)

According to the U.S. National Park Service, the Border States furnished approximately 275,000 men for the Union, while roughly 71,000 able-bodied men served the Confederacy. It was a clear and convincing statement of where their allegiances lay.[2]

After the end of hostilities, reconstruction did not apply to the Border States, as they had remained loyal to the Union throughout the war. Yet, for those living within the states' boundaries and others that settled later, there was a period of "readjustment," especially after slavery was abolished. Blacks not only became citizens but also were granted the right to vote.[3] This in itself caused significant turmoil, particularly for citizens who were diehard pro-slavery advocates before, during and after the conflict.

Those who lived through the postwar era of social and political change were men like those listed below. They just happened to outlive all the other veterans from each of the Border States. Four of the last five men were Union veterans. After the war, three of five returned to their homes in the states where they enlisted, living there until their deaths.

Delaware

Isaiah Fassett
(b. March 17, 1844, d. June 24, 1946)
Co. D, 9th Regiment, U.S. Colored Troops (USCT)

Regimental Brief: This black regiment was organized at Camp Stanton, Maryland, in November 1863. Its first duty was at Hilton Head, South Carolina, where it performed duty until April 1864. The regiment then moved to Port Royal Island, South Carolina, where it remained until June. The 9th took part in the Ashepoo expedition (May 24 through 27) and the expedition to Johns and James islands (June 30 through July 10). From August 1864 until April 1865 the 9th was involved in siege operations at Petersburg and Richmond. It also saw action at the Battle of Chaffin's Farm (September 28 through 30) and the Battle of Fair Oaks (October 27 and 28). When Richmond fell, the 9th assisted with the occupation of that city along with Petersburg and City Point until June of 1865. It was then ordered to Brazos Santiago, Texas, and remained there until July 1, when it moved to Brownsville, Texas. After duty at Brownsville, the 9th was ordered to Rio Grande, Texas, stayed until October of 1866, and from there went to New Orleans, Louisiana, where it remained until October 2. The regiment was mustered out on November 20, 1866.

Losses: an officer and 46 enlisted men killed or mortally wounded and two officers and 266 enlisted men dead from disease.[4]

Veteran's Brief: Isaiah Fassett was a slave in Virginia, a black Union soldier in Maryland, and an accomplished carpenter by profession long before he became the last commander of the Department of Delaware, GAR. How did this fascinating journey transpire?

Isaiah Fassett was born into slavery in the village of Sinepuxent along Virginia's eastern shore. During the Civil War a third of Worcester County, of which Sinepuxent was a part, was made up of slaves. On November 11, 1863, Union army recruiters arrived at Sarah A. Bruff's farm looking for slaves to fight in the war. Ms. Bruff, the owner of several slaves, allowed Isaiah Fassett, along with several of his brothers, to be released from bondage in order to serve. But it came at a price. The Union army paid Ms. Bruff $1,600 in compensation to gain their freedom.[5] After Isaiah's release, the 19-year-old joined the 9th Regiment, U.S. Colored Troops, as a private, enlisting at Berlin, Maryland. With the 9th, Fassett

Two states claimed Isaiah Fassett as their last surviving Civil War veteran but Delaware won the bragging rights (courtesy Worcester County Tourism, Snow Hill, Maryland).

fought in several major battles near war's end. From slave to captor, his black outfit was one of the first regiments to occupy the Confederate capital of Richmond. As the soldiers entered the city, they were "cheered by throngs of former slaves."[6] Not long after that, he was promoted to the rank of corporal.[7]

After his discharge on November 26, 1866, Fassett returned to Berlin (a town located on the southern boundary that forms the border between Maryland and Virginia), where he worked as a carpenter. There he married Sallie Purnell and helped raise eight children.[8] In Berlin, he joined the GAR. On December 6, 1890, he applied for and was granted a government pension for his service during the war.

Like many elderly veterans, Fassett loved to tell war stories, especially to young people who wanted to listen. One in particular deserves retelling: "I had marched and marched until I really thought I couldn't go a step farther. I got to a place where the grass was nice and green under a large tree. I says to myself, 'This is a good place to give up.' Just then I looked up higher in the tree where a buddy had been hanged and [was] dangling.

Well, I braced myself up and began marching again. I realized there was no need to stop after all and I found energy I didn't know I had."[9]

At the age of 94, Fassett, now known to many as "Uncle Zear," attended the commemoration of the seventy-fifth anniversary of the Battle of Gettysburg along with other Civil War veterans from the state. He was about the average age of the 1,845 who attended the event in July 1938.[10]

He first served as the GAR department commander in Berlin, Maryland, but the organization ultimately disbanded as the result of a dwindling membership. Later, and until his death in 1943 at the age of 102, Fassett served as department commander for the State of Delaware.[11] He had been asked to assume command to extend the life of the organization. His election was a mere formality. Though Fassett never officially lived in Delaware, citizens of the state insisted on claiming him as one of their own, especially since he was the last department commander of the Delaware GAR.

Upon Fassett's death, three state representatives paid their final respects at his funeral.[12] At a time when segregation was still an ugly norm, this show of unity and respect was truly an honor. Today Isaiah Fassett's remains lie in a segregated cemetery outside Berlin.[13]

Today, some historians say that Civil War veteran George Washington Baker, a paperhanger from Wilmington, Delaware, who served as a wagonmaster in Nield's Independent Battery, 1st Delaware Light Artillery, should receive the honor, as he lived and died in Delaware. But the assertion, incontrovertible as it is, might have fallen on deaf ears during the mid–1940s in Delaware when their beloved Isaiah Fassett was maneuvering between two states. Baker was 97 years old when he passed away. On October 18, 1940, he was buried at Riverview Cemetery in Wilmington.

Kentucky

Robert T. Barrett
(b. November 5, 1846, d. January 12, 1951)
Troop L, 17th Regiment, Kentucky Cavalry (USA)

Regimental Brief: The cavalry unit was organized at Russellville, Kentucky, on April 25, 1865. Attached to the Military Department of Kentucky, the 17th was assigned duty at Hopkinsville, Kentucky, and in southern Kentucky along the Louisville & Nashville Railroad. After slightly less than five months, the regiment was mustered out of service.[14]

Veteran's Brief: Though General Lee surrendered the Army of Northern Virginia at Appomattox Court House in April 1865, bands of Confederate guerrillas continued to offer resistance in former Rebel strongholds. Southern Kentucky was one of those areas. At the age of 18, Robert T. Barrett, as part of the 17th Regiment Kentucky Cavalry (USA), spent the next several months confronting the remnants of what had once been a formidable adversary.[15]

An ardent abolitionist for years, "Pap" (his family-given nickname) was a farmer living in western Kentucky before and after the war. He was proud to say that his father, Giles Barrett, a native of Georgia, had served in General Washington's Continental Army during the Revolutionary War. According to the *Princeton Leader*, Barrett enjoyed wartime conversations with friends. He told one group that "the Confederates always kept them "on the run and if they ever had leisure to stop and wash their clothes, he didn't remember it." Barrett was always ready to express his opinion on all subjects relating to the welfare and progress of the community.[16]

Robert Tolliver Barrett, pictured with Edward M. Coffman (courtesy Edward M. Coffman, author of *The Embattled Past* [University Press of Kentucky, 2014]; used with permission of the author).

Barrett married twice, sired 16 children and outlived ten of them. At the 1939 Black Patch Parade held in his community, he could be seen riding his mare, "Minnie," a highly spirited horse he could still handle even at his advanced age.[17] When asked how he managed to live so long, he replied, "If you want to enjoy life, don't get nervous and excited. When everything seems to go wrong, just walk off, stay awhile and whistle and sing."[18]

Three weeks before his death, Robert T. Barrett had taken ill at a son's home where he had been living for a while. Up until then, he had rarely been ill or taken medication.[19] This time whistling and singing did not help. He died in the comforting arms of his son Thomas and daughter-in-law. He was 104 years old. Barrett left three daughters, three sons, and a multitude of grandchildren and great-grandchildren. Burial took place at Liberty Cemetery in Lyon County, Kentucky.[20]

Maryland

James M. Reed
(b. April 3, 1846, d. October 20, 1946)

Co. B, 8th Regiment, Pennsylvania Volunteer Infantry,
and Co. H, 191st Regiment, Pennsylvania Volunteer Infantry

Regimental Brief for the 8th Regiment, Pennsylvania Volunteer Infantry: Organized at Camp Curtin, Harrisburg, April 23, 1861, as a three-month unit, the contingent saw duty at Chambersburg, Pennsylvania, until June 7. Subsequently, the regiment performed guard duty along the Potomac. On July 2, it guarded stores and fords at Williamsport, Pennsylvania, before being ordered to Martinsburg, Pennsylvania. The last guard duty was performed at Keyes Ford, Pennsylvania, on July 20. The regiment mustered out on July 29, 1861.[21]

Regimental Brief for the 191st Regiment, Pennsylvania Infantry: On May 31, 1864, the unit was organized in the field from veterans and recruits of the Pennsylvania Reserve Corps. It fought at the following major battles and sieges in Virginia during 1864: Cold Harbor (June 1 through 12); Bethesda Church (June 1 through 3); White Oak Swamp Bridge (June 13); the Siege of Petersburg (June 16 until April 2, 1865); Weldon Railroad (June 21 through 23); Weldon Railroad a second time (August 18 through 21); Poplar Springs Church (September 29 through October 2); Hatcher's Run (October 27 through 28); and Warren's Expedition to Weldon Railroad (December 7 through 12). In 1865 the regiment fought in the following major battles and campaigns in Virginia: Hatcher's Run (February 5 through 7); Appomattox Campaign (March 28 through April 9); and Five Forks (April 1). It was present at Appomattox Court House (April 9) for General Lee's surrender. During the first two weeks of May, the regiment marched to Washington, D.C., before taking part in the Grand Review on May 23 and was mustered out on June 28, 1865.

Losses: 1 officer and 40 enlisted men killed and mortally wounded and 161 enlisted men dead from disease.[22]

Veteran's Brief: James M. Reed (aka Reid) enlisted as a private in the 8th Regiment Pennsylvania Infantry on March 1, 1864, at New Brighton, Pennsylvania, and later with the 191st Regiment, Pennsylvania Infantry. With only a few months of military service under his belt, Reed faced heavy combat for the first time at Cold Harbor, Virginia, in a battle that proved devastating to General Grant's army. After the regiment licked its wounds—and there were plenty to lick—the men participated in the Siege of Petersburg, which included a number of major battles (see the regimental brief listed above). At the end, Reed's regiment was present at Appomattox Court House when General Lee surrendered. On May 23, 1865, he and his regiment took part in the Grand Review of the Army of the Potomac at Washington, D.C., before being discharged a little more than a month later at Harrisburg, Pennsylvania.[23]

After leaving military service, Reed found his way to Cumberland, Maryland, where he became a farmer. What took him to Maryland is uncertain. During the war, Cumberland was a federal stronghold where 6,000 to 8,000 Union troops were stationed at any given time. For security, pickets were positioned near the town, while occasional patrols surrounded the outer perimeter. But on February 21, 1865, Confederate cavalry (the majority of the men came from the Cumberland area) breached what proved to be a weak defensive position. With only limited resistance, a cavalry squad made its way to the downtown area and walked directly into a hotel where Brig. Gen. George Crook was billeted. The general was easily captured and offered no resistance. Under guard he was escorted out of the town and made a prisoner of war. Little did the raiding party realize that three other Union generals and several high ranking officers were also billeted in the same hotel. Two in particular would eventually serve their country as president of the United States: Brig. Gen. Rutherford B. Hayes and Maj. William McKinley. The clandestine operation was highly successful but proved too little too late. Southern spirits were briefly lifted by the raid, but as one clerk in Richmond noted soon after learning about the events, "This is a little affair, but [it] will make a great noise." For Southerners, any positive news at this late stage from the front brought some hope even though citizens knew it was only for a fleeting instant, as the outcome of the war now seemed evident.[24]

Somewhere along the way, Reed lost interest in farming, and it was not long before he became a boatman on the Chesapeake and Ohio Canal. On December 23, 1876, at Cumberland, Maryland, Reed married Elizabeth Clendenning. Over the ensuing years, they had seven children, five of whom would outlive him. Unfortunately, little else is known about Reed's later years.

Reed died at the home of his daughter Anna Reed. At the time of his death at the age of 100, he was a widower; Elizabeth died in 1925. James M. Reed's remains are buried at Rose Hill Mausoleum, Cumberland, Maryland.[25] He managed to outlive the last Confederate veteran, Eli Scott Dance, from Baltimore County, Maryland, by nearly a year-and-a-half. Dance served with Company C, 1st Regiment, Maryland Cavalry and passed away on May 7, 1945.[26] It is highly probable that the men crossed paths in Maryland, though no evidence has surfaced to verify the notion.

Missouri

John Hutchison
(b. March 14, 1846, d. March 18, 1951)
Co. I, 46th Regiment, Missouri Volunteer Infantry

Regimental Brief: The regiment was formed in Springfield, Missouri, from August to November of 1864, for six-month enlistments. The 46th remained in the Springfield area for the duration with the exception of detachments that saw service in Douglas County, Taney County, at Stockton, Hartsville, Neosho, Cassville, Newtonia, and Buffalo until March of 1865. Another detachment was sent to the District of Middle Tennessee until May of 1865. The regiment was mustered out March 6 through May 24, 1865.

Losses: 8 enlisted men killed and mortally wounded and 18 enlisted men dead from disease.[27]

Veteran's Brief: Though his father was James Asbury, John preferred to carry the surname of his mother's first husband: Hutchison. Why is anyone's guess. The answer could still be out there hidden in family documents and oral histories.[28]

John Hutchison's reason for joining the Union army might have had more to do with seeking vengeance then it had with his patriotic leanings. He was living near Pond Fork Creek in Missouri when, at the age of 17, he witnessed the killing of his uncle by three Confederates in a field near his home. The young boy did the only thing he could—join the U.S. Army; he entered the 46th Regiment, Missouri Infantry, as a private.[29]

The vast majority of Hutchison's service entailed the patrolling of borders between Missouri and Arkansas, as Confederate raiding parties were constantly seen in the area. While reminiscing as an aged veteran, he was asked about Revolutionary War-style muskets that were still in use during the Civil War. He left no doubt about how he felt: "The trouble with those old single ball muskets—a man was just as well off in front of them as behind them. You never knew which way they were going to shoot."[30]

Though his regiment fought mostly skirmishes, the clashes could be nearly as dangerous as fighting a battle. In one case, Hutchison remembered that while his company was patrolling an area they saw three men riding across a field. One was wearing the coat of a Union soldier. The riders looked suspicious, so several men from the company took off after them on horseback. When the Union men caught up to the riders, the one wearing the uniform turned and fired his weapon. A firefight erupted. After the three unknowns were killed, the bodies were stripped and determined to be Confederates, as one was wearing a Confederate uniform underneath the Union army coat. According to Hutchison, at least one of their men was shot, but Hutchison left no indication as to the seriousness of the wound or if the man recovered.[31]

Hutchison returned to Ozark County after the war. How he spent the remainder of his years is vague. The little known about his post–Civil War life has been retrieved from limited sources. He married Mary Faggett and the union produced eleven children. At the age of 105, while under his daughter's care, Hutchison passed away at her home in Bristow, Oklahoma, where he lived for a short while.[32] Missourians rightfully claimed him as their own, as he spent nearly his entire life in Missouri (his home state) and chose to be buried in Isabella Cemetery, Ozark County. Hutchison left an incredible number of survivors: approximately 190 grandchildren, great-grandchildren, great-great-grandchildren, and even great-great-great-grandchildren.[33]

West Virginia

Uriah Talmage Alley
(b. November 18, 1847, d. October 26, 1947)
Co. C, 6th Regiment, West Virginia Infantry

Regimental Brief: The regiment was organized at Grafton, Mannington, Cairo, Parkersburg, and Wheeling, West Virginia, between August 13 and December 26, 1861. By detachment, the men performed railroad guard duty and served on the line of the Baltimore & Ohio Railroad at various points west of Sleepy Hollow for the entire term of service. From April 1862 through June 1865, the detachments took part in a number of skirmishes. The regiment was mustered out on June 10, 1865.

Losses: 8 enlisted men killed and mortally wounded and 2 officers and 167 enlisted men dead from disease.[34]

Veteran's Brief: In his youth, Uriah Talmage Alley's family moved from Pine Grove, where he was born, to Cameron, West Virginia. The 35-mile trek brought the family closer to the western border of Pennsylvania, perhaps to find better employment opportunities for his father, John. It was in this small hamlet that Uriah learned to ride and take care of horses, a passion he followed into adulthood. Though his education ended abruptly at the third-grade level, he was able to read and write adequately to manage in life.

Like many young men during the war years, Alley *got a hankering* to join the army. He was only 17 in September 1864 when he lied about his age to gain enlistment. But only a month passed before Alley got more than he expected. According to a newspaper account, on Monday morning, November 28, 1864, over a thousand rebels attacked a fort in New Creek, West Virginia, at a place guarded by Alley's regiment. The attack came as a total surprise, as the first line of men who came into view wore Union uniforms. Within thirty yards of the fort, the disguised Confederates let out a Rebel yell and charged. The panic-stricken and badly outmanned Union soldiers ran for their lives without so much as firing a shot. Over 250 citizens and soldiers were captured, with Alley being one of them. On his march to prison, his feet became badly frozen but, fortunately, Alley managed to recover.[35] The young soldier, barely wet behind the ears, spent the balance of his short-lived military career (about four months), not fighting, but incarcerated at the infamous Andersonville Prison in Andersonville, Georgia.[36]

About the time Alley was released, the war was nearly over. He was finally discharged on June 10, 1865. Returning to Cameron, he became a livestock dealer. In 1868, he married Brucie Caroline Clouston, who was nearly twenty years his junior. On November 2, 1870, Alley applied for and was granted a government pension for his service during the war. He must have done quite well; between his business ventures and a government pension, he was able to afford a house servant.

For years, he was known affectionately as "Uncle Duck," the origin of which has yet to be answered. While in his nineties, a local newspaper described Alley as having "a very colorful life" and that he appeared to be in "unusually good health." He was also said to be in possession of a "keen memory." The statement was no vague boast. Alley could still mount and ride a horse into his nineties.

Uriah Talmage Alley mustered out at the end less than a month shy of his 100th birthday. He had gone to bed after supper one evening stating that he didn't feel well. Shortly afterward, he fell into an irreversible coma. He was survived by his son, Woodburn Bruce Alley. The old soldier's remains are buried at Cameron Cemetery in Cameron, West Virginia, alongside his beloved wife, Brucie, who predeceased him by five years.

Uriah Talmage Alley (courtesy Jay S. Hoar, *The North's Last Boys in Blue***).**

Chapter 6

The Western Territories
(as of April 1865)

After the Louisiana Purchase of 1803, which greatly expanded America's territories west of the Mississippi, additional land acquisitions, territorial boundary changes, and the formation of new states necessitated over twenty map alterations, right up until the end of the Civil War; the molding and redefining of state and territory boundaries seemed endless. Though it did reach its zenith, the growth process continued for another 90 years as territories were subdivided and new states established. The Louisiana Purchase alone made it possible for the federal government to create 15 new states out of 828,000 square miles the federal government acquired from France for $15 million.[1]

Though the federal government owned the land, legislators in Washington, D.C., were cognizant that the territories had to be settled and developed to truly become an economical investment for not only present settlers but also for future generations. The first pioneers from the East Coast had settled lands in the 1800s and early 1900s but not in great numbers, especially after being confronted by Indians whose land they were attempting to occupy. By the 1870s and 1880s America had already realized that a new and larger wave of pioneers was needed to settle and develop the territories.

Dating back to the 1850s, land grants (a government gift of real estate or the privilege to use the land) were given to the railroads.[2] Extending the privilege to railroads before giving land to private citizens proved a wise decision. After the transcontinental railroad was completed in May 1869, it became possible for people to travel faster and more conveniently from the East to the West Coast. Settlers took advantage of the opportunity and rode the rails westward. After finishing the line, the railroads sold their excess land to the influx of new settlers, usually at an exorbitant price. For newly arrived settlers, the railroads provided a ready access to manufactured goods with their ability to transport such items from the industrial cities east of the

Mississippi to settlers out West. As Americans continued to populate the West, the remoteness of the territories diminished, not in miles but in travel time. Simply put, America's lands became considerably more accessible.

It was 1871 when a young correspondent requested career advice from Horace Greeley, editor of the *New York Tribune*. Greeley responded and a phrase from his letter quickly made history: "Go West!" He said more than that, qualifying his recommendation by giving the young man some food for thought: "Can you chop? Can you plow? Can you mow?" Concluding his letter, he said, "Having mastered these, gather up your family, and Go West!"[3] Greeley knew that relocating there proved difficult and required the heartiest of souls to survive, but he also knew that the opportunities were boundless.

In 1889, prime real estate left unassigned in Oklahoma by the federal government was to be opened for settlement. About two million acres were made available and over 50,000 folks showed up to stake a claim. It came to be called the Oklahoma Land Rush. Each successful claimant was allowed up to 160 acres of land with the proviso that they not only live on the property but also improve it. If they complied, the settlers were granted a land title by the federal government.[4]

With a sense of adventure, the desire to acquire property, and a fresh start in life, many Civil War veterans and their families migrated to the West. Twenty-six years before the Oklahoma Land Rush, a Union army scout named Daniel Freeman beat everyone to the punch while the war still raged. He was leaving the Nebraska Territory for duty in St. Louis, Missouri, on January 1, 1863, when he convinced a local land clerk he met at a New Year's Eve party the night before to open his office so he could file a land claim. Everything was copasetic. The Homestead Act, signed into law by President Abraham Lincoln on May 20, 1862, allowed such claims to be filed.[5] It remains unclear how many of the following veterans (Union and Confederate) were land recipients who ultimately settled in the western territories. Certainly it had to be a very significant number.

Arizona

Parker Louis Gordon
(b. September 1, 1847, d. December 5, 1946)
Co. F, 154th Regiment, Illinois Volunteer Infantry

Regimental Brief: The regiment was formed at Camp Butler near Springfield, Illinois, and mustered in February 21, 1865. The 154th moved to Louisville, Kentucky, and then to Nashville and Murfreesboro, Tennessee

(February 24 through March 3, 1865). There it guarded the Nashville & Chattanooga Railroad until April 1865. From April until September, the 154th performed garrison duty. The unit was mustered out on September 18, 1865.

    Losses: 76 dead from disease.[6]

Veteran's Brief: On November 19, 2005, members of the Sons of Union Veterans of the Civil War, Arizona, conducted a grave-site rededication ceremony at the Greenwood Memory Lawn Cemetery in Phoenix to honor Arizona's last surviving Civil War veteran.[7] After a long and exhaustive search by the organization's members, the veteran's identity was uncovered. His name was Parker Louis Gordon.[8] Three years later a memorial marker was placed in Gordon's honor at Pioneer and Military Memorial Park in Phoenix by members of the Picacho Peak Camp-at-Large #1,

Parker Louis Gordon (*Life and Labors of Rev. Henry S. Gordon*).

Sons of Union Veterans of the Civil War (SUVCW), Phoenix, Arizona.[9]

    Born near Steeleville, Illinois, Parker Louis Gordon's father, Henry S., came from Franklin, Pennsylvania, and his mother, Rebecca Young, from England. On February 15, 1865, barely six months shy of his eighteenth birthday, he managed to enlist as a private in Co. F, 154th Regiment, Illinois Volunteer Infantry, and was initially made a drummer. Shortly after that, he was assigned duties as an infantryman.[10] According to his descendant Richard McNeil, a great-grandson, despite the regiment's short-lived history Gordon saw "much action." But in mid–May of 1865, while serving at Murfreesboro, Tennessee, he caught a severe cold that required immediate medical attention and was incapacitated for several weeks. Fortunately, and unlike many others who fell ill in his unit, he fully recovered and returned to duty before being discharged along with his regiment on September 18, 1865.[11]

    Gordon married three times: first to Emma Walters of Rockwood on November 30, 1871; then to Emma Hall of Campbell Hill in March 1883; and last to Rebecca Jane Weedon, also of Campbell Hill, on October 27, 1888. All three women lived in close proximity to his residence in Steeleville. What motivated Gordon and his family to move from his "comfortable home" at Ava, Illinois, in 1918 to Phoenix, Arizona, remains a mystery.[12] Only scant details of his later years have been found. After the family's move to

Phoenix, Gordon transitioned from farmer to grocer, an occupation that took him into retirement at the ripe old age of eighty.[13] In his mid-twenties, he fathered a child with his first wife, Emma, and later adopted two additional children while married to Rebecca.[14]

At the age of 99, Gordon passed away after a brief illness at the home of his daughter, Grace Townsend. He was survived by his wife Rebecca, a daughter, and several grandchildren and great-grandchildren.[15] His remains are entombed in a crypt at Greenwood Memory Lawn Cemetery, in Phoenix. On the front of the marble vault is embossed, "Arizona's Last Union Civil War Soldier, Parker Louis Gordon, 1847–1946, ," and underneath, "Rebecca Jane 1867–1953."[16]

Colorado

Robert T. Bryan
(b. August 29, 1848, d. January 17, 1949)
Co. D, 145th Regiment, Illinois Volunteer Infantry

Regimental Brief: The 145th was organized at Camp Butler near Springfield, Illinois, and mustered in for 100 days on June 9, 1864. It was ordered to St. Louis, Missouri, on June 12, performed duty there until September and was mustered out at Camp Butler September 23, 1864.

Losses: 40 dead from disease.[17]

Veteran's Brief: At the age of 12, Robert T. Bryan witnessed some of the Lincoln-Douglas debates that have long since gone down in history. According to Robert years later, the debates left him with a lasting impression. In the mid–1860s, his father, Alfred L., a gentleman of Scotch and Irish descent, was a personal friend of Abraham Lincoln. Ironically, Robert was not only born in a log cabin like the 16th president, he also hailed from the town of Lincoln, Illinois.[18]

Only 15 years old at the time of enlistment, Bryan served with Co. D, 145th Regiment, Illinois Volunteer Infantry, first as a driver for a 30-mule team out of a Missouri supply depot and

Robert T. Bryan (courtesy Carnegie Branch Library for Local History, Boulder, Colorado).

later as a guard at an Illinois prison that housed approximately 2,000 Confederate soldiers.[19] Because the regiment was mustered for a period of only 100 days, his military time passed quickly.

After his discharge, Bryan married Joanna Chenowith on September 6, 1865, in Lincoln, Illinois. During the next several years, he and his wife lived in Illinois, Iowa, Colorado, Kansas, and Nebraska before returning to Harlan, Iowa, were he farmed and operated a laundry.[20]

In 1925, Bryan's beloved wife, Joanna, passed away. On the invitation of his widowed daughter, Effie Clapper, a seamstress, he moved to her home in Boulder, Colorado, which became his last domicile.[21] While living in Boulder he joined the local GAR post, in which he was active. As one of the last Civil War veterans living in Boulder, Bryan participated as a featured guest in a number of patriotic parades and reviews. It is said that he never refused what he called "a good game of dominos."[22] Blessed with good eyesight, he was able to read newspapers and the Bible without glasses right up until the end.[23]

Robert T. Bryan died in Boulder at the age of 100. All five of his children survived him. Prior to his passing, Bryan requested that his body be returned to Iowa for burial. His wish was granted and his remains were interred at Thurman Cemetery in Thurman, Iowa.[24] (In 2012, the small town of Thurman, with a population of approximately 250 people, suffered devastating losses from a tornado that destroyed nearly 75 percent of its homes and businesses.)[25]

Idaho

Israel Adam Broadsword
(b. December 23, 1846, d. July 25, 1952)
Co. H, 51st Regiment, Missouri Infantry

Regimental Brief: The regiment enlisted men in St. Joseph, Missouri, from March 1 through April 14, 1865, and performed most of its duty in the St. Louis area. The 51st was mustered out on August 31, 1865.

Losses: 2 enlisted killed and 47 dead from disease.[26]

Veteran's Brief: Israel A. Broadsword was born in Ottawa, Ohio. When he joined the Union army, the war was nearly over. The few months that he did serve were with Co. H, 51st Regiment, Missouri Infantry. Despite a short enlistment, he saw action in a major battle at Lexington, Missouri, along with a number of smaller engagements.

During late 1868 and early 1869, Broadsword served as a sergeant in

Co. H, 19th Regiment, Kansas Volunteer Cavalry, during the Indian wars.[27] Many years passed before he shocked his son, George, by telling him that he rode out of Topeka, Kansas, with his regiment one day to rescue two ladies (a Miss White and a Mrs. Morgan) at Little Clear Water River in Texas. The women had been taken prisoner during an Indian raid. The rescue attempt proved successful and the Indians were driven back.[28]

In 1870, Broadsword married Viola Amy Morris from Troy, Kansas. The union produced two children. Viola died in 1900 at Kerwin, Kansas. No documents have been found relating to a second marriage, yet one source lists Broadsword as the father of nine sons, three of whom served in World War I, and a daughter.[29] During his long life, Broadsword lived in Colorado, Kansas, and Idaho while working as a frontiersman, rancher, homesteader and farmer. His occupations were discovered by reviewing U.S. Federal Census records.[30]

For many years, Israel Adam Broadsword lived in Samuels, Idaho.[31] At the age of 101 he received a Civil War service medal, presented to him by Major F.V. Smith of the University of Idaho's Reserve Officers Training program. It was given belatedly to Broadsword on behalf of the War Department, which was notified of the oversight by Abe Goff, a local state congressman. The formal ceremony drew family, neighbors, and friends, one as

Even at the age of 103, Israel Adam Broadsword was still able to tend to his fruit trees (*Scenic Idaho* 5, no. 1 [1950], in an article written by Mary E. Reeves and archived at Boise State University).

young as three, along with a few centenarians for good measure. Also present were veterans of the Spanish-American War, World War I, and World War II.[32]

According to writer Mary E. Reeves, Broadsword believed "that not only time has softened the intense hatred of those early days, but also the fact that not many people living then are alive today to cherish the old grudges."[33] Just prior to his death at the age of 105 in Spokane, Washington, he might have been transported across the state border to a veterans home or hospital. In any event, Israel Adam Broadsword's remains were brought back to Sandpoint, Idaho, for burial at Pinecrest Memorial Park.[34]

Montana

Thomas Arthur Castle
(b. October 8, 1846, d. November 25, 1943)
Co. B, 132nd Regiment, Pennsylvania Volunteer Infantry

Regimental Brief: The regiment was organized at Harrisburg, Pennsylvania, in August 1862. The 132nd moved to Washington, D.C., on August 19 and performed duty there until September 2, then took part in the Maryland Campaign (September 6 through 22, 1862) and fought at the Battle of Antietam (September 16 and 17). From there the regiment moved to Harpers Ferry, Virginia, on September 22 and performed duty there until October 30. From December 12 through 15, the unit fought at the Battle of Fredericksburg before taking part in the Battle of Chancellorsville (May 1 through 5). It was mustered out on May 24, 1863.

Losses: 3 officers and 70 enlisted men killed and mortally wounded and 40 enlisted men dead from disease.[35]

Veteran's Brief: For years, Robert A. Thornburg was considered the last surviving Civil War veteran from the State of Montana. He died on November 26, 1944; however, the author believes there were several issues with his selection. Thornburg claimed to have served in a southern Missouri local militia, but his words came without definitive proof, either verbally or in writing. Along the way, he noted that his military service records were destroyed in a fire. Also, no affidavits were ever provided by Thornburg that "conclusively" proved the legitimacy of his claim. In the final analysis, there was never any evidence he could use on his own behalf. Even though Thornburg attended Civil War reunions—

Thomas Arthur Castle's final resting place at Lakeview Cemetery, Cheyenne, Wyoming (courtesy Rick J. Fisher). Insert: the only known image of the veteran, taken during a 1914 GAR Memorial Day ceremony (*Wyoming Tales and Trails: Cheyenne Photos*).

as many imposters did—and came from an area where a high concentration of Confederate soldiers lived (a nebulous argument at best), his claim to be a veteran cannot be substantiated beyond a reasonable doubt, at least not until additional evidence surfaces.

The author has selected the next in line for the honor: Thomas Arthur Castle. But even Castle's selection comes with a bit of uncertainty, not because of his credentials but because of the short length of time the veteran lived in Montana.[36]

Castle was born in Factoryville, Pennsylvania. During the Civil War, Thomas' father, Francis, served in the U.S. Army Corps of Engineers. His service most likely influenced young Thomas to enlist as a private on August 11, 1862, despite his being underage. During his tenure in the military, Castle fought with his regiment in several major battles. On May 24, 1863, he was discharged at Harrisburg, Pennsylvania.[37]

After arriving home from the war, Castle became a miller. Later, with his father, he became a contractor and builder. Looking for adventure, both he and his father pulled up stakes and moved with Thomas's young wife to Cheyenne, Wyoming, a long and arduous trip. They traveled as far as they could by rail before joining others on a wagon train. They arrived at Cheyenne in 1867, a bit dusty but safe, as one of the first groups of settlers. There Castle set out to become a livestock rancher on land just north of Cheyenne.[38]

In 1938, with his daughter, Alice Williams, the two journeyed to Gettysburg, Pennsylvania, for the commemoration of the seventy-fifth anniversary of the Battle of Gettysburg. Attending the reunion brought Castle great pleasure. For thirty years, he was the GAR commander of the John F. Reynolds Post No. 33 at Cheyenne. He also served as junior vice commander of the GAR Department of Colorado and Wyoming and up until the last few years of his life led the Cheyenne military parade. When the assembly of veterans reached the cemetery, he was given the honor of reciting General Logan's Order No. 11 that created Decoration Day (now called Memorial Day).[39]

Thomas Arthur Castle died a widower at the age of 97 at his daughter's home in Shelby, Montana, while under her care. It was Thanksgiving morning and within minutes of feeling ill, the aged veteran expired.[40]

The debate continues as to which state can rightfully claim this man as one of its own. Though Castle lived most of his adult life in Wyoming, he did, in fact, spend his remaining time in Montana. As he died in Montana, that was his legal residence and thus why this author credited him as the last Civil War veteran from that state. However, some might disagree with this decision, especially because of the following: five days after his death Castle's remains were returned to Wyoming for burial at Lakeview Cemetery in Cheyenne, Wyoming.[41]

Nebraska

Michael Bon Doll
(b. June 6, 1849, d. December 24, 1948)
Co. F, 7th Regiment, Iowa Volunteer Infantry

Regimental Brief: Organized at Burlington, Iowa, between July 24 and August 4, 1861, the regiment's first duty stations were in Missouri, Kentucky, and Illinois respectively. After November, the unit returned to Missouri and remained there until the end of January 1862. On February 16, after moving to Tennessee, the 7th helped capture Ft. Donelson. In March the regiment fought at the Battle of Pittsburg Landing and in April at the Battle of Shiloh. Beginning the end of April 1862 the 7th spent the majority of its time in Mississippi fighting at the Battle of Iuka (September 19) and the Battle of Corinth (October 3 and 4). For the balance of the year, it was involved in several pursuits of the enemy throughout Mississippi. In March 1863 the regiment moved to Bethel, Tennessee, remaining there until the beginning of June. Until year's end, the unit was involved in a number of skirmishes. After all the heavy fighting the two previous years, the veterans were furloughed during the months of January and February 1864. Upon their return, the regiment was ordered to Tennessee until April before moving to Georgia and taking part in the Atlanta Campaign in May. On May 13 and 14, it fought at the Battle of Resaca. After an assault on Kennesaw Mountain (June 27) the regiment fought at the Battle of Atlanta and the subsequent siege of the city (July 22 through August 25). During most of October, the 7th pursued General Hood into Alabama. On December 10 through 21, it was involved in the Siege of Savannah before being ordered to take part in the Campaign of the Carolinas (January to April 1865). From March 4 through 6, it took part in an expedition to Florence, South Carolina, before moving to North Carolina, where it fought at the Battle of Bentonville (March 20 and 21). In mid–April, the regiment advanced on Raleigh and took park in its occupation. After the surrender of General Johnston's army, the unit marched to Washington, D.C., where it

There was nothing like a good cigar for veteran Michael Bon Doll (courtesy *Omaha World-Herald*).

took part in the Grand Review (May 24, 1865). It was mustered out at Louisville, Kentucky, on July 12, 1865.

Losses: 7 officers and 134 enlisted men killed and mortally wounded and 4 officers and 160 enlisted men dead from disease.[42]

Veteran's Brief: The 7th had experienced years of hard fighting before Michael Bon Doll (aka Bondoll) enlisted as an underage recruit on February 8, 1865, at the tail end of the war. It is doubtful that he saw much combat during those few months. He was fortunate in several regards. Not only did he see President Lincoln in Washington, D.C., when Bon Doll was on his way south to join his new regiment but when the war ended he also participated in the regiment's march to Washington, D.C., and the Grand Review held shortly thereafter. Along with the rest of his regiment, he was discharged shortly thereafter.[43]

After returning home, Bon Doll became a farmer. In 1875, he married Martha Ann Rumbley at Lynn, Iowa. They made their home in Wiota, Iowa, where they raised six children. Married for twenty-seven years, Martha passed away in 1902. After her death, Bon Doll moved to Colorado for several years and then to Beatrice, Nebraska, where he lived for 30 more years with his daughter, Lottie Yager.[44]

While living in Nebraska, he was an active member of the GAR.[45] When he died at the age of 99, the state command was disbanded and the records transferred to the Nebraska State Historical Society, where they reside today. Over the years, Bon Doll's cemetery plaque had sunk into the ground and was rediscovered only within the past few years. At that point the bronze marker was affixed to a new slab and adorned with an additional plaque that signified his status as the last Civil War veteran from Nebraska. On October 19, 2013, a ceremony was held at Wiota Cemetery near Wiota, Iowa, to rededicate the grave site by Daughters of Union Veterans of the Civil War and Sons of Union Veterans of the Civil War from both Nebraska and Iowa, along with Michael Bon Doll's descendants as honored guests.[46]

Nevada

William Orrin Phillips
(b. February 16, 1846, d. December 13, 1940)
Co. G, 144th Regiment, Ohio Volunteer Infantry (National Guard)

Regimental Brief: In early June 1864, shortly after muster, Company B was assigned defensive duty at Baltimore, Maryland. After being relieved in Baltimore, it took part in the Battle of Monocacy Junction in Maryland

(July 9) before moving to Washington, D.C., on July 13. In mid–July, the unit advanced to Winchester, Virginia. There it operated in the Shenandoah Valley from July 20 to mid–August. On August 13, the unit helped to repulse an attack by General John Singleton Mosby, the "Grey Ghost," and his Partisan Rangers at the small Virginia town of Berryville. It remained at Berryville until August 20. Eleven days later, the company was mustered out, on August 31, 1864.

Losses: 10 enlisted men killed and mortally wounded and 53 enlisted men dead from disease.[47]

Veteran's Brief: Born and raised in Upper Sandusky, Ohio, William Orrin Phillips enlisted in the 144th Regiment, Ohio Volunteer Infantry, at Camp Chase about four miles west of downtown Columbus, Ohio. The camp served as a staging and training facility as well as a Confederate prisoner of war compound until war's end.[48] The muster roll describes Phillips as 5'8" tall with fair completion, blue eyes and light hair. He was 18 years old and a shoemaker when he enlisted. Phillips knew when he enrolled that he would serve only 100 days. During his brief time in the army, he experienced some combat. After mustering out with the rest of the regiment, Phillips returned to Ohio and lived there for another two years.

While living in Ohio, Phillips married a divorcee named Rachel Heffelbower, a lady two years his senior. Shortly after the nuptials, he and Rachel moved to Greenleaf, Kansas, where they set up a homestead. In less than a month, Phillips constructed a 12' × 18' house—about the size of a small living room today. The structure was described as having "a shingled roof, board floor, one door and two windows of sash and glass."[49] On October 4, 1869, Phillips acquired 160 acres of land—a land-grant claim—cultivating about 23 acres while planting an orchard of 600 fruit trees. Initially he built a stable, a hog pen, and a chicken coop. Along the way, the couple had five children—a girl and four boys, the firstborn in 1869 and the last in 1883.[50] After living in Kansas for thirty-five years, Phillips moved to Reno, Nevada, where he lived with his son Frederick and daughter-in-law Mattie.[51] Phillips was now

William Orrin Phillips' cemetery monument. A photograph of the veteran has proved elusive (courtesy Lena Taylor McKee).

living on his invalid pension granted by the federal government in 1888; by 1921, he was receiving $150 a quarter. Many of his health problems in old age were attributed to diseases he contracted at Camp Parole, Maryland. After a heavy rainstorm he was afflicted with mumps and fever and eventually had his right testicle removed because of a serious infection, caused by the illness, that settled there.[52]

By 1927, and continuing for the rest of his life, the aftereffects of the war had taken a heavy toll on his body. He was diagnosed with sciatic rheumatism that at first caused numbness in his legs and later nearly a total loss of function. He was generally confined to his home. When he did go out, he walked with a cane and was regularly guided by a caregiver.[53] Even with his disability he was able to attend the commemoration of the seventy-fifth anniversary of the Battle of Gettysburg, and up until the end he managed to take part in GAR Memorial Day activities in his hometown. On December 13, 1940, Phillips died a few months shy of his 95th birthday leaving behind three children, ten grandchildren, and twelve great-grandchildren. His wife, Rachel, had predeceased him in 1928. Before his wife's death, they had lost their only daughter to injuries caused during a cyclone that struck near her home. After William Phillips' funeral, his remains were transported from Reno to Mt. James Cemetery in Greenleaf, Kansas, where he lies today.

New Mexico

William T. Scammahorn, Sr.
(b. December 16, 1846, d. September 12, 1945)
Co. C, 155th Regiment, Illinois Volunteer Infantry

Regimental Brief: The regiment was organized at Camp Butler outside of Springfield, Illinois, and mustered in on February 28, 1865. The unit's brief assignment was to guard blockhouses along the lines of the Nashville and Chattanooga Railroad. The regiment was mustered out on September 4, 1865.

Losses: 71 dead from disease.[54]

Veteran's Brief: William T. Scammahorn was the last surviving Civil War veteran from the State of New Mexico.[55] Born in Ohio, he enlisted in the 155th Regiment, Illinois Infantry, at the age of 18 while the unit was being formed. After months of guarding blockhouses, for much of his enlistment, the war was finally over. Considering its short duration of service, Scammahorn's regiment experienced a high number of deaths by illness (during the war years, disease took twice the toll of those who died in combat). He was discharged on September 4, 1865.[56]

On December 17, 1874, Scammahorn married Sarah C. Flesher. She died in Colorado on July 18, 1897. Five years later, on February 10, 1902, he married Vennie B. Baltzly, a lady also from Colorado. The marriages produced a total of ten children, six boys and four girls. Before finally settling in New Mexico, Scammahorn and his family had lived in Illinois, Indiana, Kansas, Arkansas, and Colorado.[57] For years he made his living from tilling the soil, prospecting, and tie-hacking for the railroad. There is also evidence that at one time he tried his hand at horse-trading.

William T. Scammahorn, Sr., died of hypostatic pneumonia on September 12, 1945, in the small town of Chama, New Mexico, in the northern mountainous region of the state. He was 98 years old. There is scant and unconfirmed evidence that he was part Native American. His second wife, Vennie, predeceased him in January of 1939.[58] Accord-

William T. Scammahorn at the age of 96. His grave site has been lost over time (courtesy Jay S. Hoar, from his collection).

ing to a descendant, Grace Jones (now deceased), William T. Scammahorn, Sr., "is buried under a cedar tree in the middle of nowhere" on private land in or near Chama. The interment area was covered by rock but by a 1979 account the government headstone had yet to be found.[59]

North Dakota

Dallas George Duell
(b. December 12, 1845, d. January 22, 1943)

Co. D, 72nd Regiment, Illinois Volunteer Infantry, and
Co. C and F, 66th Regiment, U.S. Colored Troops (USCT)

Regimental Brief, 72nd Regiment, Illinois Infantry: The regiment was organized at Chicago. Illinois, and became known as the first regiment of the Chicago Board of Trade. By August 1862, the entire regiment was complete and mustered into service for three years. The very day of its muster it started for Cairo, Illinois, arriving there on August 24. On September 6, the regiment was ordered to Paducah, Kentucky, where it went on post duty for eleven days before moving to Columbus, Kentucky, at which point it performed guard and picket duty until November 21. Later it found time for two expeditions: Clarkton, Missouri, when it dispersed a Confederate camp and captured a number of prisoners, horses, and supplies, and New Madrid. The regiment then made its headquarters at Memphis until January 19, 1863. While stationed there, it went on an expedition to Horn Lake Creek, where it dispersed a gang of Blythe's Confederate guerrillas. In the process, the men captured a number of Confederates. The first major battle in which the regiment engaged was at Champion's Hill. In a desperate charge at Vicksburg, Mississippi, on May 22 the regiment suffered heavy losses. On July 12, it embarked for Natchez, Mississippi, where it landed the next day, taking possession of the town while capturing a large number of prisoners, several pieces of artillery, Confederate government stores, and 5,000 head of Texas cattle. There it remained, doing provost duty, until October 17. For the next year, the regiment performed provost guard at Vicksburg. On November 29 the men became involved in a severe skirmish at Spring Hill on the road between Columbia and Franklin, Tennessee. Finally, it was actively engaged in the Siege of Spanish Fort, which was the last hostile action in which it participated. On August 6, 1865, the regiment was mustered out at Vicksburg and thence moved directly to Chicago.

Losses: 7 officers and 79 enlisted men killed or mortally wounded and 3 officers and 145 enlisted men died of disease.[60]

Regimental Brief, 66th Regiment, U.S. Colored Troops (USCT): On March 11, 1864, from the remnants of the 4th Mississippi Infantry (African

Descent), the 66th Regiment, U.S. Colored Troops, was formed. It consisted of all black enlistees with white officers only. The 66th performed post and garrison duty at Goodrich Landing and Lake Providence, Louisiana, until February of 1865. In March and July, it again saw action at Goodrich

Judge Dallas G. Duell as he appeared in the *Devils Lake* (ND) *Inter Ocean* newspaper, June 19, 1908, as a candidate for the office of state's attorney (courtesy Lake Region Heritage Center, Devils Lake).

Landing. Later the unit performed post and garrison duty at Little Rock, Arkansas, until March of 1865 and then at Vicksburg, Mississippi, for a year thereafter. The 66th was mustered out on March 20, 1866.[61]

Veteran's Brief: Born in Fulton, New York, Dallas George Duell moved with his family to Palatine, Illinois, at the age of 11. Not yet 17 years old, Duell enlisted on July 30, 1862, as a private in the 72nd Illinois Infantry.

During his time with the 72nd, Duell had many fascinating wartime experiences—both poignant and humorous—that were highlighted in his hometown newspaper, the *Devils Lake World*, beginning on March 3. 1926 (excerpts were republished years later in the North Dakota State Government Web site). As Duell noted in one of his stories, he experienced his first taste of "havoc" when he was able to view a recent battlefield upon approaching Vicksburg, Mississippi. This is what he said:

> The dead lay very thick upon the ground and the wounded who could walk were trying to get back to the field hospital. It was an awful sight, ambulances were going down the road towards the hospital and blood could be seen dripping from the cracks in the bottom of the box. In going over the field I came across a young soldier who was about my age, propped up against a tree, dressed in rebel gray who had been shot in the abdomen. I gave him a drink from my canteen and talked with him for quite a little while. He said that he knew that he was going to die, that he had been forced into the army and that it was against his will that he was fighting against the North. He said that he was not afraid to die and if only he could have seen his mother before going, he could die happy.[62]

Arguably the tragic scene had a profound impact upon Duell's psyche, as he concluded his assessment of the scene by telling the newspaper correspondent: "This conversation with the boy caused me to feel pretty creepy and wonder when my turn would come to be in the same fix that he was."[63]

At the surrender of Vicksburg, Duell remembers seeing all the "small white flags and large ones" popping up over the trenches. "In a short time," he said, "the men in blue were standing on our entrenchments and those in gray on the rebel line ... exchanging witticisms with each other as if they had not a short time previously been trying to seek each other's life."[64]

On December 26, 1863, at Vicksburg, Duell was intentionally discharged so he could accept a lieutenant's commission in the 66th Regiment, U.S. Colored Troops. With Company F of the 66th he participated in the Louisiana and Arkansas campaigns. He was ultimately discharged on March 20, 1866.[65]

After the war, General E.O.C. Ord appointed Duell as registrar of Hancock County, Mississippi, during the initial Reconstruction period. Eventually Duell returned home and pursued a career in law at Wheaton College in Illinois. While there, he met and married Delia L. Edmonds (March 19, 1868). Sometime after the wedding, he left school and took up farming. Seven years later Delia died. In 1882, he met and married Ella Viola Snider.

Between the marriages 14 children were born, seven girls and seven boys (two died in infancy). In 1885, the family moved to Devils Lake, North Dakota, where the couple claimed 160 acres of government land.[66] About this time, Duell resumed farming, while also practicing law for the first time after admission to the North Dakota Bar.

Initially life was not easy for the young Duell family, especially during the harsh North Dakota winters. As Duell's wife, Ella, explained years later, "One time we were out of wood and my husband had gone to town for supplies [he had driven an ox team with a wagonload of wheat he intended to trade for wood]. I walked to a neighbors one-and-a half miles and carried home a big armful of wood and dragged a long pole to chop up." But upon returning home Ella faced the ravages of an unexpected blizzard. For seven days, she chopped wood inside the shack doing the best she could to keep her three small children and herself warm. She went on to explain "the walls began to get white with frost and when the storm ceased, I nailed a white kitchen apron on the lath and nailed it to the corner of the shanty to call for help to care for our stock and shovel through 13-feet of snow drifts." Fortunately two neighbors took heed and came to her rescue. It was a hard life indeed. During the first few years at Devils Lake, Ella also helped her husband tar paper the shanty, build a sod stable, and dig a well.[67]

As for her husband, Dallas continued to absorb himself in the legal profession as farming took a back seat. Along the way, he was elected a Ramsey County judge, a position he held for fourteen years. During his long life, he was also elected as state's attorney and later a police magistrate for Devils Lake.[68] Adding to his credentials, in 1891 Judge Duell organized the North Dakota National Guard Company at Devils Lake and served as its first captain. As an active GAR member he, along with Ella, attended at least 45 national encampments. When his friend John Carroll died during his term as a GAR commander for North Dakota, Duell assumed the role. He was North Dakota's last veteran to serve in that capacity.[69]

Three days after he died at the age of 97, Judge Dallas George Duell was interred at the GAR Cemetery at Devils Lake. He had outlived his wife by less than seven months. His descendants continued his military legacy, serving in World War I, World War II, and the Korean Conflict.[70]

Oklahoma

William Mercer Buck
(b. June 5, 1852, d. July 10, 1950)
Scout and intelligence gatherer for the Confederacy

Regimental Brief: The last surviving veteran from Oklahoma was not affiliated with any specific Confederate regiment.

Veteran's Brief: When General Lee surrendered his troops at Appomattox, William Mercer Buck had yet to reach the age of thirteen. In this illustrious grouping of the last Civil War veterans from each state, Buck is, by far, the youngest.[71]

The reader may wonder how a boy this young became a Confederate soldier. The answer is simple. When members of the Confederate army camped near his home, Buck offered his assistance as a scout. It is said he performed his assignment so well that as time passed he was given command of a group of Southern scouts. Buck felt, however, that his greatest contribution to the war effort was helping his mother repair tattered clothing worn by troops passing through their farm.[72]

The war ended rather abruptly for the young boy. Not long afterward, he decided to move to a Confederate refuge in Van Zandt County, Texas. Here he lived for eight years. On December 4, 1872, while still in Texas, he married Anna Eliza Booth. They had twelve children over a fifty-nine-year span. For many of those years, Buck labored as a farmer before settling into a career he truly loved: carpentry.[73] Exactly when he moved to Oklahoma is unclear, but he did live there for a number of years.[74]

The citizens of the State of Oklahoma called him "General" in honor of his veteran status. To his family, he was known simply as "Pappy." Those who knew him, especially family members, said he was "a courtly old gentleman, with a keen sense of humor, a strong feeling of family closeness, proud, yet thoughtful and considerate and 'very independent.'"[75]

Beginning in 1918, Buck attended United Confederate Veteran national reunions. In October 1948 in Montgomery, Alabama, he was elected commander in chief of the UCV at the 58th annual reunion, one of his greatest honors.[76] When asked the secret to his longevity, he replied, "I never drank, never smoked or never danced in all my life. I believe in living moderately." William Mercer Buck died of heart fail-

A smiling William Mercer Buck poses for the camera (courtesy Jay S. Hoar, *The South's Last Boys in Gray*).

ure at the age of 98, a "remarkable gentleman" to the end. His earthly remains lie at Greenhill Cemetery in Muskogee, Oklahoma.[77]

South Dakota

Horace Warner Simpson
(b. April 5, 1848, d. July 20, 1945)

Co. F, 23rd Regiment, Illinois Volunteer Infantry

Regimental Brief: The 23rd was organized at Chicago, Illinois, and mustered in on June 15, 1861. Its first duty was at New Creek, Virginia— soon to become West Virginia—where the unit remained in the general vicinity until April of 1863. The regiment was involved in several skirmishes throughout the balance of the year in places like Back Creek, Petersburg Gap, Moorefield, and the Kanawha Valley. In the beginning of January until April of 1864, the regiment conducted operations in Hampshire and Hardy counties. From April until June the 23rd was on furlough. When the regiment re-formed in early July, it was ordered to Harpers Ferry. In August it became part of General Sheridan's Shenandoah Valley Campaign (August 7 through November 28) and fought in such places as Cedar Creek (August

A spry Horace Warner Simpson at the age of 96 (courtesy Jay S. Hoar, *The North's Last Boys in Blue*).

12), Winchester (August 17), and Berryville (September 3). On September 19, the regiment joined in the Battle of Winchester. On December 30, it moved to Petersburg, where it took part in siege operations against Petersburg and Richmond that lasted from January through April 1865. From March 28 through April 9, the regiment was involved in the Appomattox Campaign while pursuing General Lee and his forces (April 3 through 9). Present at Appomattox Court House on April 9, 1865, when General Lee surrendered, the 23rd remained in Virginia until July before mustering out at Richmond, Virginia, on July 24, 1865. The men were officially discharged at Chicago, Illinois, on July 30, 1865.

　　Losses: 4 officers and 50 enlisted

men killed and mortally wounded and 2 officers and 93 enlisted men dead from disease.[78]

Veteran's Brief: Horace Warner Simpson was born in Pecatonica, Illinois. Growing up, Simpson worked on the family farm in Rockford helping with the chores. He also attended a rural school and completed eight years. Reminiscing about his youth, he was proud to tell his story about listening to the Lincoln-Douglas debates when he was only 10 years old.[79]

Simpson, like so many other last surviving Civil War veterans, was underage when he enlisted in the Union army (he either lied about his age or received consent from his parents to join). Nonetheless, he was only 15 years old when he joined the 23rd Regiment, Illinois Infantry. According to Simpson, his regiment was the second unit to enter Richmond when the Confederate capital fell in April 1865. After eighteen months of service, on August 4, 1865, he received his discharge.[80]

After returning to Rockford, he married Harriet R. Davis and settled into the life of a farmer. Eleven years later, the family moved to Manchester, Iowa, where they lived for ten years before moving again to Lyons, Nebraska. After his wife died in 1897, he moved to Faulkton, South Dakota, where he continued to farm for the remainder of his life.[81]

At the age of 97, Horace Warner Simpson died suddenly at his home shortly after hoeing his garden. He was survived by six children: four girls and two boys. According to a local newspaper obituary, he was devoted "to the principles of honesty, truth and square-dealing," all of which "won him the respect and admiration of the entire community."[82] His remains were transported to Laurel, Nebraska, for burial, presumably to be interred next to his wife.[83]

Utah

Harry Ira Stormes
(b. April 3, 1847, d. October 5, 1945)
Company M, 2nd Regiment, Wisconsin Cavalry

Regimental Brief: The regiment was organized at Milwaukee, Wisconsin, between December 30, 1861, and March 10, 1862. From mid–June to mid–July 1862, the 2nd marched to Jacksonport and Helena, Arkansas, where it remained until January of 1863. On February 4 the regiment was ordered to Memphis, Tennessee, where it remained until mid–May before moving to Vicksburg, Mississippi, in June. That month, the unit was involved in the Siege of Vicksburg and the Siege of Jackson. It remained in Mississippi until the end of December. During the following year (1864), it moved between Mississippi and Louisiana, seeing action in a number of places Northerners never heard of before: Sunnyside Landings, Fish Bayou, Pearl River, Clinton, Rodney, Fayette, Port Gibson, Cole Creek, Natchez, Woodville, Ft. Adams, and Yazoo City. At the end of 1864, the regiment moved to Memphis, Tennessee, where it remained until June. The regiment continued to skirmish and take part in expeditions for the remainder of the year. In March 1865, the 2nd moved to northern Mississippi before being ordered to Alexandria, Louisiana, in June. From there, it marched to Hempstead, Texas, the better part of August and there performed duty until October. The 2nd was mustered out at Austin, Texas, on November 15, 1865.

Losses: 24 enlisted men killed and mortally wounded and 4 officers and 234 enlisted men dead from disease.[84]

Veteran's Brief: Thousands of veterans moved westward after the war. Utah, situated in the Western Territory, attracted several thousand of these veterans, all looking for better opportunities.[85] Ardis E. Parshall, a Utah historian, perhaps said it best when speaking about the state's deceased Civil War veterans: "These men are part of our Civil War heritage—not because they went out from us to serve, but because they brought the legacy of their service back to enrich the life of Utah." As Parshall tells it, most, if not all, "blended seamlessly into Utah's social and commercial fabric."[86] Harry Ira Stormes was one of these men.

A newspaper correspondent once called Stormes "witty" and "chipper."[87] That description most likely was an accurate assessment of his personality. Case in point: Stormes made national headlines when he held annual solo encampments for eleven consecutive years as Utah's last department commander and lone comrade of Utah's GAR Department.[88] His meetings went something like this: he called the meeting to order; offered

a prayer; read the previous meeting minutes; nominated and reelected himself as the state commander; saluted his secretary, Mrs. Schnell (normally the only person in atten-

Harry Ira Stormes (left) with fellow GAR comrade George William Vogel, Sr., at Salt Lake City, Utah, April 26, 1937 (courtesy George C. Vogel, George W.'s great-grandson).

dance besides himself); then adjourned the proceedings. Stormes did not conduct the affairs to seek publicity for himself but rather to perpetuate the memory of former members who had passed before him. It was a noble gesture.[89]

Born in Vermont, Stormes (who preferred being called by his middle name, "Ira," rather than Harry) made his way through several states before enlisting in the 2nd Regiment, Wisconsin Cavalry, as a private on August 1, 1864. The extent of his wartime experience is vague. Less than a year after his enlistment, he was discharged on June 12, 1865, at Memphis, Tennessee.

Stormes married an Englishwoman seven years younger than he named Jennie Tachell. They had three children, two girls and a boy. Jennie died on January 14, 1931.[90] Although his greatest pleasure was smoking a pipe, Stormes also enjoyed cigars, so much so that he created a business of manufacturing them for the retail market. Unlike the majority of cigars that are sold today, his were handmade. Nobody is certain how long he lasted in the trade, but when cigar-making machines were introduced in the mid–1910s, it probably impacted his business. Ironically, though he enjoyed tobacco, he professed to smoking only three cigarettes during his lifetime. Turning to prospecting to earn a living, Stormes mined for gold and silver in the foothills of Nevada and Montana. Achieving only limited success with this endeavor, he decided to move to Salt Lake City, Utah, and settle down.[91] What he did to earn a living after his prospecting days is uncertain. Perhaps he joined the industrial revolution and returned to cigar making but this time using machinery instead of his hands.

Unlike many of the last Civil War veterans, Stormes was more of a fatalist. When asked the secret of his old age, he replied, "Some people have a long life and some a short one. All anyone can

"Ira" Stormes, as he preferred to be called, is pictured in the brochure *Proceedings of the Fifty-Ninth Annual Encampment, Department of Utah, Held at Newhouse Hotel, Salt Lake City, Utah, May 15, 1941* (author's collection).

do is live the Golden Rule and believe in the Creator. Habits, near as I can tell, don't make a difference."[92]

Ira Stormes was making plans to attend the National GAR Convention in Des Moines, Iowa, when he suddenly became ill. He passed away a short time later at the age of 98 after suffering from heart failure, leaving his daughter Jennie Elizabeth Berryman as his sole survivor. His remains lie alongside his wife in Wasatch Lawn Memorial Park, Salt Lake City, Utah.[93]

Washington

Hiram Randall Gale
(b. November 8, 1846, d. March 15, 1951)
Co. K, 46th Regiment, Wisconsin Volunteer Infantry

Regimental Brief: Formed at Madison, Wisconsin, on March 2, 1865, the regiment was mustered in March 2, 1865. The 46th moved to Louisville, Kentucky, from March 5 through 10, and then to Athens, Alabama, from

Hiram Randall Gale (center, wearing a wide-rimmed Grand Army of the Republic hat) inspects a newspaper that was hot off the press. Gale's son is the tall gentleman standing in the background (courtesy Museum of History and Industry, Seattle, Washington).

April 22 through 24. There it performed duty along the Nashville and Decatur Railroad until September. It was mustered out on September 27, 1865.

Losses: 20 dead from disease.[94]

Veteran's Brief: Like Harry Ira Stormes, Hiram Randall Gale hailed from Vermont. Born in Waterbury (12 miles northwest of Montpelier) to parents who hailed from Washington County, Vermont, the family moved westward during Hiram's early years. While living in Wisconsin, he enlisted on January 25, 1865, as a private with the 46th Regiment, Wisconsin Infantry (the unit did not officially muster until early March). On September 27, 1865, after less than six months of service, it was disbanded at Nashville, Tennessee. Hiram was discharged as a corporal.[95] It is doubtful that any of the soldiers within his unit ever saw combat.

Gale married three times: first to Laura Ann Perkins on August 10, 1870; second to Ida Rose Burdick in 1882; and third to Catherine A. McCumber on September 1, 1927. The first marriage produced four children, three boys and a girl, and the second a girl.[96]

In 1870, Hiram lived in Gale, Trempealeau County, Wisconsin, where he worked as a grocer. (The village of Gale was founded by George Gale, most likely an ancestor of Hiram.) It remains unclear when Gale departed for the State of Washington, but U.S. Federal Census records and other pertinent documents show him residing at Tacoma in 1892, Olympia in 1900, and Bremerton in 1920.[97] He most likely had been living in the State of Washington prior to 1887, as he and his two sons, Edgar and Charles, founded the *Bremerton News* while simultaneously buying out a few other newspaper companies in the area and operating them as well. Selling the newspaper business in 1920, instead of retiring he continued working, this time as a real estate agent. By 1930, Gale was living in Seattle and by 1940 in Edgewood. For several years, he served as the department commander for the GAR of Washington and Alaska. Later, he was elected commander in chief of the GAR, serving in that capacity from 1945 to 1946.[98]

Hiram Randall Gale died at the Veterans Administration Hospital in the town of American Lake, Washington, at the age of 104 and is buried at Evergreen-Washelli Memorial Park, Seattle, Washington.[99]

Wyoming

Hiram Alonzo Hunkins
(b. October 17, 1844, d. March 4, 1947)
Co. K, 48th Regiment, Wisconsin Volunteer Infantry

Regimental Brief: Near the close of the war, the 48th Regiment, Wisconsin Volunteer Infantry, was organized at Camp Washburn in Milwaukee, Wisconsin. During the year, the regiment of eight companies split into separate detachments in order to build fortifications, construct bridges, and erect buildings, all with the intent of protecting against Confederate guerrillas. Company K left Wisconsin on March 8 and arrived at Fort Scott, Kansas, on April 28. Five months later, the company marched to Fort Zarah, also in Kansas, arriving there on September 26. Later the unit was assigned garrison duty at Fort Lyon, Colorado, until December 1865. After a year, all the companies were mustered out of service on March 24, 1866, at Fort Leavenworth.

Losses: 16 dead from disease.[100]

Veteran's Brief: Hiram Alonzo Hunkins was the oldest of six children born in New Berlin Township, New York. Growing up he was pleased to learn of his distinguished heritage: his great-grandfather Robert Hunkins fought in the French and Indian War and was also a captain in Stark's Green Mountain Boys at Bennington, Vermont, and Saratoga, New York; his grandfather Hiram Hollister fought in the War of 1812; and his father, Benjamin, became Wisconsin's first territorial legislator. Eventually, Hiram

Left: As a 19-year-old private, Hiram Alonzo Hunkins appears ready to serve (courtesy Orin Hunkins, Hiram's great-grandson).

Right: Hiram Alonzo Hunkins in his senior years (courtesy Orin Hunkins, Hiram's great-grandson).

Alonzo Hunkins also added to his family's legacy of dedicated service to America, both civic and military.[101]

Tired of farming, on March 23, 1865, Hunkins enrolled in the 48th Regiment, Wisconsin Volunteer Infantry, and soon was assigned to Company K. During his year of service, he saw little if any action and his personal experiences seemed quite mundane: overseeing the Indian population in the area but never seeing any trouble; coal mining for fuel while in the field; and killing buffalo for rations. About buffalo hunting, Hunkins gave an interview to a newspaper reporter that was printed in the *Greeley Tribune* on November 5, 1934, in which he was quoted as saying "young buffalo tasted better than beef."[102]

When the conflict ended, Hunkins returned home to live with his parents but soon left for southeastern Nebraska. There he met a schoolmistress who became his bride, Cytherea Stearns. They married in Lincoln, Nebraska, sometime in 1869. It was back to farm living after he and his wife became homesteaders on eighty acres of former government land. But in 1889, Cytherea died unexpectedly, which must have been a terrible blow. Hunkins did the only thing he knew how to preserve her memory. He continued to farm the land for several decades while maintaining his strong Christian values: he never smoked, drank, or swore. But his age ultimately caught up to him. Nearing his ninetieth birthday, he wisely pulled up stakes and moved to Colorado to be near his daughter, Annis C. Barnes.[103]

An extremely intelligent man, he was a dedicated student of the economy. "People owe too much money," he once confided, "and the stream of interest is going from those who can't afford to pay to those who have plenty."[104] Hunkins was not only perceptive but light-years ahead in his thinking, especially when it came to finances. Throughout his life, he was most proud of his voting record, having cast a ballot in every election since 1868.[105]

The last three weeks of Hiram Alonzo Hunkins' life was spent at the Cheyenne VA hospital in Cheyenne, Wyoming.[106] His passing in that hospital gave him the title as the last Civil War veteran from Wyoming despite having lived for several years in Colorado. He was 102 years old. In another twist, Hunkins was laid to rest at Leland Cemetery, Cordova, Nebraska. His finally burial site should not come as a surprise, as that is where his beloved wife is interred.[107]

Before closing this section, it is worth mentioning that all too often we tend to think of veterans solely as aged warriors. That perception is dreadfully misleading. Take for example a brief account given to the author by Orin Hunkins, who remembers as a young child reading and reciting nursery rhymes with his great-grandfather. Hiram Alonzo Hunkins, the last Civil War veteran from Wyoming, was 98 years old at the time. Orin Hunkins would never forget the experience and the soft spot that resided in his great-grandfather's heart, nor would Judy Miller, who is pictured in an earlier brief sitting on the lap of her great-grandfather Daniel A. Clingaman doing exactly the same thing.[108]

Chapter 7

The Territories of Alaska and Hawaii

Alaska

Few people associate the State of Alaska with the Civil War, but there is a connection. Though many believe that the last shots of the war were fired in Brownsville, Texas, the final shots actually came from cannons on the deck of the CSS *Shenandoah* off the coast of Alaska.

The *Shenandoah* was built in "neutral" Great Britain for the Confederate navy and transported to the Confederacy in a stealth rendezvous near the African coast. Its primary mission "was to disrupt Union shipping and commerce." After burning Union vessels in the south Atlantic and the Indian Ocean, the *Shenandoah* and her crew headed for the Bering Sea. There the crew burned and pirated whalers, whose cargo of oil was an essential commodity in America during the nineteenth century. In just a single year, the *Shenandoah* was credited with the capture or destruction of 38 Union ships while taking 1,000 prisoners. Amazingly, the record was achieved without a single casualty on either side. When much of the marauding was accomplished, the Confederacy was near collapse. After hearing the news of General Lee's surrender at Appomattox, and to escape the distinct possibility of hanging, the crew sailed to Liverpool, England, where they surrendered to the Royal Navy. The vessel's flag was lowered for the last time on November 5, 1865. Today, the CSS *Shenandoah's* battle flag is on display at the Museum of the Confederacy in Richmond, Virginia.[1]

Though a number of Civil War veterans from both sides of the conflict migrated to Alaska and became prospectors during the Yukon gold rush, most returned to the United States with little to show for their chilling adventure. Those hardy souls who remained set up permanent homesteads throughout the territory. Some continued to prospect, others became clerks, cooks, farmers, lawyers, store proprietors, teachers, trappers, and woodcutters. As the years moved forward, the few remaining veterans slowly passed away and were buried in the wilderness near their shacks or in cemeteries in Anchorage or Fairbanks. Today, only a scant number of stone monuments are visible. Nearly all are difficult to decipher, a state caused by Alaska's long and harsh winters. The inscriptions—if the stone monuments had any—were in most cases obliterated decades ago by the elements. Burial records to determine where Civil War veterans are interred are practically nonexistent. An unknown number of veterans were buried on family plots with graves marked by simple wooden planks inserted into the soil. The markers rotted away in less than a decade or two and in most cases remote grave sites in the wilderness were never officially recorded.

The author believes that the last surviving Civil War veteran from Alaska is John N. Conna, who died 38 years before Alaska achieved statehood on January 3, 1959.

Alaska's Last Civil War Veteran

John Newington Conna
(b. c.1836, d. October 11, 1921)
1st Regiment, Louisiana Native Guards, USA/Corps d'Africa

Regimental Brief: Organized in New Orleans, Louisiana, in 1862 the 1st Regiment, Louisiana Native Guards, U.S.A./Corps d'Africa, became one of the first all-black combat units during the war. The Union contingent mustered some 1,000 blacks of which a number originally served in the Louisiana Confederate Militia. The Native Guard was primarily employed as a labor detail from September 1862 until May of 1863 after which the men guarded rail lines around the city. In June of the same year, the regiment was reorganized into the 1st, 2nd, and 3rd Corps d'Afrique. The regiment's first taste of combat came at Port Hudson, Louisiana. The unsuccessful charge resulted in 37 deaths, 155 wounded and another 116 captured. Port Hudson eventually fell a month later. Because of widespread racism and substandard living conditions that resulted in a high rate of desertion, the Corps d'Afrique was abruptly dissolved. The remaining men were transferred into the newly formed 73rd and 74th regiments of the U.S. Colored Troops.[2]

Veteran's Brief: A product of a mixed marriage (an Irish immigrant and an unknown black female), John Newington Conna was born a slave in San Augustine, Texas. By the time the Civil War commenced, Conna had already gained his freedom. Seeking adventure, he joined the 1st Regiment, Louisiana Native Guards, USA/Corps d'Africa. Before his enlistment expired,

A detail of the cover of a Civil War era music sheet titled "Hymn of the Freedman."

he had fought in three major battles: the Siege at Port Hudson and the battles of Milliken's Bend and Tonica Bayou.

After the war, Conna moved first to New York City and soon afterward to Hartford, Connecticut. In 1870 he married Mary L. Davis. Nine years later he, his wife and their seven children moved to Kansas City, Kansas. While there, he again joined the military and became a lieutenant in the Missouri National Guard, which came to be known as the "American Rifles." Upon expiration of his enlistment and seeking better opportunities for a black man, he moved his family to Tacoma, Washington, a frontier town that consisted of "muddy streets, 30 saloons, 7 churches, and a brewery." The Connas were the first black family to reside in Tacoma. Using some of his money from his Civil War pension and personal savings, he was able to operate a profitable 160-acre farm obtained through a government land grant. In 1890, after several years of hard work, Conna became a successful real estate broker, which in time enabled him to purchase his own real estate firm. Also during that period he became a lawyer. It is said that he always encouraged blacks to move to the State of Washington; however, this is not to say that racism did not hinder his own efforts for social acceptance and equality.

While in Tacoma, Conna was actively involved in local and state politics. In the late 1800s he was elected president of the John Brown Republican Club and the Washington State Protective League. He was also a member of the Afro-American League (predecessor of the NAACP). It was not long before he was named the first sergeant at arms of the Washington State Legislature, thus becoming the state's first African American political appointee.

At the age of 64, Conna, like so many others, caught the "gold fever." In 1900 he travelled with his friend James Wickersham, a Tacoma attorney and later a federal judge, to Fairbanks, Alaska, but not before he and his wife donated 40 acres of land to the city of Tacoma as a Christmas present. Though he never achieved the fortune he was seeking while gold prospecting, Conna was able to establish a real estate, mining and investment firm along with owning and operating a secondhand furniture store. Both ventures proved highly profitable.

John Conna died at an estimated age of 85 (his exact birth date is uncertain) from the effects of diabetes after losing a leg to the illness. A heart condition also contributed to his demise. Mary, his wife, had predeceased him by 14 years. His remaining children (as many as 16 survived out of 19) were said to be scattered throughout the

Though he never found the riches he dreamed of in Alaska, John N. Conna still managed to succeed as a businessman (courtesy Tacoma Public Library).

land, one as far away as China. Conna's remains rest in the Clay Street Cemetery in Fairbanks.[3]

Hawaii

The Kingdom of Hawaii was a sovereign nation in April 1861 when the first shots were fired in America's Civil War. Almost immediately Hawaii declared itself neutral. The war was being fought over 5,000 miles away, and for average Hawaiians it was probably the farthest thought from their minds. Yet the Hawaiian monarchy and many islanders believed the outcome of the war could have a profound economic impact on their nation, especially considering that the new monarch was seeking a revised trade agreement with the United States. Though neutral throughout the conflict, Hawaii remained decidedly pro–Union.[4]

Seemingly overlooked in the annals of American Civil War history, an estimated fifty to a hundred Hawaiians fought for the North and South during the Civil War. Hawaiian-born Henry Ho'olulu Pitman was a Union private serving with Co. H, 22nd Regiment, Massachusetts Volunteer Infantry, when he died at Camp Parole, Annapolis, Maryland, from the ill effects of captivity at Richmond's Libby Prison.[5] And there was part-Hawaiian James Bush, who served in the Union navy. Another two dozen students from the Punahou School in Honolulu enlisted in the Union army. Before the war was over, five sacrificed their lives for the Union. And, yes, there were also Hawaiian-born Confederate seamen—twelve in total—who served onboard the CSS *Shenandoah*. Regrettably, scores of others, along with their names, have long since been forgotten.[6]

After the war, veterans from states north and south found Hawaii both alluring and enchanting; thus, they joined former mainland Americans who had settled there during the early to mid-nineteenth century. The tropical climate, comforting trade winds, tranquil waters, and welcoming natives, all of which contributed to a utopian paradise, were far too compelling to resist. But perhaps, there was also another reason the war veterans moved to the islands: Hawaii afforded them the tranquility they had long been seeking.

During the ensuing years, the transplanted veterans from the North established their own Grand Army of the Republic post. It consisted of 110 members and lasted but four short decades. Today, one of the final resting places for 34 Civil War veterans can be seen at the GAR plot in Oahu Cemetery. The burial ground resides on an upslope adjacent to the cemetery's main road. In the center of the plot is a flagpole. Sitting upright are four cannon muzzles used as boundary markers at each corner. Unlike the cemeteries in Alaska, all 34 interments are easily identifiable by name and regiment etched in each stone. Buried on the plot is James Devlin, resting at peace alongside his wife Sarah. When the Civil War ended, Devlin was only 17 years old. He is recognized as Hawaii's last surviving GAR Civil War veteran.

Twenty-three years after Devlin's passing, Hawaii was granted statehood. The date was August 21, 1959.

Hawaii's Last Civil War Veteran

James Devlin
(b. December 28, 1848, d. January 19, 1932)
Co. C, 10th Regiment, Tennessee Cavalry (USA)

Regimental Brief: Organized at Nashville, Tennessee, in August 1863, the regiment initially performed duty in north central Kentucky until January of 1864. The troop then rode to Nashville and Pulaski, Tennessee, where they guarded rail lines of the Nashville and Chattanooga Railroad and the Nashville and Northwestern Railroad until November 1864. From May 2 through 12 its soldiers served as scouts in Hickman and Maury counties. On August 21, 1864, the men skirmished at Rogersville. In August, the cavalry proceeded to Greenville then Blue Springs. For the remainder of 1864, they patrolled in Alabama and Tennessee. In mid–

The final resting place of James Devlin (courtesy Ralph Thomas Kam). Insert: an obituary notice that includes a rare image of James Devlin. Devlin's death was reported on January 19, 1932, in the *Honolulu Star-Bulletin* (Nanette Napoleon Collection, Hawaii State Library, Honolulu).

December, the unit was present at the Battle of Nashville where they pursued General Hood's army to the Tennessee River. From February 6 to March 10, 1865, the cavalry unit moved to Vicksburg, Mississippi, and then to New Orleans, Louisiana. There they were ordered to Natchez, Mississippi, and shortly thereafter to Rodney, Mississippi, where they served until May 25. From there, they patrolled in Nashville before riding to Johnsonville, Tennessee, where they remained until August. On August 1, 1865, the 10th Regiment, Tennessee Cavalry, was mustered out of service.

Losses: an officer and 24 enlisted men either killed or mortally wounded and an officer and 181 enlisted men dead from disease.[7]

Veteran's Brief: If James Devlin were alive today, he probably would have had a hearty laugh about the number of ways his simple Irish name was misspelled. Try these examples: Darlin, Denver, Derlin, and Develin. There might have been others. During his lifetime, Devlin needed to lighten the mood, as a major calamity at war's end probably had a lasting effect on his mental well-being. Years later, shortly before his death, an unintentional slight caused him considerable emotional pain, if not downright anger. It was something he did not deserve as the last surviving Civil War veteran from Hawaii. These are the incidents he had to endure: the first was major, the second minor.

James Devlin was coming home at last. He had served faithfully in Co. C, 10th Regiment, Tennessee Cavalry (USA), and was happy to be traveling back to Tennessee where family, friends and neighbors were anxiously awaiting his return. The last months of the war had not been easy for him. As a prisoner of the Confederates, he had been deprived of the basic necessities of life: sufficient and palatable food, suitable clothing, and adequate medical care. But now that the war had ended and after his release, his prospects had brightened. One can only imagine Devlin's thoughts after surviving his prison ordeal as he waited to board a side-wheel river steamboat that would take him home at last. From Vicksburg the vessel planned to travel northward up the Mississippi River with stops at Memphis, Cairo, Evansville, Louisville, and Cincinnati. But when the vessel arrived on April 24, 1865, to pick up passengers and cargo, an engineer noticed that the ship's boilers were leaking. While the boilers were being repaired, the captain allowed passengers to board—and board they did. An estimated 2,000 war veterans (50 others were nonveterans) filled every nook and cranny: the hurricane deck, all the cabins, the Texas deck, even the pilothouse despite the fact that the vessel was legally registered to carry a maximum of 376 passengers and crew.

Though the captain feared the overcrowding, he knew the overabundance of passengers generated a huge increase in revenue, as the federal government reimbursed the steamship line five dollars per enlisted man and ten dollars per officer.[8] It was the kind of money few steamboat captains could ignore.

With the boilers repaired, the vessel departed. The next 48 hours were uneventful. After docking in Memphis, another boiler leak had to be fixed. After the repair, the vessel departed around midnight on the 26th but not before taking on coal. As a result of the added weight, the serious over-crowding, and the stiff current, both the paddle wheels and the boilers were seriously overtaxed.

Suddenly and seemingly out of nowhere, at 2:00 a.m. on April 27, 1865, and just seven miles north of Memphis, three of the four boilers exploded, sending jagged pieces of shrapnel, wood fragments and hot coals, along with human bodies, flying through the air. The vessel had nearly been blown apart. What remained afloat was on fire and those clinging to what was left of the decks dove into the water. Some survived but many perished from severe burns. Others drowned because they could not swim or were too fragile from their imprisonment to tread the frigid waters. According to one survivor, "shrieks and cries for mercy were all that could be heard."[9]

The vessel's name was the *Sultana* and it would go down in history as the worst 19th-century steamboat disaster in American annals.[10] The exact number of losses will never be known but a fair estimate places the count at around 1,450. James Devlin was extremely fortunate. He was one of the approximately 600 survivors, of which about 200 died in nearby hospitals

A photograph of the steamboat *Sultana* the day prior to the shocking disaster.

An illustrator's depiction of the steamboat *Sultana* shortly after the explosion showing disabled soldiers fighting for their lives in the Mississippi River (*Harper's Weekly*, May 20, 1865, Library of Congress).

within weeks of sustaining their injuries. Devlin was rescued by the crew of the steamboat *Pocahontas* and taken to Adams Hospital in Memphis suffering from chills, what today is called exposure.[11] After his recovery, he found his way home, perhaps by another mode of transportation and not by steamboat. Devlin was officially discharged in June 1865, most likely on a surgeon certificate; his pension record shows he was suffering from an inguinal hernia among other ailments.

In 1880 Devlin, now a disabled veteran, migrated to Hawaii—a sovereign nation when the first shots were fired at Ft. Sumter—with his wife Sarah, whom he had married two years earlier. For several years he had been working as an engineer in a San Francisco mill. A logical man might assume that he had seen enough of steamboats; but ironically, and perhaps intentionally, after settling in Hawaii Devlin became an interisland steamship engineer and worked on repairing and maintaining boilers. In February 1901 he was granted a chief engineering license after passing an intensive examination.[12] He finally retired when he was 69 years old.

On Decoration Day, May 30, 1931, Devlin woke early and prepared himself to attend the parade and ceremony. He was one of Hawaii's last surviving veterans of the war and he wanted badly to honor his deceased fellow war veterans. He waited … and he waited, but no one came to pick him up to take him to the event. As his wife Sarah related later, "He was terribly disappointed."[13]

James Devlin, the man who survived the *Sultana* disaster and later was forgotten at the 1931 Oahu Decoration Day ceremony did not live to see the next commemoration. He died seven-and-a-half months later at Pearl Harbor Hospital at the age of 83. As far as can be determined by the author, Devlin was the last Civil War veteran from the islands. Today his remains lie at peace in the GAR plot at Oahu Cemetery (previously called Nuuanu Cemetery).[14] Here his tent is pitched alongside thirty-four fellow veterans from the George W. De Long Post No. 45 who faithfully answered the final muster.

Chapter 8

The "Last of the Last"

If you are wondering what happened to the inclusion of the last surviving veterans who died in the states of Alabama, New York, and Minnesota, look no further. They are listed here and for good reason: they truly are "the last of the last."

The Confederacy's Last Surviving Civil War Veteran

Alabama's Pleasant Riggs Crump
(b. December 23, 1847, d. December 31, 1951)

Co. A, 10th Regiment, Alabama Infantry

Regimental Brief: The regiment was organized in June 1861 at Montgomery, Alabama. A month after its formation the infantry unit was ordered to Virginia. It fought under J.E.B. Stuart at Dranseville, Virginia, before being reassigned to General Wilcox, Perrin, Sanders and W.H. Forney's brigade. The infantry regiment sustained 129 casualties at the Battle of Gaines' Mill and 83 at the Battle of Frayser's Farm (also known as the Battle of Glendale). In early to mid September of 1862 during the Maryland Campaign (also known as the Antietam Campaign), 10 were killed and 53 were wounded. Of the 311 engaged at the Battle of Gettysburg, 34 percent were reported killed, wounded, or missing. In 1864 the regiment was also engaged at the Battle of Cold Harbor, where General Grant suffered a stunning defeat. The 10th also fought against the Union at Petersburg and during the Union assault near Appomattox at the end of the war.[1]

Veteran's Brief: In an article titled "Last U.S. War Veterans: Ordinary Men in Extraordinary Times," Len Barcousky of the *Pittsburgh Post-Gazette* put it thusly: "Determining the identity of the last Confederate veteran has proved to be a sometimes controversial task. In the post-war South, many service records were destroyed, looted or discarded. As a result, a baker's dozen of Southern men, all of whom died in the 1950s have been proposed as the last surviving Confederate veteran." Agreeing with Barcousky's assessment, B. Frank Earnest, commander of the Army of Northern Virginia Sons of Confederate Veterans, added this: "[B]ecause of incomplete and lost records, there always will be disputes over who was the last veteran."[2]

After analyzing the available evidence, this author, along with several other Civil War historians, feel that the last surviving Confederate veteran was a gentleman named Pleasant Riggs Crump. Born in the small hamlet of Crawford's Cove near Ashville, Alabama, Pleasant Riggs Crump grew up to become a farmer like his dad. But life on a farm was mundane for a young boy looking for adventure. Crump was only 16 years old in November 1864 when he decided to join a young neighbor like himself and venture to the front at Petersburg, Virginia. There they enlisted as privates in Co. A, 10th Regiment, Alabama Infantry. With the opportunity for a total Confederate victory steadily slipping away, Confederate regiments did little to adhere to age requirements of potential recruits. The boys enlisted and fought in several battles during the Siege of Petersburg. Decades later Crump recalled how he was just across the road from the McLean House at Appomattox, Virginia, when he was ordered to stack arms during Gen. Lee's surrender.[3]

Sitting next to his grandniece Celia B. Milam is the last Confederate veteran Pleasant Riggs Crump (courtesy Celia B. Milam).

After Crump's parole, he returned to St. Clair County, Alabama, and farmed. In 1871 he married Mary Hall of Lincoln. The newlyweds settled on 38 acres of land that had been given to them by Mary's father. Crump built a house on the property, where he continued to reside uninterrupted for 78 years. Over time, the Crumps had five children. On December 31, 1901, Mary died. Four years later, Crump married Ella Wallis of Childersburg. It was during his second marriage that he applied for a pension in Talladega, Alabama. The date was June 26, 1915, and it was subsequently approved. In July 1942, Ella died.[4]

For over seventy years, Crump had been a deacon at the Refuge Baptist Church. He had read his bible "cover to cover seven times and could quote many passages."[5] Prior to his passing, he lived with his grandson. It was about the same time that the United Confederate Veterans honored him with the title "Colonel." Days before his passing, he said, "I have placed my life in the hands of the Lord. He has been unusually good to me, for there are not many who have seen as much life as I have."[6] At the age of 104, he passed away, precisely fifty years to the day after his first wife died. He had lived to witness 23 United States presidents and the only president the Confederate States of America ever had: Jefferson Davis. Pleasant Riggs Crump's remains rest at Hall Cemetery (formerly Refuge Cemetery) in Lincoln, Alabama.[7]

The Union's Last Surviving Civil War "Combat" Veteran

New York's James Albert Hard
(b. July 15, 1843, d. March 12, 1953)
Co. E, 32nd Regiment, New York Volunteer Infantry

Regimental Brief: Organized at Staten Island, New York, the regiment was mustered in on May 31, 1861. Sent to Alexandria, Virginia, the soldiers performed reconnaissance before advancing to Manassas, where they took part in the first major conflict of the Civil War: the Battle of Bull Run (July 21). After the Union defeat, the regiment stampeded back to Washington to regroup and defend against a Confederate attack that never materialized. The regiment remained there until March of 1862. On April 22, it was ordered to Virginia, where it took part in a massive Union operation devised by General McClellan to overtake Richmond that came to be known as the Peninsula Campaign. During the campaign, the regiment took part in sieges and battles, most notably these: Siege of Yorktown (April 24 through May 4), Gaines' Mill (June 27), and Malvern Hill (July 1). By mid–August, most of the Union forces had regrouped at Harrison's Landing. From there the regiment moved to Fortress Monroe and Centreville, Virginia, where it remained until the end of August. In September it took part in the Battle of Antietam (September 16 and 17) and later the Battle of Fredericksburg (December 12 through 15). Along with other regiments that participated in the debacle at Fredericksburg, the regiment was involved in the infamous "Mud March" a month later. After the two major battles, the unit remained in Falmouth, Virginia, until late April 1863 before fighting at the Battle of Chancellorsville (April 27 through May 6). After a few other operations, the soldiers from the unit mustered out on June 9, 1863, upon expiration of their term of service. Those with longer enlistments (three-year men) were transferred to the 121st Regiment, New York Infantry.

Losses: 5 officers and 37 enlisted men killed and mortally wounded and an officer and 53 enlisted men dead from disease.[8]

Veteran's Brief: James Albert Hard participated in a number of major engagements during his two-year enlistment with Co. E, 32nd Regiment, New York Volunteer Infantry. While serving to preserve the Union, he might have felt it impossible to survive the devastating ordeal; yet, miraculously, he did. He had fought at Bull Run, during the Peninsula Campaign, at Chancellorsville, Antietam, and Fredericksburg. There are also lesser battles in which he participated that are too numerous to mention.[9]

Born in Victor, New York, the third of thirteen children and the son of a stagecoach driver, Hard spent his boyhood in the town of Windsor. Growing up he had little formal schooling, but he did learn to read and write.[10] According to Hard's own account, republished years later, "life was much harder in those days than it is now, but we had a lot of fun." Reminiscing about his youth, he said, "To show you how things have changed, we used to think it was a wonderful Christmas if we got a doughnut and a stick of candy and a few nuts of some kind."[11]

Hard remembers working at a sawmill near Syracuse when "a lot of fellows came by in a wagon. They were making a lot of noise and they stopped at the mill. When I asked what all the racket was about they told me the President had issued a call for volunteers and they were going to enlist." That was enough for the young man in his late teens. Hard, too, enlisted in the 32nd Regiment, New York Volunteer Infantry, at Dryden, New York. It was four days after the Confederate attack at Ft. Sumter. Hard was 19 years old at the time.[12]

During his tour of duty, he had the thrill of meeting President Lincoln, not once but on two occasions. His first meeting took place at a White House reception at the outbreak of the war before he was issued a uniform. While approaching the president after standing in a long reception line, he was greeted with these words: "Well, son, you look like you would make a good soldier. Why don't you join up?" Hard told the president that he was already in the army and Lincoln smiled and made a brief remark that, regrettably, the young soldier soon forgot. But the smile and handshake afterward was something he always remembered. "Whenever he spoke to anyone he had a wonderful smile," Hard related, adding that his "grip ... nearly crushed my hand."[13] The second opportunity came at Bailey's Cross Roads, where the president was inspecting troops. Hard again was afforded the pleasure of shaking Lincoln's hand. Years later, when asked to describe Lincoln's appearance, he reminisced about a time in the field when he saw the president from a distance, saying that he remembered him as "a comical looking fellow on horseback." Sometime later Hard also felt privileged to shake the hand of General Ulysses S. Grant. But all was not sublime. At the Battle of White House Landing on the York River during the Peninsula Campaign, he witnessed his commanding officer, Cpt. L. C. Grown, killed while standing next to him.[14]

Three years after the war, Hard married but his wife (given and maiden name undetermined) died prematurely in 1879, leaving a daughter, Alberta, and Hard as her sole survivors. In 1884 he married Anna E. Hart. The second marriage lasted until 1929 when she passed away.[15]

Like so many other males prior to the war, Hard was a farmer. When he was mustered out after his enlistment expired while the war continued unabated, Hard became a government railroad worker. But after the war, and for reasons unknown, he decided to become a carpenter. Perhaps seeking a better opportunity, he ultimately established a pension business that thrived for the next 38 years. In 1882 he moved to Rochester, New York, where he remained for the rest of his life.[16] When asked how he managed to live so long, he said. "Work hard, don't worry, and smoke plenty of cigars." Nearing the end of his life, he was blind, though he served in a ceremonial capacity as the New York department commander and the junior vice commander in chief of the GAR.[17]

At the final GAR encampment held at Indianapolis, Indiana, in 1949, he half kiddingly stated, "I have been in perfect health today and I may reach the 200 mark."[18] Several years later, as he smoked his usual cigar just months before his passing, he drew laughter when he said, "I'll keep on

James A. Hard had lost his sight shortly before his death, but not his patriotic fever (from an original wire service photograph credited to Wide World Photos, titled "Surviving Civil War Veterans," author's collection).

living as long as I can keep on puffing." A fighter all his life, the end did not come easily. Months shy of his 110th birthday, Hard was admitted to Rochester General Hospital on February 13, 1953, where, because of circulatory problems, his right leg was amputated just above the knee. He lived for another eleven days after surgery. Initially he rallied before taking a turn for the worse. When he died, the city of Rochester mourned his passing by affording him a state funeral. The streets of the city were lined with thousands of citizens honoring the memory of their beloved veteran. For the first time since V-J Day, the city hall bell tolled 13 times, in tribute to James Albert Hard. It was a fitting tribute to the last combat soldier who fought in the Civil War. After church services, a large procession brought him to his final resting place at Mt. Hope Cemetery, where he was interred next to his second wife.[19]

America's Last Surviving Civil War Veteran

Minnesota's Albert H. Woolson
(b. February 11, 1847, d. August 2, 1956)
Battery C, 1st Regiment, Minnesota Heavy Artillery

Regimental Brief: The regiment was organized at St. Paul and Rochester, Minnesota, between September 1864 and February 1865. The batteries were

ordered to Chattanooga, Tennessee, as fast as they were organized. There the men performed garrison duty until September of 1865. The regiment mustered out on September 27, 1865. It is doubtful that any of the men saw combat.

Losses: 87 dead from disease.[20]

Veteran's Brief: Arguably, the death of the "last surviving Civil War veteran marked the climax of a historic period in our nation's history. Regardless of the side he allied—Union or Confederate—or his past contribution to the war effort, his death brought a sense of melancholy to all Americans. Along with his passing, America had lost its last tie to a distant past, not of war per se, but in a larger sense, its childlike innocence, thoughtful simplicity, ele-

Albert H. Woolson as a young Union soldier who never saw combat (public domain).

gant manners, strong religious convictions, high moral standards, youthful idealism, steadfast determination, unwavering chivalry, and abundant sacrifices that so distinguished the period.

Indeed, the Civil War was a horrendous event in our nation's history. According to authors Ken and Ric Burns, those who lived through the era experienced "the most horrible, necessary, intimate, acrimonious, mean-spirited, and heroic conflict the nation has known."[21] In the end, those lucky enough to have survived the war became the sounding board for future generations. As one spectator at a 1903 Civil War gathering noted, "The world will never see their like again."

Although a number of books and Internet articles tell the story of the last surviving Civil War veteran, a visit to Gettysburg National Military Park at Gettysburg, Pennsylvania, can provide a visual experience not soon forgotten. Located south of downtown Gettysburg on Hancock Avenue in Ziegler's Grove stands a bronze monument erected in tribute to the Grand Army of the Republic and the last surviving GAR veteran of the Civil War. At the monument's dedication in 1956, Col. Frederic G. Bauer, com-

Albert H. Woolson could still play the drums as an aged veteran (courtesy H.N. [Bert] Woolson Collection on Albert Woolson, 1881–1964, WCMss12, Whitman College and Northwest Archives).

mander in chief of the Sons of Union Veterans, spoke these touching words:

> We dedicate today a statue of Albert Woolson. He was the last of the Grand Army of the Republic and he was also a son of a veteran. This statue is in many ways unique. Usually statues are dedicated to great and noble men, great military leaders, or men who have given their lives for their country. Here we have a statue of a man who was none of these things. We note that the front of the statue does not bear his name. It bears the wording "In Memory of the Grand Army of the Republic." Comrade Albert Woolson symbolizes all the great virtues of the common, ordinary citizen, the citizen who becomes a soldier and then returns to ordinary life.[22]

Bauer's assessment is accurate in every regard. Albert Woolson, formerly of Battery C, 1st Regiment, Minnesota Heavy Artillery, is considered to be the undisputed final survivor of the conflict by a large majority of Civil War historians. Because Woolson symbolized "all the great virtues of the common, ordinary citizen" it seemed fitting that he be the last to represent the hundreds of thousands from both sides of the conflict who went before him. And in the end, as you shall see, he represented them with pride, honor, and dignity.

Woolson was born in the small hamlet of Antwerp, New York. Albert's father, Willard, was a cabinetmaker, painter, and furniture builder. He was also a musician. When the war broke out, Willard enlisted with other musicians in Co. I, Fourth Regiment, Minnesota Infantry. After a year of not receiving any correspondence from him, the family traced his whereabouts to an army general hospital in Minnesota. He had been badly wounded in the leg at the Battle of Shiloh. By the time the family was reunited with him, Willard's leg had to be amputated. He died shortly thereafter. Young Albert was devastated by the loss and wanted to join the Union army to rectify the damage inflicted by the enemy upon his family. Although Albert was underage, his mother signed a consent form allowing him to enlist at the age of 17, on October 10, 1864, in Battery C, 1st Regiment, Minnesota Heavy Artillery. He first served as a rifleman but was later assigned as a drummer and finally a bugler. The battery he served was designated a reserve unit and remained at Lookout Mountain near Chattanooga, Tennessee, for the spring and early summer of 1865. In August the unit was mustered out, and in September Woolson received his discharge. He never fired a shot at the enemy.[23]

In 1868 Woolson married Sarah Jane Sloper. After her death in 1901 he married Anna Haugen three years later. Woolson worked in several capacities after moving permanently to Duluth in 1905. He worked in mills and logging camps and in the end as a stationary engineer before retiring at the age of 85.[24]

Even before he learned that he was the last Civil War veteran in the nation, Woolson relished his role as an ambassador for the GAR. He attended numerous school, church, and civic functions and took part in patriotic ceremonies, wearing his finely tailored uniform whenever the opportunity arose. He especially enjoyed being in the company of children. Near the end he became a bit of a celebrity and was interviewed by newspaper, radio, and television reporters. During one interview he summarized his thoughts about war in simple terms when: "The business about war is all nonsense."[25]

According to correspondent Raymond Wilcove, around 1949 Woolson took out a five-year subscription to the *National Tribune* (a veteran's newspaper established in 1877 by the GAR). Woolson wrote the editor, Edward K. Inman: "When my subscription runs out, I want to renew it for another five years." At the last GAR reunion, Woolson found the strength to travel to Indianapolis and participate in the event. Seven years later at the unimaginable age of 109, he developed lung congestion and was hospitalized at St. Luke's Hospital in Duluth, Minnesota, for nearly nine weeks before lapsing into an irreversible coma. He died five days later with family members at his bedside. Woolson was survived by six daughters and two sons. His second wife, Anna, died in 1949.[26]

Woolson's funeral, much like Albert Hard's, turned into an elaborate affair, with messages of condolences coming from not only local and state dignitaries but President Dwight D. Eisenhower as well. Some 1,500 persons attended the funeral and hundreds more lined the city streets. Another 2,000 family, friends, and dignitaries attended the final funeral oration at Park Hill Cemetery in Duluth. As the coffin was about to be lowered, a fife and drum corps slowly turned and marched away. In the distance the only sound to be heard was the fading music of "The Battle Hymn of the Republic."[27] Albert Woolson thus became the "last of the last" of a rare breed of Union and Confederate veterans to participate in the final muster.[28]

Near the end of a truly remarkable era, Congress provided that upon the deaths of the last Civil War veterans from the Grand Army of the Republic and the United Confederate Veterans their remains would be graciously accepted for burial at Arlington National Cemetery, that is if their next of kin approved. As you have read, neither Pleasant Riggs Crump's nor Albert Woolson's relatives chose this option and the ensuing honor it bestowed. Perhaps at some point the veterans had expressed a desire to be buried in their home states near family and friends. In the end, Alabama and Minnesota became the benefactors of not only the remains but also the memories of two soldiers who served their respective nations with pride, dignity, and honor.

Upon Albert Woolson's passing, all existing GAR records were removed to the Library of Congress. Battle flags, military collectibles and other "remaining items" were entrusted to the Smithsonian Institution.

Chapter 9

Is This the Final Chapter?

During 1951, citizens in fifteen states observed with heartfelt sorrow the passing of their last Civil War veteran that left but four states that could boast veterans from the war still living within their boundaries. The remaining veterans were Union men having a combined average age of approximately 108. In 1952 the last veteran from Idaho died. In 1953 California and New York buried their last veterans, and then three years later Albert Woolson of Minnesota, "the last of the last," was laid to rest. But did Woolson's passing finally close the chapter in this epic journey? If the past decade is any indication, though the physical presence of Civil War veterans is no longer upon this earth the memory of these noble people and their enduring sacrifice continues to resonate throughout the free world. History, now as always, never dies. Sometimes, however, its fire needs to be rekindled.

Today, Civil War reenactors realistically portray the men and women who lived during that period while silently honoring the memory of those veterans long since departed. But this is not the only reminder. Television documentaries continue to inform us about the war years and its men, women, and families who suffered the hardships and devastation that only war can inflict. Old photographs freshly analyzed have revealed some startling surprises. For example, in a recently analyzed photograph, President Abraham Lincoln can be seen in the distance riding a horse on the grounds of the Evergreen Cemetery in Gettysburg, Pennsylvania, prior to delivering his famous address. In Charleston, South Carolina, a Confederate submarine, the CSS *H.L. Hunley*, was discovered in 1995 and raised from the ocean depths. Since 2000, a painstaking effort is being made to restore the vessel for permanent exhibition. Reburials of the remains found onboard the submarine have been carried out in a solemn ceremony deserving of these fearless young men. Even 150 years later, belated burials of Civil War soldiers are not unusual. On occasion, farmers tilling the soil near battlefields or long-abandoned soldiers' encampments continue to excavate bones of fallen soldiers, both Union and Confederate. These are but a few examples of how this war and the men who fought it continue to live on in the twenty-first century.

Recently another Civil War reminder has grabbed the attention of the nation: the flying of the Confederate Battle Flag. The contradiction associated with displaying the Southern flag has not diminished over time and has sadly reawakened old wounds. To Confederate descendants of loyal and valorous soldiers, the flag is viewed with a sense of pride that is permanently etched in their heritage. But to African Americans whose ancestors suffered the degradation of slavery for over 200 years the flag is perceived as an affront to human dignity. The long-lived and polarizing issue has been difficult to resolve. Someday, and soon, it's to be hoped, the nation will be able to bind its wounds and find an acceptable solution to satisfy all.

There is one final point. Whether the author has made the right choices in identifying the last Civil War veteran from each state is in many ways a moot point. What matters most is not who died first or last, but that all veterans who participated in this cataclysmic event are recognized and remembered. To each and every veteran of the military, past and present, there is no greater honor.

To learn about the last survivors of major events or significant milestones relating to the Civil War the reader is invited to review Appendix E.

Appendices

A: The Last Civil War Veteran from Each State

Veteran (U = Union) (C = Confederate)	Last Residence	Regiment or Duty Assignment	Age at Death	Date of Death
Albert W. Woolson, U	Minnesota	1st Minnesota Heavy Artillery	109	August 2, 1956
James Albert Hard, U	New York	32nd New York Infantry	109	March 12, 1953
William Allen Magee, U	California	12th Ohio Cavalry	106	January 23, 1953
Israel Adam Broadsword, U	Idaho	51st Missouri Infantry	105	July 25, 1952
Pleasant Riggs Crump, C	Alabama	10th Alabama Infantry	104	December 31, 1951
Alfred Blackburn, C	North Carolina	Manservant to John Augustus Blackburn of the 21st North Carolina Infantry	109	December 15, 1951
George Washington Keith, C	Florida	West Florida Home Guard Co.	99	November 7, 1951
Martin Luther Peters, C	Virginia	26th Battalion, Virginia Infantry	102	October 28, 1951
Lansing A. Wilcox, U	Wisconsin	4th Wisconsin Cavalry	105	September 29, 1951
Joseph Haden Whitsett, C	Texas	Shelby's Escort Co. of Shelby's Missouri Cavalry	103	August 15, 1951
Joseph Clovese, U	Michigan	63rd U.S. Colored Troops	107	July 13, 1951
John Greene Chisum, C	Arkansas	45th Arkansas Cavalry Regiment	103	June 11, 1951
Thomas Wiley Guinn, C	Mississippi	Mississippi Home Guards	102	April 7, 1951
James W. Smith, U	Oregon	Olney's Detachment of the Oregon Cavalry	108	March 22, 1951
John Hutchison, U	Missouri	46th Missouri Infantry	105	March 18, 1951
Hiram Randall Gale, U	Washington	46th Wisconsin Infantry	104	March 15, 1951
Daniel A. Clingaman, U	Ohio	195th Ohio Infantry	104	February 18, 1951
Charles W. Bailey, U	Kansas	47th and 5th Wisconsin Infantry	102	January 29, 1951
Robert T. Barrett, U	Kentucky	17 Kentucky Cavalry	104	January 12, 1951
Vernon Emerson Lifrage, C	South Carolina	South Carolina State Reserves	102	August 4, 1950
William Mercer Buck, C	Oklahoma	Scout and intelligence gatherer	98	July 10, 1950
James Marion Lurvey, U	New Hampshire	40th Massachusetts Infantry and 4th Massachusetts Heavy Artillery	102	April 7, 1950
Lewis Fablinger, U	Illinois	16th, 140th, and 96th Illinois Infantry	103	March 14, 1950
Charles Douglass, U	Connecticut	15th Connecticut Infantry	102	January 29, 1950
James Patterson Martin, U	Iowa	1st Wisconsin Heavy Artillery	101	September 20, 1949
Burrell Maricle, C	Louisiana	6th Louisiana Cavalry	105	May 25, 1949
Charles H. Duckworth, U	Pennsylvania	18th Pennsylvania Cavalry and 3rd Pennsylvania Provisional Cavalry	102	April 10, 1949
William Jasper Brown, C	Georgia	22nd Battalion, Georgia Light Artillery	103	March 2, 1949

Veteran (U = Union) (C = Confederate)	Last Residence	Regiment or Duty Assignment	Age at Death	Date of Death
John Christian Adams, U	Indiana	17th West Virginia Infantry	101	February 17, 1949
Robert T. Bryan, U	Colorado	145th Illinois Infantry	100	January 17, 1949
Michael Bon Doll, U	Nebraska	7th Iowa Infantry	99	December 24, 1948
William Nelson Morgan, U	Tennessee	7th Tennessee Mounted Infantry	104	October 17, 1948
James Albert Spicer, C	D.C.	7th Regiment Virginia Cavalry	103	February 9, 1948
Zachary Taylor McLaughlin, U	Maine	12th Maine Infantry	98	November 7, 1947
Uriah Talmage Alley, U	West Virginia	6th West Virginia Infantry	99	October 26, 1947
George Riley, U	Massachusetts	U.S. Navy	97	October 10, 1947
Hiram Alonzo Hunkins, U	Wyoming	48th Wisconsin Infantry	102	March 4, 1947
Parker Louis Gordon, U	Arizona	154th Illinois Infantry	99	December 5, 1946
James M. Reed, U	Maryland	8th and 191st Pennsylvania Infantry	100	October 20, 1946
Isaiah Fassett, U	Delaware	9th U.S. Colored Troops	102	June 24, 1946
George Ashby, U	New Jersey	22nd and 45th U.S. Colored Troops	102	April 26, 1946
Harry Ira Stormes, U	Utah	2nd Wisconsin Cavalry	98	October 5, 1945
William T. Scammahorn, U	New Mexico	155th Illinois Infantry	98	September 12, 1945
Horace Warner Simpson, U	South Dakota	23rd Illinois Infantry	97	July 20, 1945
Gilbert Charles Lucier, U	Vermont	1st Vermont Heavy Artillery and the Veterans Reserve Corps	97	September 22, 1944
Thomas Arthur Castle, U	Montana	132nd Pennsylvania Infantry	97	November 25, 1943
James Henry Riley, II, U	Rhode Island	2nd Rhode Island Infantry	101	May 7, 1943
Dallas George Duell, U	North Dakota	72nd Illinois Infantry and 66th U.S. Colored Troops	97	January 22, 1943
William Orrin Phillips, U	Nevada	144th Ohio Infantry (National Guard)	94	December 13, 1940
James Devlin, U	Hawaii	10th Tennessee Cavalry	83	January 19, 1932
John Newington Conna, U	Alaska	1st Louisiana Native Guards, U.S.A./Corps d'Africa	85	October 11, 1921

B: The Last Ten Civil War Nurses

Name	Side Served	Last Residence	Location and Type of Nursing Service (Remarks)	Date of Death
Hattie Carter	Confederate	Greenburg, PA	Food and ammunition carrier to soldiers in Richmond, VA (slave and Civil War widow)	January 9, 1956
Sarah Frances Pearce Rockwell	Union and Confederate	Danbury, CT	Primarily nursed Confederates but also some Union soldiers at Libby Prison (her birth date has been disputed)	November 23, 1953
Jennie Overton	Union and Confederate	Paducah, KY	Home front nurse	February 13, 1951
George Winfield Tyner	Confederate	West Monroe, LA	Private in 22nd Louisiana Infantry. Served as a local hospital nurse	August 14, 1949
Lavinia Mount Kingsbury Johnson Minton	Union	Highlands, NJ	Home front nurse near Red Bank, NJ	May 28, 1948

Name	Side Served	Last Residence	Location and Type of Nursing Service (Remarks)	Date of Death
Susan Haines Clayton	Union	Talent, OR	Camp Carrington, Indianapolis, IN	March 7, 1948
Emma Louise Becker Nagle	Union and possibly Confederate	Bethlehem, PA	Civilian Volunteer Nurses Corps, Winchester, VA	November 26, 1946
Mary Courtney Ward Ray	Union and Confederate	Hinton, OK	Home front nurse in Alabama	January 17, 1946
Harriet Hinkson Holmes	Union	Primarily Montpelier, VT	Home front nurse	August 5, 1945
Hannah Beavis Randle Walters	Union and Confederate	Birkdale, Lancashire, England	Nursed wounded at Battle of Gettysburg from July 5 through July 14, 1863	March 20 1943

Source: *The North's Last Boy's in Blue* (vol. 2) by Jay S. Hoar. Used with author's permission.

C: The 1890 U.S. Census and Veterans Schedule

Article 1, Section 2, of the U.S. Constitution mandates that an official count be taken of every resident in the United States. The initial legislation required only that the census be a population count and that it be conducted every ten years. The first U.S. Census was conducted less than three years after Congress first assembled. Since 1790, a census has been conducted faithfully every ten years during a year ending in zero.

Why the need for a census? A census is required for two primary reasons: the first is to ascertain and allocate the number of seats each state is entitled to in the U.S. House of Representatives based upon its population; and second (also using population data) is to determine how billions of dollars of federal funds are to be distributed among states and local municipalities. As the years passed, the need to learn more about the U.S. population and its economy became more apparent. During the nineteenth century the number of census questions continued to increase, and by the twentieth century hundreds of topics were included in the enumeration. Because of the multiplicity of information required by the government and the growing complexity of making sense out of all the data, on March 6, 1902, Congress enacted legislation creating a permanent Census Office within the Department of the Interior. Today, the responsibility is delegated to the U.S. Census Bureau, an agency attached to the U.S. Department of Commerce.

Through the years, historians and genealogists alike have found census records to be an invaluable aid while conducting their research. Names of family members and their residences at the time of the enumeration, birth years (sometimes with the month), birthplaces and occupations the time, along with other pertinent data, comprise only the tip of the iceberg, especially as census data-gathering requirements grew over the decades.

For the 1890 U.S. Census, the Census Bureau felt a need to learn more about its military veterans. A special enumeration was conducted that coincided with the decennial census required for that year. It came to be called the 1890 Veterans Schedule (the name used in this book), though the correct document title is the *Special Schedule—Surviving Soldiers, Sailors, Marines, and Widows, Etc.* The Census Bureau felt it was important to assist veterans in locating comrades in arms to testify in pension claims and also to verify the number of survivors and widows for future pension legislation. Some congressmen also believed that the information would be useful in determining whether various types of military service impacted veterans' longevity. Using their own files and records obtained from the U.S. War Department, the Census Bureau prepared a list of veterans' names to assist in the enumeration process. The superintendent of the Census Bureau, with the backing of Congress, planned to publish the veterans' data and place copies in public libraries and at headquarters of various veterans' organizations. The plan never came to fruition due to inadequate funding and the complexity of manually sorting through all of the findings.

While conducting the primary census in 1890 enumerators had been previously trained to produce the Veterans Schedule (also referred to as the Special Schedule) if a person identified himself as a veteran after that question was asked. A positive response resulted in additional service-related questions: name, rank, company, regiment or vessel, date of enlistment, date of discharge, and length of service. The enumerator also asked for a post office address, whether any disabilities were incurred in the service and, of course, whether the veteran had any remarks.

The census was successfully conducted and eventually filed away in the basement of the Commerce Department building located in Washington, D.C. But the unexpected happened. On January 10, 1921, a fire destroyed most of the 1890 census records. (At least one author has taken exception to this theory, saying that the administrative records had not supported the conclusion that fire destroyed the documents.) Regardless of the method of loss, the records were all but destroyed, leaving researchers devastated by the tragic loss of such vital research and irreplaceable data especially as it related to military veterans, the majority either Union or Confederate Civil War survivors recorded by the enumerator. The paucity of surviving veterans who fought in the War of 1812 or the Mexican War was also revealed. Eventually fragments of some records were found; however, schedules for Alabama through Kansas and approximately half of Kentucky's records were lost. In 1943 the National Archives was able to preserve some of the fragments and cataloged them in their files. The fragmented records that did survive contain some valuable information and were eventually transferred to microfilm, thus making them available to researchers.

For those readers interested in a more detailed account about the 1890 U.S. Census and the accompanying Veterans Schedule, the reader is advised to peruse the U.S. National Archives and Records Administration publication *First in the Path of the Firemen: The Fate of the 1890 Population Census* 28, no. 1 (Part 2, Spring 1996).

D: Union and Confederate Veterans Who Resettled Overseas

As one might imagine, a small minority of veterans returning from the war decided to return to their native lands. Some were immigrants and longed for their motherland, perhaps missing relatives and friends, their distinctive culture, and a slower-paced lifestyle than that of America. Others may have left to seek greater adventures. They traveled back to countries like Australia, British Honduras, Canada, England, France, Germany, Japan, Ireland, Italy, New Zealand, Russia, and Scotland. But there was a contingent of veterans who departed the continental United States for entirely different reasons, as was the case with a few fragmented groups of Confederate veterans who immigrated to South America.

Straggling home after the war, former Confederate veterans were not only disheartened but downright humiliated by what they found: cities, towns, and villages laid waste; homes and farms burnt to the ground; lives lost; families scattered; savings wholly depleted; and few, if any, work opportunities to start anew. After four years of heavy fighting, these veterans beheld a South that had been thoroughly devastated both economically and emotionally. To a number of Confederate veterans conditions appeared so appalling on the home front that reconstruction of the South seemed unachievable, at least during their lifetimes. And, to an even smaller contingent, because of their unremitting allegiance to the "Cause," reconciliation with the Union was completely unacceptable. For these diehard former Confederates, the dreadful indignity of having to live the remainder of their years as "reconstituted Yankees" under federal occupation was simply too much to bear. Many had already solidified their position at war's end when an estimated 270,000 Confederates refused to take the Union loyalty oath and sign a Federal offer of parole.

Not long after their arrival home, thousands of immensely proud and adamant Confederate veterans acted upon their personal feelings in the most drastic way. Looking elsewhere for territory that they could colonize without having to renounce their Southern beliefs and ideals, groups of men accompanied by their families established small colonies in Mexico, Venezuela, and British Honduras. By far the largest migration was to Brazil, a country that during the war had been allied with the Confederacy.

Colonizing Brazil appeared attractive, at least on the surface. Land was fertile, with soil already being tilled by existing slave labor. The soon-to-be expatriates felt it a perfect opportunity to move beyond the disastrous loss at the hands of the Union and forge ahead with a new way of life. With a promise of citizenship, the opportunity to manage a semi-independent agricultural cooperative including subsidies and tax breaks, and transportation assistance, all of which was promised by Emperor Dom Pedro II, exile from the defunct Confederacy seemed a wise decision. Yes, Pedro II was kindhearted in his offer but he also was looking out for his own country's self-interest. With cotton sales at record highs, Brazil could enter the picture with experienced cotton growers from America.

Traveling in separate groups, the self-exiled former Confederates and their families embarked on their long journey to Brazil onboard small ships and sailboats. Hailing from Alabama, Arkansas, Florida, Georgia, Louisiana, Kentucky, Mississippi, North Carolina, South Carolina, Tennessee, Texas, and Virginia, they hoped to rekindle the lifestyle they had cherished so deeply while living in the South. After their arrival, several of the groups settled in the southeastern area of Brazil along the coastline, though some found refuge inland and much farther north. For the most part, the former Confederates and their families were Irish, Scottish, English, Welsh, Scandinavian, Dutch and German. Citizens of Brazil soon found a name for them: Confederados.

The initial migration of "war refugees" (as some called themselves) totaled about 4,000; but before two decades had passed, the total ranged from 10,000 to 20,000 expatriates, depending on the source a person wishes to believe. Most settled in Sánta Barbara d'Oeste and Americana, so named by the natives because of the number of Americans who chose to live there. As the years progressed, life was more difficult than first envisioned and scores returned to the States; how many is unknown. Those more hardy and adventurous who chose to remain renounced their U.S. citizenship and became official Brazilians.

In the end, both the Brazilian government and "the lost colony of the Confederacy" (as some called it) achieved their mutual objectives. The Confederados introduced modern agricultural techniques and expanded the variety of crops with the introduction of watermelons and pecans. They also introduced southern-fried chicken into the Brazilian diet.

Today, descendants of the Confederados still live in Americana. Though they were a solid majority in the late nineteenth century, they now make up a mere 10 percent of the city's population. Over the past 150 years descendants of the Confederados have settled throughout Brazil. Of those who remain, a striking number still bear Anglo-Saxon surnames, offering additional proof of their ancestry. English as their primary language lasted for three generations but now Portuguese is the language of choice. English can occasionally be heard from a Confederado descendant but with a noticeable Brazilian accent.

Today a number of Confederados belong to the Fraternity of American Descendants, a cultural group that dedicates itself to preserving their mixed American and Brazilian heritage. Annually the Confederados hold what they call Festa Confederada. Profits realized from the event are used to maintain the Campo Cemetery where most Confederados are interred. The festival draws many onlookers and participants (all descendants from former Confederate veterans who settled in Brazil). The men are attired in Confederate uniforms and the ladies wear hoop skirts. Food that is served has an American southern flair with a touch of Brazilian flavor thrown in for good measure. Those observing the festivities cannot help but notice the Confederate flag on the back of the stage where dancers frolic and entertain their guests. There is one big difference: after 150 years of living in South America, present-day Confederados frown on discussing past slavery issues. Obviously proud of their heritage, they are not in the least bit interested in resurrecting old wounds that have proven so painful for so many.

A cultural and ethnic subgroup of exiled Confederate veterans and their families also settled in British Honduras (today called Belize). Like Brazil, British Honduras was sympathetic to the Confederacy, if not in spirit then certainly in the profits the country realized for supplying arms to the South during the war. One advantage British Honduras had over Brazil was that the population was an English-speaking colony. But unlike Brazil, the inhospitable climate and predatory insects became unbearable. A large majority of exiles eventually returned to the States, fed up with the high heat and humidity and the wretched insect manifestation.

According to federal pension records, in 1899 over 350 Union veterans lived in England. A recent estimate placed the number of Union and Confederate veterans buried there at approximately 1,000. If the number is accurate, as many as two-thirds of those veterans were not on the federal pension roles or were former Confederates. In September 20, 1910, the London Branch of American Civil War Veterans was organized by a former Englishman and American Civil War veteran John Davis. While maintaining strong feelings of loyalty to both America and England, Davis decided to organize the group. Initially the organization of Union veterans counted fewer than 100 members on its roles. Eventually the membership rose to a high of 150 comrades. Though exclusively a Union fraternity, the organization invited former Confederates living in England to reminisce at a local restaurant in 1913. The London Branch of American Civil War Veterans lasted until 1933, when it officially disbanded, presumably just before the last member died. In 1945 an unidentified Oklahoma newspaper supposedly reported that an American Civil War veteran was still living in England.

On August 9, 1939, a gentleman named George Wilson Edwards, formerly with Co. I, 25th New York Cavalry, died in Australia at the age of 96. To date, he appears to be the last man from America's Civil War to live, die and be buried in Australia. His remains lie in Northern Suburbs Cemetery, New South Wales, Australia. Nobody knows for certain how many Union and Confederate veterans returned to or resettled in Australia. What is known is that contemporary researchers have found the burial sites and accompanying monuments of over a hundred Civil War veterans throughout Australia and New Zealand. The interments include a predominate number of Union soldiers and sailors along with a sprinkling of Confederate veterans.

Today, American Civil War buffs from Australia have a number of organizations that continue to perpetuate the memory of the conflict. Besides the American Civil War Roundtable of Australia and its associated groups and the William Kenyon Australian Confederated Sons of Confederate Veterans (SCV) Camp 2160, there are also reenactors like the 63rd New York Zouaves (New South Wales), the 2nd Virginia Living History Group (Victoria), the Blue and Gray (Victoria), and the Australian American Civil War Reenactors Forum.

For an enjoyable read, visit the Internet site "The Brazilian Town Where the American Confederacy Lives On," by Mimi Dwyer. The article is highly entertaining and the accompanying photographs that embellish the story add an appropriate and distinctive zest to the discussion (http://www.vice.com/read/welcome-to-americana-brazil-0000580-v22n2).

To learn more about the exiled Confederates in British Honduras the author recommends Donald C. Simmons' book *Confederate Settlements in British Honduras*.

E: Last Survivors of Major Events or Milestones Before, During and After the Civil War

The reader might find it interesting to learn about the last survivor of many of the major events and milestones achieved that are directly or indirectly tied to America's Civil War, hence this addition. The author believes that thinking about the times in terms of just five years (1861–1865) does the subject a grave injustice. Much happened prior to, during, and following the war that contributed to making the Civil War one of the most read about and researched times in our nation's history.

Though their contributions were both heroic and significant, the soldiers and sailors are but one voice in the war's epic struggle. In consonance with the theme of this book, "the last veteran," the author included the following section to recognize other individuals who directly participated in or unexpectedly witnessed historic events unfold before their eyes. In so doing, the author has made the assumption that the reader has a general knowledge of the historical events and milestones presented here, as it is not within the scope of this book to reiterate the entire story.

Last Survivor of the Raid at Harpers Ferry

On October 15, 1859, the night of the attack on the U.S. Federal Arsenal and Rifle Works at Harpers Ferry, Virginia, Owen Brown, the third son of radical abolitionist John Brown, was left behind at a Maryland farmhouse called Kennedy Farm that served as the raiders' headquarters. His duty was to guard the horses in preparation for a swift escape. The raid was orchestrated by his father with the intended result of causing a major insurrection among the slaves and arming them with weapons captured during the attack. But the mission failed miserably. John lost two of his sons in the shootout and he himself was wounded, eventually tried for treason and hanged. The

Owen Brown (courtesy West Virginia Archives and History Division, Charleston, West Virginia, from the Boyd B. Stutler Collection).

insurrection he had envisioned never transpired. Shortly after receiving news that the raid had failed, Owen managed to escape the hot pursuit of Union soldiers.

Owen Brown eventually found his way to California. On January 8, 1889, after staying out of the limelight for a number of years, he died of pneumonia at the age of 64 at the residence of his brother-in-law, Henry Thompson, of Pasadena, California. Owen Brown is acknowledged as the last surviving participant of the infamous raid, despite his minuscule contributions that night.

To learn more about the raid at Harpers Ferry, the author recommends Tony Horwitz' riveting book, *Midnight Rising: John Brown and the Raid That Sparked the Civil War*.

Last Witness to the Siege of Ft. Sumter

Civil War enthusiasts are acutely aware that the first shots of the war took place on April 12–13, 1861, at Fort Sumter, which is located in the harbor of Charleston, South Carolina. But how many know the name of the last surviving witness to the bombardment of the Union fort by the Confederates?

Before the war Roger Atkinson Pryor, a lawyer from Virginia, joined the editorial staff of the *Washington Union* and later the *South*, a newspaper he helped establish. In 1857, Pryor, a Democrat, was elected to the U.S. House of Representatives and served until March 1861. A strong advocate of slavery and states' rights, he agitated for the secession of Virginia. When

Roger Atkinson Pryor.

Virginia refused to act, he travelled to South Carolina and, along with others, urged an attack on Fort Sumter. All of them thought that this aggressive action would force Virginia to secede from the Union. Shortly after, Pryor, along with his wife, was invited to embark on the last manned boat of South Carolinians in order to witness the planned attack on the Union fortification. When asked to fire the first shot, he declined, saying, "I could not fire the first gun of the war" (Pryor's declination has been referenced in many books published after the war).

Of the participants present at the fort those two days in April, Pryor has come to be recognized as the last surviving witness to the bombardment. During the war he became a colonel with the 3rd Regiment, Virginia Infantry, ultimately rising to the rank of general. Eventually he commanded the "Florida Brigade" and later assumed command of Maj. Gen. Richard H. Anderson's Division in Longstreet's Corps. But in battle, Pryor proved inept and eventually resigned his commission. Surprisingly, he reenlisted as a private and scout in a Virginia cavalry regiment before being captured and eventually paroled by President Lincoln.

A few years after the conflict, he moved to Brooklyn Heights, New York, and established a law firm working with clients like Benjamin F. Butler, the former Union general hated by many Southerners for his actions in Baton Rouge, Louisiana. How sentiments do change so quickly when earning a living takes precedence. Not long after Pryor settled with his family in New York, he came to be called a "Confederate carpetbagger," as opposed to the more well-known usage of the term during Reconstruction: "Northern carpetbagger." After an illustrious career in politics, he was appointed as justice of the New York Supreme Court, serving from 1894 to 1899 before retiring.

Roger Atkinson Pryor died at the age of 90 on March 14, 1919, in New York City and was laid to rest at Princeton Cemetery, Princeton, New Jersey.

To learn more about the life of Roger Atkinson Pryor, the author recommends three informative books: *The Confederate Carpetbaggers* by Daniel E. Sutherland; *Surviving the Confederacy: Rebellion, Ruin and Recovery; Roger and Sara Pryor During the Civil War* by John C. Waugh; and *Adapt or Perish: The Life of General Roger A. Pryor* by Robert S. Holzman.

Last Veteran to Fight at the Battle of Bull Run, During the Peninsula Campaign, the Battle of Antietam, and the Battle of Chancellorsville

The last soldier to have taken part in the above battles and campaign has been previously acknowledged in one of the last sections of this book: James Albert Hard of Co. E, 32nd Regiment, New York Volunteer Infantry.

Last Veteran at the Battle of Gettysburg

According to the U.S. National Park Service, James Marion Lurvey, Co. A, 40th Regiment, Massachusetts Volunteer Infantry, is "most likely" the last surviving veteran of the Battle of Gettysburg and the last living link to Gen. George G. Meade's army. Lurvey's distressing story about his duty at a

Union field hospital on the battlefield has been told earlier in this book. Lurvey was also the last Civil War veteran from the State of New Hampshire.

Last Naval Veterans in the Clash between the USS Monitor and the CSS Virginia

On March 9, 1862, in the harbor at the mouth of the James River in Hampton Roads, Virginia, two ironclad gunships, the USS *Monitor* and the CSS *Virginia,* fought a history-making naval battle. Because it was the first clash between ironclads, the confrontation ushered in a new era of naval warfare.

Originally part of the Union naval fleet, the *Virginia* was initially christened the USS *Merrimack.* A conventional steam frigate, it was salvaged by men of the Confederacy in Norfolk Navy Yard after the Union abandoned the vessel. The wooden ship was converted into an ironclad vessel by removing the top structure, installing an armored revolving gun turret and cladding the entire vessel in sheets of iron.

When the *Virginia* opened fire at 8:00 a.m. on the nearby USS *Cumberland* and the USS *Congress,* crowds of Union and Confederate supporters were already lined up on the decks of other ships to watch the ensuing action. The Confederate ironclad quickly managed to sink the two wooden hulls while also inflicting heavy damage on the USS *Minnesota*, but nightfall prevented her from finishing off the vessel. The next day, the *Monitor* appeared and prevented the *Virginia* from completing the destruction of the *Minnesota.* Soon the hard fighting commenced between the ironclads. When the smoke cleared, neither vessel had inflicted significant damage on the other. At 12:30 P.M., the *Virginia* turned and headed for its navy yard. The battle was over.

After a four-and-a-half-hour standoff produced no clear winner, each navy claimed victory. For both the Union and the Confederacy the naval battle was a major morale booster for citizens back home. Later the naval engagement became known also as the Battle of Hampton Roads.

When the Confederates evacuated Norfolk on May 9, 1862, to prevent the capture of the *Virginia* by the Union navy, the vessel was destroyed by its own crew. The *Monitor* would also suffer a devastating fate, but not at the hands of the Confederacy. On December 31, 1862, an unexpected gale off the coast of Cape Hatteras, North Carolina, sank the vessel. The remains of the *Monitor* were discovered after many years, and in 2002 part of the ship was salvaged from the deep. A gun turret and other artifacts were recovered and later refurbished.

According to the *Philadelphia Inquirer* of June 14, 1921, the last Union volunteer and survivor of the *Monitor* was Ireland-born, 82-year-old John

Ambrose Driscoll, who had died at the U.S. Naval Home of heart disease the previous day. According to the newspaper account, Driscoll and his crewmembers were devastated when only the ship's designer, John Ericsson, came to wish the sailors safe seas when the ironclad set sail on its maiden voyage from the Brooklyn Navy Yard.

Today, John Ambrose Driscoll lies at peace in a naval plot at Mt. Moriah Cemetery in Philadelphia. Surrounded by low-income housing, the once picturesque cemetery has long since been in serious disrepair, though efforts to clean up the grounds have recently been initiated.

The last Confederate survivor of the *Virginia* is said to be John Patrick Kevill, who died at the age of 95 on January 3, 1941. After his wartime service, Kevill became a store clerk. His remains lie at Cedar Grove Cemetery at Norfolk, Virginia. Little else is known about the veteran.

Over the years numerous books have been published dealing with the well-known Civil War naval battle. There are a plethora of good reads among the many and, while not wishing to limit the reading choices, the author recommends a recently published book about the battle the reader might find engaging: *The CSS* Virginia: *Sink Before Surrender* by John V. Quarstein.

Last Veteran of Pickett's Charge

According to newspaper correspondent Herbert T. Ezekiel in an article published in the *Richmond Virginia Times-Dispatch* of September 28, 1936, titled "Pickett's Last Man," a Confederate soldier with Co. A, 56th Regiment, Virginia Volunteer Infantry, was "so far as is known" the last surviving veteran to have participated in the ill-fated Pickett's Charge of July 3, 1863. His name is Cpt. Frank Walker Nelson and he was one of the countless men who made the futile assault at Cemetery Hill during the Battle of Gettysburg, Pennsylvania. It is said that the veteran officer talked about the charge for years. No wonder. Who could forget such carnage?

Frank Walker Nelson died on November 9, 1936, at the age of 93. He is buried in Hollywood Cemetery, Richmond, Virginia, along with many other Confederate military heroes, veterans, and dignitaries. His gravestone is engraved simply at the top with the word "Father"; inscribed on the bottom there is a religious sentiment: "In Certain Hope of a Resurrection in Christ."

Last Veteran to Participate in the Assault on Ft. Wagner

Organized in March 1863, the 54th Massachusetts Volunteer Infantry accepted Eli George Biddle—who told the army recruiting officers he was

17 when in truth he was only 16 years old—as a private. Biddle was not only one of the first to enlist in the African American regiment—the first of its kind in the North—but over a century later became the last surviving member.

Officially called the 54th Massachusetts Volunteer Infantry, the enlisted ranks consisted exclusively of African Americans. In keeping with the times, the entire staff of officers was white. The regiment had something to prove: when given the opportunity, they could fight as well as white Union soldiers. And fight they did, garnering well-earned and hard-fought respect for their bravery under fire.

The heroic and compelling tale about the 54th Regiment's assault on Ft. Wagner has been retold numerous times including on the silver screen in the movie *Glory*, which has been rerun on television more times than most care to remember. For those few who are unfamiliar with the story or in need of a refresher, a shortened version of it follows.

The Rev. E. G. Biddle.

On July 16, 1863, the 54th saw its first action, on James Island, where it lost forty-five of its men. Two days later, the regiment was ordered to lead the attack on Ft. Wagner at tiny Morris Island in the harbor off the coast of Charleston, South Carolina. Led by Colonel Robert Gould Shaw, the regiment's young and dashing commander, the assault proved both ill-advised and ill-fated. The well-fortified and firmly entrenched Confederates rained a merciless stream of bullets and cannon fire upon their adversaries that instantly killed Col. Shaw and ultimately resulted in the loss of over half of the regiment's troops (killed, wounded, and missing). Despite overwhelming odds and a slim chance of victory after the initial assault, the regiment never retreated while awaiting reinforcements that never arrived. Though the battle proved a resounding victory for the Confederates, it also reinforced, quite convincingly, what African Americans already knew: they were more than willing to fight for their freedom even if it meant an untimely death.

As for the last survivor of the assault on Ft. Wagner, Eli George Biddle was lucky to survive the assault, as he was wounded twice. In 1882 he became an ordained deacon and later served as the chaplain of the Department of Massachusetts GAR. The Reverend Biddle died on April 8, 1940. His remains are interred at Mt. Hope Cemetery at Forest Hills, Boston, Massachusetts.

The author highly recommends that the reader view the Massachusetts Historical Society Internet article titled "54th Regiment!" In it can be found fifteen images of African Americans and three white officers, of which Col. Robert Gould Shaw is one, all members of the 54th. Links to digitized images are also provided that allow access to 108 photographs of men in the regiment. The article, photographs, and additional links can be found at http://www. masshist.org/online/54thregiment/essay.php?entry_id=528.

Last Survivor of the "Immortal Six Hundred"

Perhaps one of the least known stories from the annals of the Civil War deals with a group of courageous Confederate officers who came to be called the "Immortal Six Hundred." The following is an abridged version of the story.

In late summer of 1863, Union Maj. Gen. Quincy A. Gillmore dispatched a message to Confederate Gen. P.G.T. Beauregard stating his intention to fire into the business and residential areas of Charleston, South Carolina, as he considered them military targets. The hail of artillery shells was to commence on August 22. Beauregard protested on the basis that he had insufficient time to evacuate civilians from the city. Gillmore disregarded the excuse and the shelling commenced early the next morning from Union-occupied marshes between Morris Island and James Island, four miles distant from the city. As the shelling continued, the city of Charleston looked every bit a war zone, with shell craters everywhere and animals decomposing in the streets.

As the siege continued, both sides of the armies changed command: Union Maj. Gen. John Gray Foster replaced Gillmore and Confederate Maj. Gen. Samuel Jones relieved Beauregard, who had been reassigned to North Carolina. Foster quickly realized he lacked the means to overtake the well-fortified Confederate city and, therefore, continued with the siege. Jones had a similar problem as the Yankees: he, too, lacked the resources to defeat the enemy. Knowing he had to do something, as the citizens of Charleston were nearing their wits' end, Jones asked Jefferson Davis on June 1, 1864, for 50 Union

Lt. (and the Rev.) Thomas Stewart Armstead (from *The Immortal Six Hundred* by Maj. J. Ogden Murray, 1911).

prisoners he could place in various parts of the city that would put them in direct line of the Union guns. Davis approved the transfer and on the twelfth of June, prisoners of war arrived by trains from a camp in Macon, Georgia. All were officers: five were brigadier generals and the rest lower ranking. As envisioned, the prisoners were placed under guard in an area of Charleston occupied by noncombatants. Jones notified Foster of what he had done.

In retaliation, Foster did the same. He requested fifty Confederate prisoners of war be sent to him to be placed in front of the Union forts on Morris Island. Foster informed Jones of his counter move. Needless to say, Jones was incensed and shot back a reply that the Union move was "antichristian, inhuman, and utterly indefensible by any law, human or divine." Even President Lincoln became involved, trying to defuse the situation by approving an exchange of prisoners that had previously been suspended. The plan eventually unraveled for various reasons: much had to do with outside factors relating to conducting a prisoner exchange so late in the war and the general mistrust and animosity each commanding officer felt toward the other.

As a result of General Sherman's capture of Atlanta, 600 Confederate prisoners were brought to the stockade on Morris Island on the seventh of September. The men were seriously mistreated from the start, and for the balance of the month they were exposed to the summer elements and all the fleas and mosquitoes that went along with it, flying shrapnel from premature exploding Union shells fired over their heads from Ft. Wagner, and their own friendly fire artillery rounds that flew over the stockade. Eighteen rounds landed in the stockade; all were duds. Luckily no prisoner was harmed but several Union guards were hit by shrapnel.

On October 8 the captives were moved inland to other cities. But for many, the shellfire continued for another 45 days, until they were transferred to Ft. Pulaski at Savannah, Georgia. The transfer did not lessen their misery. With bitter cold throughout the winter, 13 men died of disease. When March 1865 arrived, the survivors were removed to Ft. Delaware, fifteen miles south of Wilmington, and that became their final destination. Here another 25 died. The final release of prisoners happened in July 1865.

In 1905, J. Ogden Murray, former Confederate major and one of the six hundred captives, wrote a book about his group's trials and tribulations. Murray appropriately titled his work *The Immortal Six-Hundred*. Since the book's publication, the title has been used interchangeably with the men who lived through the ordeal, certainly a fitting tribute to these brave Confederate men.

And who was the last of the Immortal Six Hundred? His name is Thomas Stewart Armstead (aka Armistead), a former Confederate lieutenant who served with Co. E, 8th Regiment, Florida Volunteer Infantry, during the war. Later he became a Methodist circuit preacher delivering God's word throughout Alabama, Florida, and Georgia until his passing on November 16, 1922.

A number of Internet articles about the "Immortal 600" have been posted within the past few years that should satisfy the casual reader's curiosity. Those who desire to read a more comprehensive account about the dramatic tale can certainly find it in the book *The Immortal 600: Surviving Civil War Charleston and Savannah* by Karen Stokes.

Last Surviving Veteran Incarcerated at Andersonville Prison

George Wilsman, a private in Co. H, 42nd Regiment, Indiana Volunteer Infantry, is purported to be the last surviving Union soldier confined at the infamous Andersonville Prison in Andersonville, Georgia. Born in Cincinnati, Ohio, he enlisted in the Union army at the age of 18.

During the Battle of Chickamauga he and several others from his regiment were taken prisoner.

A captive for fourteen months, ten of which were spent at Andersonville Prison, he was exchanged in March of 1865. Like so many other veterans, after the war Wilsman became a farmer and tilled the soil. Early on he married Louise Schaaf Dale and had two sons. Louise died in 1923.

When asked about his imprisonment, he never blamed the camp commander. Wilsman believed Cpt. Heinrich Hartmann Wirz (better known as Henry Wirz) was unjustly convicted and hanged. The real villains, he said, were men he was incarcerated alongside: "My own comrades inside the pens fought me for food, clothes and trinkets. Men were killed for their skillets and battered drinking cups."

Prior to his passing he had been living with his daughter, Mrs. Lloyd V. Heady, at Evansville, Indiana. Fifty years of early-morning rising and tiresome farming finally caught up with him. After a year's illness, George Wilsman died on August 16, 1940, and was buried at the Santa Claus United Methodist Church Cemetery at Santa Claus, Indiana.

No one knows for certain when or where Wilsman told his associates about his incarceration at Andersonville Prison, but the statements he purportedly made were reprinted in an Indiana newspaper obituary without attribution.

Last of the Libby Prison Tunnel Diggers

Libby Prison was located in a three-story brick warehouse along the waterfront of the James River in Richmond, Virginia. Used as a jail before the war, the warehouse was leased by Cpt. Luther Libby and his son George and it was there they operated a ship's chandlery and grocery business. Affixed to the outside of the building was an advertising sign that read: "L. Libby & Son, Ship Chandlers." When the Confederacy hurriedly took over the building to use as a hospital, the sign was never removed. In 1862, the second and third stories of the building were used to confine captured Union officers. The name "Libby" stuck, perhaps to the chagrin of its former occupants, Luther and George.

The lack of food, scarcity of supplies, inadequate sanitation, and inability to control seasonal fluctuations in temperature and conditions, coupled with general overcrowding, all combined to inflict a heavy toll on the officers. Initially 700 Union officers were imprisoned, but by 1863 over 1,000 were held in the facility. Disease became rampant and death commonplace.

The men finally arriving at a point when conditions became absolutely intolerable, an elaborate escape plot was hatched. Seven men were selected to dig a fifty-five–foot tunnel under the building and its walls so that they could exit far enough away from the prison to offer the escapees a fighting chance at survival. From there, it was to be every man for himself.

John Mitchell.

Seven officers were selected as diggers, and all were sworn to secrecy. Only a select few of the prisoners had an inkling of what was planned. One guard who worked inside the warehouse was ultimately bribed. He was promised $1,000 from each of the diggers if they successfully made it to freedom. The men commenced work using only their hands and some pocketknives a few had concealed when they first arrived. The work proved not only lengthy in time but also extremely demanding. John Mitchell, 78th Regiment, Illinois Volunteer Infantry, from Pomeroy, Washington, was one of the diggers. He became so exhausted one day while digging the tunnel that he fell into a state of delirium and had to be pulled out and taken to the prison nurse.

According to Mitchell's later account, the nurse saved his life. When he regained his wits weeks later, Mitchell learned that the night escape on February 9, 1864, proved as successful as possible under the circumstances: of the 109 who escaped, 48 were recaptured and two drowned in the James River. All six diggers Mitchell worked alongside made it to Union lines. Reported in *Confederate Veteran* 27 (1909), Mitchell is quoted as saying, "Of the men who dug that tunnel, I am the only one living. The last of the other six has been dead several years."

John Mitchell died on January 23, 1918, at Yamhill County, Oregon. He rests in peace at Pomeroy City Cemetery at Pomeroy, Washington.

To learn more about the escape, the author recommends reading the enlightening book *Libby Prison Breakout: The Daring Escape from the Notorious Civil War Prison* by Joseph Wheeler.

Last Union and Confederate Generals of the War

Brig. Gen. Aaron Simon Daggett (b. June 14, 1837, d. May 14, 1938) was the last Union General of the war, dying at the age of 100 in West Roxbury, Massachusetts. He served with the 5th Regiment, Maine Volunteer Infantry,

Brig. Gen. Aaron Simon Daggett.

Maj. Gen. Felix Huston Robertson (*Confederate Veteran* XXXVI, no. 10 [October 1928], author's collection).

and later the 16th U.S. Infantry, seeing considerable combat as a high-ranking officer. After the Civil War, he also saw action in the Indian Wars, the Spanish–American War and later in China and the Philippines.

Brig. Gen. Felix Huston Robertson (b. March 9, 1839, d. April 20, 1928) was the last Confederate general of the war and the only native-born general from Texas to serve in the Confederacy. According to author William C. Davis, "Felix Robertson ... was almost without doubt the most reprehensible man in either army to wear the uniform of a general." According to several accounts, at the Battle of Saltville scores of African American cavalry troops were slaughtered in their beds. Davis wrote, "Only by the narrowest of margins did he escape being tried by his own government for what later generations would call war crimes." Brig. Gen. Robertson passed away in Waco, Texas, and is buried at Oakwood Cemetery in the city where he died.

Last Witness to Abraham Lincoln's Assassination

As a young man, the author remembers viewing a CBS television game show called *I've Got a Secret* (a New York studio production that premiered in 1952 and was broadcast until 1967). The show's premise was straightforward: a team of celebrity panelists tried to determine a contestant's secret: something unusual, amazing, embarrassing, or humorous about that person. Many times, after a number of unsuccessful guesses, the contestant walked away the winner, although during the early days of television the prize money was not a substantial amount. Still, the audience was entertained, including yours truly.

On February 9, 1956, the contestant, a feeble 95-year-old man in failing health, had to be helped to a chair situated next to the show's moderator, Gary Moore, before being subjected to a genial line of investigative questioning. On this particular evening, Samuel James Seymour's secret was quickly uncovered by the second panelist: Seymour was the last surviving person present, as a five-year-old boy, at Ford's Theater on the night Abraham Lincoln was assassinated.

Seymour's godmother, Mrs. George S. Goldsboro, had taken young Samuel to see the play *Our American Cousin*. According to Seymour's account, they sat in a balcony seat opposite Lincoln's box. Although he did not see the assassination (nor did anyone else in the audience), he did remember seeing John Wilkes Booth leap from the balcony onto the stage below. He also remembered feeling bad for the man who hurt himself after a hard landing on the stage. Despite Seymour's losing the game, Gary Moore awarded him the $80 in prize money. In lieu of a carton of cigarettes normally extended to each contestant by the show's sponsor, Moore gave him a can of pipe tobacco, as Seymour did not smoke cigarettes.

For most of his life, Seymour lived in Baltimore, Maryland, where he worked as a carpenter and contractor. Later he moved in with his daughter Irene (Horn) Hendley of Arlington, Virginia. Approximately two weeks after his 96th birthday and only a few months after his appearance on the game show, he passed away. Samuel James Seymour is interred at Loudon Park National Cemetery in Baltimore.

Fortunately the February 9, 1956, episode featuring Samuel James Seymour was preserved on film and later digitized. Though blurry, it can be viewed at https://www.youtube.com/watch?v=-jgGX1v4YFo. Seymour had a black eye at the time, the result of a fall he took at his hotel days before the live show was to be filmed. It is a video worth watching.

Last Witness to the Capture and Death of John Wilkes Booth, Abraham Lincoln's Assassin

According to his own account, John Henry Coghill, an ex-slave, was living across the street from the Garrett farm in Caroline County, Virginia, when he witnessed the capture and ultimate death of John Wilkes Booth. Coghill was 13 years old at the time. His statement about the incident was published in John E. Washington's book *They Knew Lincoln*. Today the original 1942 edition is considered a much-sought-after collector's item and on some Internet sites has been offered for sale in the range of $250 to $450.

According to Coghill's personal statement "there were no white people around, only soldiers" when the tobacco barn where Booth was hiding was set ablaze. He didn't hear the subsequent shot that felled the assassin, but he clearly remembered seeing the soldiers carry the mortally wounded man outside into the night air.

Exactly when and where John Henry Coghill died and is buried remains somewhat of a mystery. One source lists the year of his death as 1942 and his place of interment as Baltimore, Maryland. As for being the last witness to John Wilkes Booth's capture and death, nobody as yet has come forward with credible evidence to dispute the claim.

Last Surviving Ex-Slave

Many have claimed, or been designated by others, as the last ex-slave born in America. In fact, some 28 others have been named who surpass the lady's date of death mentioned below. Without proper documentation, none of the claims can be authenticated. Of the 28 alleged ex-slaves, 22 were said to be over 110 years old, with one claiming to be as old as 130. It seems almost inconceivable that any of them experienced such longevity, though statistically it is humanly possible. Sadly, unless additional evidence is found, none of these claims can be taken seriously.

Eliza Moore was born a slave in Montgomery County, Alabama, in 1843, and during the Civil War she was owned by a Dr. Taylor. After careful analysis of all available data, Eliza is considered by many historians as the last certifiable African American ex-slave in America. Though many other purported ex-slaves have claimed to be the last, Eliza is the only person to date whose claim can be supported by adequate documentation.

Eliza is said to have married a gentleman named Asbury Moore, also a former slave. Upon emancipation, the Moores became sharecroppers and remained in the state of Alabama. During their marriage they had two children. Asbury died in 1943 and is said to have been more than 100 years old at the time. When Eliza died on January 21, 1948, her death was reported five days later in the *Montgomery (AL) Advertiser*. The obituary stated she had succumbed at the residence of Charlie Brown, Jr., in Gilchrist Place, Montgomery County, Alabama. Reportedly, Eliza was 105 years old and had lived on the estate for nearly 70 years.

Last Widow to Receive a Civil War Pension

As best as can be determined, Maudie Celia (Acklin) Hopkins from Arkansas was the last surviving widow of a Civil War veteran. Maudie was 19 years old when she married Confederate veteran William M. Cantrell on February 2, 1934. He was 86. Marriages of convenience, commonly called May-December weddings, were commonplace during the Great Depression: the bride gained a steady income from her husband's pension and the groom received the proper care and attention he so desperately needed in his twilight years. Surprisingly, many of these couples had children.

William M. Cantrell enlisted as a private at the age of 16 in Pikeville, Kentucky, and served in French's Battalion of the Virginia Infantry. Captured in 1863, he was released after an exchange of prisoners. His first wife died in 1929. Maudie married William in 1937 and shared in his small pension, but only for a short time because William died just ten days after the nuptials. Later that year she remarried. Before her life ended, she married two more times. In total, she had three children. Maudie was not allowed to keep her first husband's small pension for any length of time, as a state law prohibited her from doing so. The 1939 Arkansas amendment to an existing law closed the so-called loophole. The law stated that Civil War veteran widows born after 1870 were no longer eligible to collect their deceased husband's pensions.

Maudie Cantrell, later Maudie Hopkins, died in a nursing home on August 17, 2008, in Lexa, Arkansas, at 93 years of age.

Last Child to Receive a Civil War Pension

According to a May 10, 2014, article in the *Wall Street Journal*, Irene Triplett, then age 84, is the last child of a Civil War veteran still receiving a monthly pension check from the Department of Veteran Affairs. Her father, Mose Triplett, first served as a Confederate private with the 53rd North Carolina Infantry before transferring to the 26th North Carolina Infantry. On June 26, 1863, while suffering from fever in a hospital at Danville, Virginia, he deserted. Months later he enlisted in the Union army. Though it might sound unusual, many folks living in the western part of North Carolina during the war held a strong allegiance to the Union. Triplett may have felt pressured to join the Confederacy, as several of his friends did so, but later had second thoughts, hence his change of uniform colors from butternut to blue. He joined the 3rd North Carolina Mounted Infantry (USA), served out his enlistment and qualified for a federal government pension.

Triplett was married twice. His first wife, Mary, died in the 1920s. Apparently there were no children. Years later he married his second wife, Elida Hall, nearly 60 years his junior. But Elida suffered from mental disabilities along with her daughter, Irene, who was born in 1930. According to the *Wall Street Journal*, Irene told reporter Michael M. Phillips that she "didn't care for neither one of them, to tell you the truth, about it. I wanted to get away from both of them. I wanted to get me a house and crawl in it all by myself." She also confided to Phillips that kids in school made fun of her and called her father a traitor. At home and at school, she suffered severe beatings. Despite making it to the sixth grade, her learning disabilities caused her removal from the classroom.

Mose Triplett died on July 18, 1938, and is buried in Wilkes County, North Carolina. At the age of 13, Irene and her troubled mother were committed to a mental institution. Elida apparently died at the facility. As best as can be determined Irene is still alive. She has been institutionalized in one facility or another for the better part of 70 years.

Last Civil War Veteran Elected
President of the United States

Twenty-six of our nation's forty-four presidents served in the military, six of whom were Civil War veterans—all army men: Ulysses S. Grant (18th

U.S. president); Rutherford B. Hayes (19th U.S. president); James A. Garfield (20th U.S. president); Chester A. Arthur (21st U.S. president); Benjamin Harrison (23rd U.S. president); and William McKinley (25th U.S. president). Hayes was a general and served the Union cause with distinction. Garfield raised troops for an Ohio volunteer regiment and eventually fought in Kentucky and at the Battle of Shiloh. He served as a quartermaster and never left the state of New York. Harrison served in the Atlanta Campaign. McKinley was the last of the Civil War veterans to become a U.S. president. He served in an Ohio regiment and fought with honor at the Battle of Antietam, which resulted in a battlefield commission as second lieutenant. During the war, McKinley became a staff officer to future president Rutherford B. Hayes, a colonel at the time.

Born in Niles, Ohio, William McKinley joined the 23rd Ohio Regiment, Volunteer Infantry, serving as an enlisted soldier before rising to the honorary rank of brevet major. He remained friends with Hayes, his mentor, throughout the years. After the war McKinley became a lawyer. Finding politics to his liking, he won a congressional seat and in 1889 became chair of the powerful House Ways and Means Committee. In 1891 he ran for and became governor of Ohio. Three years later he was reelected to that office. Known as an accomplished and well-liked politician in the Republican Party, McKinley ran for the presidency, was elected and took office on March 4, 1897. Only six months into his second term, President McKinley was mortally wounded on September 6, 1901, by an assassin's bullet while he was shaking hands inside a pavilion at the Pan-American Games held

in Buffalo, New York. The president lasted until September 14 before succumbing to his wound. His assassin was steelworker and American anarchist Leon Czolgosz. Twenty years earlier, Civil War veteran and president James A. Garfield was also assassinated. On July 2, 1881, at the Baltimore and Potomac Railroad Station in Washington, D.C., President Garfield was only four months into his first term in office when he was shot by Charles J. Guiteau, who had previously been declared insane by his own family. Garfield died eleven weeks later, on September 19, 1881. (All four U.S. presidents assassinated in office were military veterans. Besides Garfield and McKinley, Abraham Lincoln (16th president) fought in the brief 1832

President William McKinley.

Black Hawk War and John F. Kennedy (35th president) was a highly decorated World War II veteran who received the Navy Cross).

Last National Commander of the Grand Army of the Republic

Organized on April 6, 1866, at Decatur, Illinois, by Dr. Benjamin F. Stephenson, the Grand Army of the Republic (GAR) was a fraternal organization consisting of Civil War military veterans that patriotically incorporated military traditions into its proceedings. At its peak in 1890, the GAR boasted 490,000 members. At the last National Encampment held in Indianapolis, Indiana, in 1949, only a few members were well enough to attend. The small gathering voted to retain the incumbent officers until the organization was officially dissolved. Theodore Augustus Penland of Portland, Oregon, was the national commander at the time and thus became its last.

Penland enlisted as a private in Co. A, 152nd Regiment, Indiana Volunteer Infantry, during the war. Serving only as guards along the Potomac River, the regiment never saw combat. Penland's father and brothers did, however. Penland's father was wounded at the Battle of Stones River (aka Second Battle of Murfreesboro) and died shortly thereafter at a Union field hospital. Adding to the family's misery, two of Penland's brothers died while imprisoned at Andersonville.

After his discharge, Penland literally walked from Indiana to California before moving on to Wyoming and Nevada. After returning briefly to Indiana, he again felt the urge to travel. Before his days were numbered, he had resided in Michigan; Los Angeles and San Diego, California; and Portland, Oregon, making the last destination his final residence. Wishing to see more of the world, not just the United States, Penland, now entering the golden years of his life, travelled to Australia and New Zealand. The highly adventurous, well-travelled and admired veteran died on September 13, 1950, in Vancouver, Washington. Today his ashes rest at the Portland Memorial Mausoleum located in Portland, Oregon.

Because the Association of United Confederate Veterans (UCV) consisted of nine

Theodore Augustus Penland.

loosely knit veterans associations throughout the South, the organization never had a headquarters' position similar to that of the GAR.

The Last Navy Veteran

An article by Roger W. Kuchera, titled "The Last Naval Veterans of the War of the Rebellion" identified Henry Doll as the last naval veteran of the conflict. Kuchera found records showing that Doll served as a Union sailor aboard the USS *Portsmouth* and the USS *Brooklyn*. He also served aboard Admiral David G. Farragut's flagship, the USS *Hartford,* and that is where he was wounded, the extent of his injury remaining unclear. Only 14 years old when he joined the navy, much of his service was tied to performing duties as a "powder monkey," a derogatory term used to describe a young boy who hauled leather boxes filled with dry gunpowder from the ship's stores to the gunner.

Doll was born in Louisiana on January 22, 1848. It remains a mystery why or when he moved to Pennsylvania. What is known is that after leaving the navy, he married Etta Waters. The couple had four children, three girls and a boy. For 50 years he worked for the Pennsylvania Railroad to support his family, first as a mechanic, then as a fireman, and finally as an engineer.

In 1947 at the age of 99, Doll was a resident-patient at the Philadelphia Naval Hospital. Nearing the end of his life, he told a correspondent that he never saw President Abraham Lincoln, unlike many army men. "The closest I ever got to him," he said, "was seeing his picture." Doll was described as having an amazing memory and could recall names, dates and places effortlessly.

Naval veteran Henry Doll died on February 8, 1947, and is buried at Westminster Cemetery at Bala Cynwyd, Montgomery County, Pennsylvania.

Henry Doll and daughter Jeanette Amour (courtesy Sheila Maudsley).

Last Veteran to Die of Combat Wounds

Forty-nine years, eight months and two days after being wounded by a ricocheting minié ball fired by a Confederate soldier during the Siege of Petersburg, Bvt. Brig. Gen. Joshua Lawrence Chamberlain, formerly with the 20th Regiment, Maine Volunteer Infantry, finally died from the devastating injury, at least according to the attending physician who pronounced him dead on February 24, 1914, in Portland, Maine. The wound was one of six Chamberlain sustained while fighting for the Union; but this injury—if you accept the doctor's postmortem assessment, ultimately caused Chamberlain's death.

Joshua Lawrence Chamberlain won the Medal of Honor for his regiment's staunch defense and his own unflappable leadership at Little Round Top on the second day of the Battle of Gettysburg. Many believe Chamberlain's actions saved the day, if not the entire Union. Whatever a person wishes to believe, no one can rightly contest the bravery of the 20th Regiment, Maine Volunteer Infantry, that hot summer day in July 1863.

Bvt. Brig. Joshua Lawrence Chamberlain, MOH (Library of Congress).

Nearly a year later, at Petersburg, Chamberlain suffered a catastrophic groin injury. A Confederate bullet struck him in the right hip. En route through his body, the round severed arteries, broke his pelvis, and ripped open his bladder and urethra. The wound caused massive damage, and surgeons who attempted to repair the wound gave Chamberlain little hope for a full recovery, if not survival. Though he did survive, he never fully recovered. As time passed, he faced four additional operations, though none were able to resolve the issues he was having with incontinence, impotency, bladder infections, and bone disease.

Joshua Lawrence Chamberlain spent nearly the next fifty years in constant pain. Even if the Petersburg wound did not cause his demise, there is every reason to believe it might have been one of the contributing factors.

Last Veterans to Serve in the U.S. Senate (Union and Confederate)

Born in Hinsdale, Massachusetts, on June 20, 1844, Francis Emroy Warren enlisted as a Union private in the 49th Regiment, Massachusetts Volunteer Infantry, and later was promoted to a noncommissioned officer. He received the Medal of Honor for his gallantry during the Siege of Port Hudson in Louisiana. After his discharge from the army in 1868, he moved to Wyoming (at the time, part of the Dakota Territory). In February of 1885, President Grover Cleveland appointed him governor of the Territory of Wyoming. He was later elected to the U.S. Senate, as a Republican, where he served from 1890 until 1893. A popular figure in Wyoming, Warren was elected six more times and served until his death in Washington, D.C., on November 24, 1929. Francis Emroy Warren rests in peace at Lakeview Cemetery, Cheyenne, Wyoming.

Charles Spaulding Thomas was born on December 6, 1849, at Darien, Georgia. According to his biography, he served only briefly in the Confederacy. After the war he received a law degree from the University of Michigan. Suffering from tuberculosis, he moved to

Sen. Francis E. Warren (courtesy Wyoming State Archives, Sub. Neg. 19423).

Denver to improve his health and in due course it did improve. In Denver he established a law practice before marrying Emma Gould Fletcher. In 1898 he was elected governor of Colorado. Later, Thomas was elected to the U.S. Senate and served from 1913 until 1921.

On June 24, 1934, Charles Spalding Thomas died in Denver. His ashes lie at Fairmount Cemetery. Thus, the former Confederate was the last Civil War veteran to serve in the U.S. Senate.

Charles Spaulding Thomas (U.S. Senate Historical Office).

Last Veteran to Serve on Active Duty

Thousands of underage boys enlisted as soldiers during America's Civil War. Born in Newark, Ohio, on August 13, 1851, and one of thirteen children, John Joseph Klem (aka Johnny Clem) left home at the age of nine to join the Union army not long after his mother was killed in a train accident. Rejected by an Ohio recruiter, he was ultimately mustered into the 22nd Regiment, Michigan Volunteer Infantry, as a musician. Many exploits concerning young Clem's bravery were published during and after the war. Some have no basis in fact. A story circulating at the time suggested that Clem nearly lost his life at the Battle of Shiloh. In fact, the regiment was yet to be organized.

At Horseshoe Ridge during the Battle of Chickamauga Clem was said to have shot a Confederate officer from his horse with a musket that had the barrel cut down to fit his diminutive size. Soon afterward he was promoted to sergeant, thus becoming the youngest noncommissioned officer in the Union army. From that supposed incident, the 12-year-old boy's reputation grew by leaps and bounds. In the North he became a national hero and was hailed as "The Drummer Boy of Chickamauga." It was during this period that he changed his name to John Lincoln Clem. The change of his middle name was because he admired President Lincoln and the replacement of the "K" in his surname was to make it appear more Americanized than German (his ancestry).

In October 1863, while detailed as a train guard, Clem was captured by a Confederate cavalry troop. His cap, with three bullet holes, attested to his ill-fated encounter with the enemy. Because of his tender age, he was soon exchanged but not before the Confederates had a propaganda blitz to show how desperate the Union army had become "when they have to send out their babies to fight us."

On September 19, 1864, after serving as a mounted orderly on Maj. Gen. George H. Thomas's staff, Clem was discharged. Soon after that, Clem was appointed by President Ulysses S. Grant to the U.S. Military Acad-

Johnny Clem, the young Civil War celebrity.

emy at West Point, but he failed the entrance exam. He was then extended a commission as a second lieutenant and assigned to the 24th U.S. Infantry. His two wounds from the war and his celebrity status as a young war hero most assuredly played in his favor. In 1875 Clem married Anita Rosetta French, who died twenty-four years later. In 1903 he married Bessie Sullivan, the daughter of a Confederate veteran; because of her lineage Clem took pleasure in claiming he was "the most united American" in the United States.

In due course, Clem rose to the rank of colonel and in 1903 he became assistant quartermaster general. On August 13, 1915, when he reached the army's mandatory retirement age, he had already been promoted to brigadier general. Following retirement, Clem and his family lived in Washington, D.C., before finally settling in San Antonio, Texas. During life's journey the Clems had three children.

On August 29, 1916, a year after his official retirement, a special act of Congress allowed Clem to be promoted to the rank of major general, thus affording him the honor of being called "the last active duty soldier from America's Civil War." As best as can be determined, Clem lobbied for the action. John Lincoln Clem, "The Drummer Boy of Chickamauga," died in San Antonio on May 13, 1938, at the age of 85. His remains rest in peace at Arlington National Cemetery, Arlington, Virginia.

Chapter Notes

Introduction

1. Speaking of Pictures, "These 68 Veterans Are All That Survive of the 3,000,000 Young Soldiers Who Wore the Blue or the Gray in the Great War That Ended 84 Years Ago," *Life*, May 30, 1949, pp. 8–10.

2. Speaking of Pictures, "These Are the Last Five Veterans of the Civil War," *Life*, June 1, 1953, pp. 2–5.

3. The Fine Arts Museums of San Francisco is in possession of Larry Rivers' 1961 painting, *The Last Civil War Veteran*, which depicts the image described in the text.

4. The monument can be viewed on several Internet sites by searching "Soldiers and Sailors of the Confederacy Monument."

5. William Marvel, "The Great Imposters," *Blue and Gray* 8 (February 1991), 32.

6. Richard A. Serrano, *Last of the Blue and Gray* (Washington, DC: Smithsonian Books, 2013), 43–60.

7. Marvel, "The Great Imposters," 32.

8. Martin F. Graham, Clint Johnson, Richard A. Sauers, and George Skoch, *The Civil War Chronicle* (Lincolnwood, IL: Publications International, 2004), 403.

9. *Ibid.*

10. See http://www.archives.gov/publicati ons/prologue/2010/spring/civilwarpension. html.

11. See http://www.findagrave.com/cgi-bin/ fg.cgi?page=gr&GRid=49607043.

12. See http://www.virginiamemory.com/ blogs/out_of_the_box/2010/10/06/generaljoh n-salling-virginias-last-confederate-veteran/.

13. Jay S. Hoar, *The North's Last Boys in Blue*, vol. 2 (Salem, MA: Higginson, 2007), 996.

14. *Ibid.*

15. *Somerset Daily American*, May 30, 1952.

Chapter 2

1. William J. Miller and Brian C. Pohanka, *An Illustrated History of the Civil War: Images*

of an American Tragedy (New York: Time Life, 2000), 13.

2. *Ibid.*, 14.

3. *Ibid.*, 36.

4. See http://www.soldierstudies.org/blog/ 2011/06/what-happened-to-civil-war-soldiers-after-the-war/.

5. *Ibid.*

6. See http://www.nps.gov/civilwar/search-battle-units-detail.htm?battleUnitCode=UOH 0012RC.

7. According to author Thomas Fox in his book, *Drummer Boy Willie McGee: Civil War Hero and Fraud*, a gentleman named William McGee living on the West Side of New York City passed himself off as a Civil War veteran from the 33rd Regiment, New Jersey Volunteer Infantry. He not only claimed to be a former soldier but also a Medal of Honor recipient awarded for bravery while capturing a Confederate gun emplacement in Tennessee. In truth, McGee was nothing more than a scam artist and a drunk. Eventually his lies caught up with him. In 1892, he died at the age of 45. It is doubtful that California's William Allen Magee, who was the real McCoy, ever heard of the man, as they lived on different sides of the continent.

8. Jay S. Hoar, *The North's Last Boys in Blue*, vol. 1 (Salem, MA: Higginson, 2006), 479.

9. *Ibid.*, 867.

10. See http://www.findagrave.com/cgi-bin/ fg.cgi?page=gr&GRid=8540222.

11. *Ibid.*

12. See http://www.nps.gov/civilwar/search-battle-units-detail.htm?battleUnitCode=UCT 0015RI.

13. C. Stewart Peterson, M.A., *Last Civil War Veteran in Each State* (Baltimore: Self-published, 1951), 6.

14. Jay S. Hoar, *New England's Last Civil War Veterans* (Arlington, TX: Seacliff Press, 1876), 153.

15. Peterson, *Last Civil War Veteran in Each State*, 6.

16. *Ibid.*

17. Hoar, *New England's Last Civil War Veterans*, 153–154.

18. See http://www.nps.gov/civilwar/search-battle-units-detail.htm?battleUnitCode=UIL0021RI.

19. See http://www.nps.gov/civilwar/search-battle-units-detail.htm?battleUnitCode=UIL0140RI.

20. See http://www.nps.gov/civilwar/search-battle-units-detail.htm?battleUnitCode=UIL0090RI.

21. See http://www.findagrave.com/cgi-bin/fg.cgi?page=gr&GRid=42199287 (the article was posted on Ancestry.com, rootsweb, and was written by Glenice A. Fablinger under the title, *History of the Fablinger Family, 1813–1997*).

22. See http://www.findagrave.com/cgi-bin/fg.cgi?page=gr&GRid=42199287.

23. Peterson, *Last Civil War Veteran in Each State*, 11.

24. See http://www.findagrave.com/cgi-bin/fg.cgi?page=gr&GRid=42199287.

25. *Chicago Daily Tribune,* October 11, 1949.

26. Peterson, *Last Civil War Veteran in Each State*, 11.

27. *Ibid.*

28. *Daily Illini,* March 16, 1950.

29. See http://www.findagrave.com/cgi-bin/fg.cgi?page=gr&GRid=42199287.

30. See http://www.nps.gov/civilwar/search-battle-units-detail.htm?battleUnitCode=UWV0017RI.

31. See http://suvcw.org/in/JCAdams.html.

32. *Ibid.*

33. *Ibid.*

34. *Ibid.*

35. See http://www.nps.gov/civilwar/search-battle-units-detail.htm?battleUnitCode=UWI0001RAH.

36. *O'brien County Bell,* September 28, 1949.

37. A brief family history was given to the author in an e-mail message by descendant Sandra Williamson on August 13, 2015.

38. Peterson, *Last Civil War Veteran in Each State*, 13.

39. See http://suvcw.org/past/jpmartin.htm.

40. Peterson, *Last Civil War Veteran in Each State*, 13.

41. *O'brien County Bell,* September 28, 1949.

42. See http://suvcw.org/past/jpmartin.htm.

43. *Ibid.*

44. *Ibid.*

45. See http://suvcw.org/past/jpmartin.htm.

46. *O'brien County Bell,* September 21, 1949.

47. See http://www.nps.gov/civilwar/search-battle-units-detail.htm?battleUnitCode=UWI0047RI.

48. See http://www.nps.gov/civilwar/search-battle-units-detail.htm?battleUnitCode=UWI0005RI.

49. Hoar, *The North's Last Boys in Blue*, vol. 2, p. 824.

50. *Ibid.*

51. A few particulars about Charles W. Bailey's life were abstracted from the January 30, 1951, newspaper edition of the *Topeka Daily Capital,* with the heading, "Charles W. Bailey, Dies at Age of 102."

52. Hoar, *The North's Last Boys in Blue*, vol. 2, p. 825.

53. See http://www.nps.gov/civilwar/search-battle-units-detail.htm?battleUnitCode=UME0012RI.

54. Hoar, *New England's Last Civil War Veterans*, 140.

55. *Ibid.*

56. *Ibid.*

57. *Ibid.,* 140–141.

58. *Ibid.,* 137.

59. Patricia Ann Carlson, ed., *Literature and Lore of the Sea* (Amsterdam, The Netherlands: Rodopi, 1986), 69–70.

60. Hoar, *New England's Last Civil War Veterans*, 138–139.

61. See http://remeberjamaicaplain.blogspot.comsearch?q=riley.

62. *Ibid.*

63. *Ibid.,* 139.

64. *Ibid.,* 127–132.

65. See http://lestweforget.hamptonu.edu/page.cfm?uuid=9FEC38F1-0E31-6A6F-9C4758132E191A92.

66. See https://jubiloemancipationcentury.wordpress.com/2013/05/27/memorial-day-greetings-remembering-joseph-clovese-of-the-usct-and-the-gar/.

67. Hoar, *The North's Last Boys in Blue*, vol. 2, p. 841.

68. *Everett Daily Herald,* July 14, 1951. Clovese's newspaper obituary is reprinted on an Internet site under the title, "Pvt Joseph Clovese (1844–1951)–Find a Grave Memorial."

69. See https://jubiloemancipationcentury.wordpress.com/2013/05/27/memorial-day-greetings-remembering-joseph-clovese-of-the-usct-and-the-gar/.

70. *Ibid.*

71. *Ibid.*

72. Hoar, *The North's Last Boys in Blue*, vol. 2, p. 842.

73. See http://www.nps.gov/civilwar/search-battle-units-detail.htm?battleUnitCode=UMA0040RI.

74. See http://www.nps.gov/civilwar/search-battle-units-detail.htm?battleUnitCode=UMA0004RAH.

75. See http://www.findagrave.com/cgi-bin/fg.cgi?page=gr&GRid=17981778.

76. Hoar, *New England's Last Civil War Veterans*, 155.

77. *Ibid.*

78. *Ibid.*, 157.

79. *Ibid.*

80. *Manchester (NH) Union,* October 26, 1903. A photograph of James M. Lurvey in his early- to mid-fifties is included in the article titled "Six Years, Not More than Ten."

81. *Ibid.*

82. *Ibid.*

83. *Ibid.*

84. Hoar, *New England's Last Civil War Veterans,* 158–159.

85. See https://npsgnmp.wordpress.com/tag/last-gettysburg-veteran/.

86. Hoar, *New England's Last Civil War Veterans,* 159.

87. See http://www.nps.gov/rich/historyculture/22ndusct.htm.

88. See http://www.findagrave.com/cgi-bin/fg.cgi?page=gr&GRid=16750849.

89. *Ibid.* Also see Hoar, *The North's Last Boys in Blue,* vol. 1, p. 409. Information about the 22nd Regiment, USCT, taking part in President Lincoln's funeral procession and the subsequent hunt for John Wilkes Booth was extracted from a New Jersey State Library Internet brief of February 21, 2014. It documented a presentation given by author Joseph Bilby about New Jersey's African American soldiers during the Civil War.

90. *Ibid.*

91. See http://www.findagrave.com/cgi-bin/fg.cgi?page=gr&GRid=16750849.

92. Hoar, *The North's Last Boys in Blue,* vol. 1, p. 409.

93. See http://www.nps.gov/civilwar/search-battle-units-detail.htm?battleUnitCode=UOH0195RI.

94. See http://image2.findagrave.com/cgibin/fg.cgi?page=sh&GRid=9750487&.

95. *Ibid.*

96. *Ibid.*

97. *Ibid.*

98. *Ibid.*

99. Today the Columbia River Gorge encompasses nearly 300,000 acres, running from the mouth of the Sandy River to the mouth of the Deschutes River and spanning southern Washington and northern Oregon.

100. See http://offbeatoregon.com/o1111c-black-sheep-of-union-army-last-oregon-vet.html.

101. Theodore A. Penland, the last commander in chief of the Grand Army of the Republic, was initially considered the last surviving veteran from Oregon until James W. Smith's past was rediscovered. Though the honor has been transferred to Smith, it seems unfortunate considering the dubious record of Smith's detachment and Penland's distinguished service to the Union and later the GAR.

102. *The Lebanon Express,* March 27, 1951.

103. *Ibid.*

104. *Portland Oregonian,* March 23, 1951.

105. See http://www.nps.gov/civilwar/search-battle-units-detail.htm?battleUnitCode=UPA0018RC.

106. See http://www.findagrave.com/cgi-bin/fg.cgi?page=gr&GRid=55708896.

107. Hoar, *The North's Last Boys in Blue,* vol. 2, p. 755.

108. *Ibid.*

109. *Ibid.*

110. U.S. Federal Census records (1870 through 1930).

111. Hoar, *The North's Last Boys in Blue,* vol. 2, p. 755.

112. See http://www.findagrave.com/cgi-bin/fg.cgi?page=gr&GRid=55708896.

113. See http://www.nps.gov/civilwar/search-battle-units-detail.htm?battleUnitCode=URI0002RI.

114. *Providence Journal,* May 8, 1943.

115. H. Crandall and A.D.C., *Annual Report of the Adjutant General of the State of Rhode Island, for the Year 1865.* (Providence: Providence Press, 1866), 41.

116. Material for this story was garnered from an interview between Lloyd Lincoln Colvin, along with his wife, Barbara, and the author on January 15, 2015.

117. See http://www.nps.gov/civilwar/search-battle-units-detail.htm?battleUnitCode=UVT0001RAH.

118. See http://vtdigger.org/2014/03/30/state-veteran-gilbert-lucier-embodied-vermonts-deep-passion-civil-war/.

119. *Ibid.*

120. Hoar, *New England's Last Civil War Veterans,* 95.

121. See http://vtdigger.org/2014/03/30/state-veteran-gilbert-lucier-embodied-vermonts-deep-passion-civil-war/.

122. *Ibid.*

123. Hoar, *New England's Last Civil War Veterans,* 95.

124. *Ibid.*

125. See http://vtdigger.org/2014/03/30/state-veteran-gilbert-lucier-embodied-vermonts-deep-passion-civil-war/.

126. See http://www.nps.gov/civilwar/search-battle-units-detail.htm?battleUnitCode=UWI0004RC.

127. See http://www.suvcw-wi.org/last_soldier/chippewa.shtml.

128. *Ibid.*

129. *Ibid.*

130. *Ibid.*

131. *Ibid.*

132. *Ibid.*

133. See http://www.usgennet.org/usa/wi/county/clark/5data/104/110.htm.

134. *Thorp Courier,* October 4, 1951.

135. See http://www.suvcw-wi.org/last_sol dier/chippewa.shtml.

Chapter 3

1. http://www.nps.gov/civilwar/search-battle-units-detail.htm?battleUnitCode=CVA 0007RC.
2. Frank S. Walker, Jr., "James Albert Spicer and His Mill by the Rapidan." *Orange County Historical Society Newsletter* 37, no. 2 (December 2006), 2.
3. *Washington Post*, February 11, 1948.
4. *Ibid.*
5. *Ibid.*
6. *Ibid.*, 3.
7. *Ibid.*, 2–3.
8. *Washington Post,* February 11, 1948.
9. Peterson, *Last Civil War Veteran in Each State*, 8.
10. *Ibid.*

Chapter 4

1. See http://www.nps.gov/civilwar/facts. htm. The reader is also encouraged to read *Nation of Nations: A Narrative History of the American Republic* (vol. 1, to 1877), in which many of these statistics were first published.
2. See http://en.wikiquote.org/wiki/The_ Civil_War_%28documentary%29.
3. To learn more about the Confederados, see the following Internet sites: http://www. odditycentral.com/travel/the-confederate-south-still-lives-in-brazil.html; http://www. confederados.com.br/title.htm; and http://en. wikipedia.org/wiki/Confederados (this site provides a listing of books about the Confederados that may be of additional interest to the reader).
4. See http://www.archives.gov/research/ military/civil-war/confederate/penstion.html.
5. See http://www.elderweb.com/book/ex port/html/2823.
6. See http://www.civilwaronthewestern border.org/content/price%E2%80%99s-misso uri-expedition-or-price%E2%80%99s-raid.
7. Marvel, "The Great Imposters." *Blue and Gray*, 32.
8. Hoar, *The South's Last Boys in Gray*, vol. 2, p. 475.
9. *Ibid.*, 474.
10. *Ibid.*, 475.
11. Gary Victor Hill, *America's Last Civil War Veterans and Participants: An Investigation* (Armidale, Australia: Frisky, 2015), 129.
12. Hoar, *The South's Last Boys in Gray*, vol. 21, p.1672.
13. *Ibid.*
14. http://freepages.genealogy.rootsweb. ancestry.com/~keuttaqhg/kssarahegc.htm.

15. Hoar, *The South's Last Boys in Gray*, Vol. 21, p. 1673.
16. The CCC existed from 1933 to 1942 and was part of President Franklin Delano Roosevelt's New Deal to get Americans back to work during and after the Great Depression.
17. http://freepages.genealogy.rootsweb. ancestry.com/~keuttaqhg/kssarahegc.htm.
18. See https://familysearch.org/learn/wiki/ en/Wauchilla_Militia,_Florida_%28Confeder ate%29.
19. Hoar, *The South's Last Boys in Gray,* vol. 21, p. 1610.
20. *Ibid.*
21. *Ibid.*
22. *Ibid.*, 1611.
23. *Ibid.*
24. Hoar, *The South's Last Boys in Gray*, vol. l, p. 476.
25. Hill, *America's Last Civil War Veterans and Participants: An Investigation*, 132.
26. *Statesboro Herald*, "Surviving Veteran Guest of Honor Monday," April 29, 1937.
27. Hoar, *The South's Last Boys in Gray*, Vol. 21, pp. 1577–1578.
28. *Ibid.*
29. *Ibid.*, 1578.
30. *Statesboro (GA) Herald*, "Surviving Veteran Guest of Honor Monday," April 29, 1937.
31. Hoar, *the South's Last Boys in Gray*, vol. 21, p. 1580.
32. *Ibid.*
33. *Statesboro Herald*, April 29, 1937.
34. http://www.nps.gov/civilwar/search-battle-units-detail.htm?battleUnitCode= CLA0006RC.
35. Marvel, "The Great Imposters," *Blue and Gray*, 32, and Serrano, *Last of the Blue and Gray*, 74–76.
36. Hoar, *The South's Last Boys in Gray*, 431–432.
37. *Ibid.*, 431.
38. Randy DeCuir, et al., *Remembering Rapides' Rebels: Portraits of Confederates and Other Civil War Figures of Rapides Parish, Louisiana* (Rapides, LA: Self-published, no date), 203.
39. *Ibid.*, 382.
40. *Ibid.*
41. *Ibid.*
42. *Ibid.*, 381–382.
43. *Ibid.*, 382.
44. See http://www.findagrave.com/cgi-bin/ fg.cgi?page=gr&GRid=5048503.
45. See http://www.datasync.com/~jtaylor/ msbarhg.htm.
46. Peterson, *Last Civil War Veteran in Each State*, 22.
47. Hoar, *The South's Last Boys in Gray*, 447.
48. Peterson, *Last Civil War Veteran in Each State*, 22.

49. See http://www.findagrave.com/cgi-bin/ fg.cgi?page=gr&GRid=53099293.
50. Hoar, *The South's Last Boys in Gray*, vol. 1, pp. 447–448.
51. See http://www.findagrave.com/cgi-bin/ fg.cgi?page=gr&GRid=53099293.
52. *Hattiesburg American*, April 7, 1951.
53. *Ibid.*
54. See http://www.findagrave.com/cgi-bin/ fg.cgi?page=gr&GRid=53099293.
55. See http://www.nps.gov/civilwar/search-battle-units-detail.htm?battleUnitCode=CNC 0021RI.
56. See http://en.wikipedia.org/wiki/Alfred_ %22Teen%22_Blackburn.
57. Hoar, *The South's Last Boys in Gray*, Vol. 21, 1681.
58. See http://en.wikipedia.org/wiki/Alfred_ %22Teen%22_Blackburn.
59. *Ibid.*
60. Hoar, *The South's Last Boys in Gray*, vol. 21, p. 1681.
61. See http://www.findagrave.com/cgi-bin/ fg.cgi?page=gr&GRid=105671883.
62. See https://familysearch.org/learn/wiki/ en/4th_Regiment,_South_Carolina_State_Tro op_Junior_Reserves.
63. Marvel, "The Great Imposters." *Blue and Gray*, 32.
64. Hoar, *The South's Last Boys in Gray*, 479.
65. See http://scscv.com/the-last-confeder ate-soldier-of-south-carolina/.
66. *Ibid.*
67. Hoar, *The South's Last Boys in Gray*, 419.
68. *Ibid.*, 419–420.
69. *Ibid.*, 420.
70. *Ibid.*
71. *Ibid.*
72. See http://www.findagrave.com/cgi-bin/ fg.cgi?page=gr&GRid=42200847.
73. Peterson, *Last Civil War Veteran in Each State*, 38.
74. *Ibid.*
75. *Ibid.*
76. *Ibid.*
77. *Ibid.*
78. Hoar, *The South's Last Boys in Gray*, vol. 21, p. 1466.
79. See http://www.nps.gov/civilwar/search-battle-units-detail.htm?battleUnitCode=CMO 0012RC.
80. Hoar, *The South's Last Boys in Gray*, 451 and 452.
81. *Ibid.*, 452.
82. *Ibid.*
83. *Ibid.*
84. *Ibid.*
85. *Dallas Morning News*, August 16, 1951.
86. *Ibid.*
87. *Ibid.*
88. See http://www.nps.gov/civilwar/search-battle-units-detail.htm?battleUnitCode=CVA 0026BI.
89. Hoar, *The South's Last Boys in Gray*, 459.
90. *Ibid.*
91. *Ibid.*
92. Hoar, *The South's Last Boys in Gray*, vol. 21, p. 1679.
93. Hoar, *The South's Last Boys in Gray*, 459 and 460.

Chapter 5

1. See http://www.nps.gov/resources/story. htm?id=205 (Amy Murrell Taylor's essay was extracted from *The Civil War Remembered*, published by the National Park Service and Eastern National, no date).
2. *Ibid.*
3. See https://en.wikipedia.org/wiki/Bor der_states_(American_Civil_War).
4. See http://www.nps.gov/rich/historycul ture/9thusct.htm.
5. Michael Morgan, *Ocean City: Going Down the Ocean* (Charleston, SC: History Press, 2011) 41.
6. *Ibid.*
7. See http://visitworcester.org/printables/ Fassett.pdf.
8. Morgan, *Ocean City: Going Down the Ocean*, 41.
9. See http://taylorhousemuseum.org/his tory/isaiah-fassett/.
10. Morgan, *Ocean City: Going Down the Ocean*, 41.
11. See http://visitworcester.org/printables/ Fassett.pdf.
12. See http://taylorhousemuseum.org/ history/isaiah-fassett/.
13. Morgan, *Ocean City: Going Down the Ocean*, 41.
14. See http://www.nps.gov/civilwar/search-battle-units-detail.htm?battleUnitCode=UK Y0017RC.
15. *Princeton Leader*, January 18, 1951.
16. *Ibid.*; also see Hoar, *the North's Last Boys in Blue*, vol. 2, p. 821.
17. See http://archiver.rootsweb.ancestry. com/th/read/BARRETT/1999-10/0939523848.
18. *Ibid.*
19. *Ibid.*
20. *Princeton Leader*, January 18, 1951.
21. See http://www.nps.gov/civilwar/search-battle-units-detail.htm?battleUnitCode=UPA 0008RI.
22. See http://www.nps.gov/civilwar/search-battle-units-detail.htm?battleUnitCode=UP A0191RI.
23. Hoar, *The North's Last Boys in Blue*, vol. 1, p. 445.
24. Daniel Carroll Toomey, *The Civil War*

in Maryland (Baltimore: Toomey, 1983), 145–147.

25. Peterson, *Last Civil War Veteran in Each State*, 18.

26. Hoar, *The South's Last Boys in Gray*, vol. 21, p. 1377.

27. See http://www.nps.gov/civilwar/search-battle-units-detail.htm?battleUnitCode=UMO0046RI.

28. See http://www.watersheds.org/history/hutchinson.htm. Inell McMillon used two sources when writing about John Hutchison's life on this Internet site: *Springfield Leader and Press; Springfield News and Leader* of March 1951, and a book titled *A Reminiscent History of the Ozark Region* (Chicago: Goodspeed, 1894), 724–725. The book is a compilation of tales by a number of authors.

29. See http://www.wateersheds.org/history/hutchinson.htm.

30. *Ibid.*

31. *Ibid.*

32. See http://worldconnect.rootsweb.ancestry.com/cgi-bin/igm.cgi?op=GET&db=seeeye&id=17433.

33. See http://www.wateersheds.org/history/hutchinson.htm.

34. See http://www.nps.gov/civilwar/search-battle-units-detail.htm?battleUnitCode=UWV0006RI.

35. Hoar, *The North's Last Boys in Blue*, vol. 2, p. 627.

36. *Cameron News*, October 30, 1947.

Chapter 6

1. See http://www.history.com/topics /louisiana-purchase.

2. See http:en.wikipedia.org/wiki/Land_grant.

3. See http://www.gilderlehrman.org/history-by-era/development-west/resources/horace-greeley-%E2%80%9Cgo-west%E2%80%9D-1871.

4. See http://en.wikipedia.org/wiki/Land_Rush_of_1889.

5. See http://www.archives.gov/education/lessons/homestead-act/.

6. See http://www.nps.gov/civilwar/search-battle-units-detail.htm?battleUnitCode=UIL0154RI.

7. Arizona achieved statehood on February 14, 1912.

8. See http://azrebel.tripod.com/2005–2006.html.

9. See http://www.suvcwaz-campt1.org/graves-registration/.

10. Peterson, *Last Civil War Veteran in Each State*, 2.

11. David Swanson (camp commander),

"Last Civil War Soldier Project ... We Need Your Assistance" *Camp Newsletter* (Phoenix: Sons of Union Veterans of the Civil War, Picacho Peak Camp #1, Arizona Camp-at-Large, October 2004), 2.

12. The Rev. Geo. A. Gordon, *Life and Labors of Rev. Henry S. Gordon, Founder of the First Baptist Church in Southern Illinois* (Campbell Hills, IL: Self-published, 1901), 34.

13. Peterson, *Last Civil War Veteran in Each State*, 2.

14. Gordon, *Life and Labors of Rev. Henry S. Gordon,* 34.

15. *Arizona Republic*, December 6, 1946.

16. See http://www.findagrave.com/cgi-bin/fg.cgi?page=gr&GSln=gordon&GSfn=parker&GSiman=1&GScid=57026&GRid=60228815&.

17. See http://www.nps.gov/civilwar/search-battle-units-detail.htm?battleUnitCode=UIL0145RI.

18. Peterson, *Last Civil War Veteran in Each State*, 5.

19. *Ibid.*

20. *Ibid.*

21. Colorado achieved statehood on August 1, 1876.

22. See http://www.dailycamera.com/ci_15136424.

23. Peterson, *Last Civil War Veteran in Each State*, 5.

24. *Ibid.*

25. See http://www.huffingtonpost.com/2012/04/14/thurman-iowa-75-percent-destroyed-tornado_n_1426261.html.

26. See http://www.nps.gov/civilwar/search-battle-units-detail.htm?battleUnitCode=UMO0051RI.

27. Peterson, *Last Civil War Veteran in Each State*, 10.

28. Mary E. Reeves, "Idaho's Last Civil War Vet," *Scenic Idaho* 4, no. 1 (1950), 26–27.

29. *Ibid.*

30. Peterson, *Last Civil War Veteran in Each State*, 10.

31. Idaho achieved statehood on July 3, 1890.

32. Reeves, "Idaho's Last Civil War Vet," 28.

33. *Ibid.*, 27.

34. See http://www.findagrave.com/cgi-bin/fg.cgi?page=gr&GRid=42198920.

35. See http://www.nps.gov/civilwar/search-battle-units-detail.htm?battleUnitCode=UPA0132RI.

36. Montana achieved statehood on November 8, 1889.

37. Peterson, *Last Civil War Veteran in Each State*, 45.

38. *Ibid.*

39. *Ibid.*, 45–46.

40. *Ibid.*, 45.

41. See http://www.findagrave.com/cgi-bin/ fg.cgi?page=gr&GRid=29164497.

42. See http://www.nps.gov/civilwar/search-battle-units-detail.htm?battleUnitCode=UIA 0007RI.

43. *Beatrice Daily Sun*, December 24, 1948.

44. *Ibid.*

45. Nebraska achieved statehood on March 1, 1867.

46. See http://www.rootsweb.ancestry.com/ ~nesuvcw/MBONDOLL.htm. Information about the rededication ceremony found at this Internet site was originally provided by the Department of Nebraska, Sons of Union Veterans of the Civil War.

47. See http://www.nps.gov/civilwar/search-battle-units-detail.htm?battleUnitCode=UO H0144RIN.

48. Camp Chase was named in honor of former U.S. senator and 23rd governor of Ohio who, during the war, served as President Lincoln's secretary of the treasury. After the war, Chase became a chief justice of the Supreme Court. Camp Chase was dismantled shortly after the war and all that remains is an adjacent cemetery where 2,260 former Confederate prisoners are buried.

49. Diane E. Greene, AG, *Nevada's and Clark County's Last Civil War Veterans* (Boulder City, NV: Self-published, 2006), 2.

50. *Ibid.*

51. Nevada achieved statehood on October 31, 1864.

52. *Ibid.*, 2–4.

53. *Ibid.*, 4–5.

54. See http://www.nps.gov/civilwar/search-battle-units-detail.htm?battleUnitCode=UIL0 155RI.

55. New Mexico achieved statehood on January 6, 1912.

56. Peterson, *Last Civil War Veteran in Each State*, 28–29. For a detailed accounting of Civil War losses, see *The Republic of Suffering: Death and the American Civil War* by Drew Gilpin Faust.

57. *Ibid.*

58. *Ibid.*

59. Hoar, *The North's Last Boys in Blue*, vol. 1, p. 376. One account places Scammahorn's burial site 26 miles west of Highway 84 south of Chama toward Park View and near the El Vado District. A lake and a dam can be seen off to its south. Though not an exact location, it is a starting point for an adventurous soul hoping to find the burial site.

60. James Stewart, Jr., et al., *The Union Army: A History of Military Affairs in the Loyal States 1861–65*, vol. 21: *New Jersey, Indiana, Illinois and Michigan* (Madison, WI: Federal, 1908), 302.

61. See https://www.google.com/?gws_rd= ssl#q=66th+regiment%2C+u.+s.+colored+ troops.

62. See http://ndstudies.gov/content/civil-war-era-north-dakota-8.

63. *Ibid.*

64. *Ibid.*

65. Peterson, *Last Civil War Veteran in Each State*, 31.

66. North Dakota achieved statehood on November 2, 1889.

67. Lake Region Chautauqua Corporation, *Ramsey County Centennial Book*, vol. 21 (Dallas: Taylor, 1982), 38.

68. *Ibid.*

69. *Ibid.*, 32.

70. *Ibid.* Also see http://www.findagrave. com/cgi-bin/fg.cgi?page=gr&GRid=112503194.

71. Hoar, *The South's Last Boys in Gray*, 415.

72. *Ibid.*

73. *Ibid.*, 415–417.

74. Oklahoma achieved statehood on November 16, 1907.

75. *Ibid.*, 417–418.

76. *Ibid.*, 417.

77. See http://www.findagrave.com/cgi-bin/ fg.cgi?page=gr&GRid=87005429.

78. See http://www.nps.gov/civilwar/search-battle-units-detail.htm?battleUnitCode=UIL 0023RI.

79. *Laurel Advocate*, July 25 and August 1, 1945.

80. *Ibid.*

81. *Ibid.*; South Dakota achieved statehood on November 2, 1889.

82. *Laurel Advocate*, July 25 and August 1, 1945.

83. *Ibid.*

84. See http://www.nps.gov/civilwar/search-battle-units-detail.htm?battleUnitCode=UW I0002RC.

85. Utah achieved statehood on January 4, 1896.

86. Ardis E. Parshall, "Living History: Civil War Veterans Became Part of Utah's Heritage," *Salt Lake Tribune*, October 9, 2011.

87. *Dansville (NY) Breeze*, May 10, 1945.

88. Parshall, "Living History: Civil War Veterans Became Part of Utah's Heritage."

89. Hoar, *The North's Last Boys in Blue*, vol. 1, p. 380.

90. See http://www.findagrave.com/cgi-bin/ fg.cgi?page=gr&GRid=78006550.

91. Hoar, *The North's Last Boys in Blue*, vol. 1, pp. 380–381.

92. *Dansville (NY) Breeze*, May 10, 1945.

93. See http://www.findagrave.com/cgi-bin/ fg.cgi?page=gr&GRid=78006550.

94. See http://www.nps.gov/civilwar/search-battle-units-detail.htm?battleUnitCode=UW I0046RI.

95. See http://vermontcivilwar.org/get.php?

input=81865; also see Hoar, *The North's Last Boys in Blue*, vol. 2, p. 831.

96. See http://wc.rootsweb.ancestry.com/cgi-bin/igm.cgi?op=GET&db=miscsea&id=1775.

97. Washington achieved statehood on November 11, 1889.

98. See http://wc.rootsweb.ancestry.com/cgi-bin/igm.cgi?op=GET&db=miscsea&id=1775.

99. *Ibid.*

100. See http://www.wisconsinhistory.org/Content.aspx?dsNav=N:4294963828–4294963805&dsRecordDetailS=R:CS2082.

101. Hoar, *The North's Last Boys in Blue*, vol. 2, p. 593.

102. *Ibid.*

103. *Ibid.*, 593–594.

104. *Ibid.*

105. *Ibid.*, 594.

106. *Ibid.*

107. See http://www.findagrave.com/cgi-bin/fg.cgi?page=gr&GRid=60606599.

108. E-mail from Orin Hunkins to the author on July 26, 2015.

Chapter 7

1. See http://alaskaweb.org/maritime/shenadoah.htm; also see http://www.adn.com/article/20110416/civil-wars-last-shots-were-fired-bering-sea.

2. See http://www.blackpast.org/aah/1st-louisiana-native-guard-usa-corps-d-afrique-1862-1863.

3. Two Internet articles by Douglas Q. Barnett, a descendant of John N. Conna, were used to prepare the veteran's brief: http://www.historylink.org/index.cfm?DisplayPage=output.cfm&file_id=7111 and http://www.blackpast.org/aaw/conna-john-n-1836-1921.

4. See http://opinionator.blogs.nytimes.com/2013/08/13/the-civil-war-and-hawaii/?_r=0.

5. Pitman (birth name, Timothy Henry Pitman) is interred at Mt. Auburn Cemetery in Cambridge, MA.

6. See http://www.nps.gov/cwwindepth/StateByState/Hawaii.html and http://the.honoluluadverstiser.com/article/2010/May/31/In/hawaii5310346.html.

7. See http://www.nps.gov/civilwar/search-battle-units-detail.htm?battleUnitCode=UTN0010RC.

8. James Robertson, *The Untold Civil War: Exploring the Human Side of War* (Washington, D.C.: National Geographic Society, 2013), 324.

9. See http://www.rootsweb.ancestry.com/~genepool/sultana.htm.

10. Naval History Division, Navy Department, *Civil War Naval Chronology, 1861–1865* (Washington, D.C., U.S. Government Printing Office, 1971), V-94.

11. See http://research.archives.gov/description/615651.

12. *Honolulu Republican*, February 6, 1901.

13. Ralph Thomas Kam, "Commemorating the Grand Army of the Republic in Hawaii: 1882–1930," *Hawaiian Journal of History* 44 (2009).

14. *Honolulu Star-Bulletin*, January 19, 1932.

Chapter 8

1. See http://www.nps.gov/civilwar/search-battle-units-detail.htm?battleUnitCode=CAL0010RI.

2. *Pittsburg Post-Gazette*, May 29, 2011.

3. Hoar, *The South's Last Boys in Gray*, 464–465.

4. See http://archiver.rootsweb.ancestry.com/th/read/OBITUARIES/2009-06/1245924826.

5. Hoar, *The South's Last Boys in Gray*, 465.

6. See http://www.thepostnewspapers.com/strongsville/local_news/witness-at-appomattox/article_dceaabb6-ab2f-59b2-b295-4dfaa9a6f25e.html.

7. See http://archiver.rootsweb.ancestry.com/th/read/OBITUARIES/2009-06/1245924826.

8. See http://www.nps.gov/civilwar/search-battle-units-detail.htm?battleUnitCode=UNY0032RI.

9. Peterson, *Last Civil War Veteran in Each State*, 30.

10. *Ibid.*

11. See http://www.suvcw.org/nygarcommanders/GARhard2.htm.

12. *Ibid.*

13. See http://suvcw/org/ny/gar/cinnabders/GARhard2.htlm.

14. Peterson, *Last Civil War Veteran in Each State*, 30.

15. *Ibid.*

16. *Binghamton Press*, March 13, 1953.

17. *Ibid.*

18. Hard's quote was recorded by Raymond Wilcove, a Central Press correspondent. He later shared Hard's sentiments in a Washington, D.C., newspaper article.

19. *Binghamton (NY) Press*, March 13, 1953.

20. See http://www.nps.gov/civilwar/search-battle-units-detail.htm?battleUnitCode=UMN0001RAH.

21. Geoffrey C. Ward, et al., *The Civil War: An Illustrated History* (New York: Alfred A. Knopf, 1990), xix.

22. See http://gettysburgsculptures.com/albert_woolson_monument.

23. See http://thedailyhatch.org/2011/05/02/ronald-wilson-reagan-part-80who-was-last-civil-war-veteran/.

24. *Duluth News-Tribune*, August 3, 1956.

25. *Ibid.*

26. See http://thedailyhatch.org/2011/05/02/ronald-wilson-reagan-part-80who-was-last-civil-war-veteran/.

27. *Ibid.*

28. See https://www.youtube.com/watch?v=5Td4xzS6r2E to view a short colorized video of Albert Woolson dressed in his GAR uniform.

Bibliography and Further Reading

Books

Ayling, Augustus D., Adj. Gen. *Revised Register of Soldiers and Sailors of New Hampshire in the War of the Rebellion (1861–1865)*. Concord, NH: Ira C. Evans, 1895.

Carlson, Patricia Ann, ed. *Literature and Lore of the Sea*. Amsterdam, The Netherlands: Rodopi, 1986.

Chadwick, Bruce. *1858: Abraham Lincoln, Jefferson Davis, Robert E. Lee, Ulysses S. Grant and the War They Failed to See*. Naperville, IL: Sourcebooks, 2008.

Chamberlain, Joshua L. *The Passing of the Armies*. New York: Putnam, 1915.

Chambers, John H. *Hawaii*. Northampton, MA: Interlink, 2006.

Chenery, William H. *The Fourteenth Regiment, Rhode Island Heavy Artillery (Colored)*. Providence, RI: Snow and Farnum, 1898.

Coffman, Edward M. *The Embattled Past: Reflections on Military History*. Lexington: University Press of Kentucky, 2014.

Crandall, H., and A.D.C., Acting Adj. Gen. *Annual Report of the Adjutant General of the State of Rhode Island, for the Year 1865*. Providence: Providence Press, 1866.

Craughwell, Thomas J. *The Greatest Brigade: How the Irish Brigade Cleared the Way to Victory in the American Civil War*. Beverly, MA: Fair Winds, 2011.

Dabney, Virginius. *The Last Review: The Confederate Reunion, Richmond, 1932*. Chapel Hill, IN: Algonquin, 1984.

Davidson, James West, et al. *Nation of Nations: A Narrative History of the American Republic*. Vol. 1, to 1877. New York: McGraw-Hill Higher Education, 2008.

DeCuir, Randy, et al. *Remembering Rapides' Rebels: Portraits of Confederates and Other Civil War Figures of Rapides Parish, Louisiana*. Rapides: Self-published, no date.

Faust, Drew Gilpin. *The Republic of Suffering: Death and the American Civil War*. New York: Vintage, 2009.

Gordon, Geo. A. (Rev.). *Life and Labors of Rev. Henry S. Gordon, Founder of the First Baptist Church in Southern Illinois*. Campbell Hills, IL: Self-published, 1901.

Graham, Martin F., et al. *The Civil War Chronicle*. Lincolnwood, IL: Publications International, 2004.

The Grand Army Blue-Book: Rules and Regulations of the G.A.R. Philadelphia: Lippincott, 1896.

Groene, Bertram Hawthorne. *Tracing Your Civil War Ancestor*. Winston-Salem: John F. Blair, 1995.

Head, Natt. *Report of the Adjutant-General of the State of New Hampshire, for the Year Ending June 1, 1866*. Concord, NH: George E. Jenks, 1866.

Hill, Garry Victor. *America's Last Civil War Veterans and Participants: An Investigation*. Armidale, Australia: Frisky, 2015.

Hoar, Jay S. *Montana's Last Civil War Veterans*. Temple, ME: Bo-Ink-um, 2010.

_____. *New England's Last Civil War Veterans*. Arlington, TX: Seacliff, 1976.

_____. *The North's Last Boys in Blue*. Vol. 1. Salem, MA: Higginson, 2006.

_____. *The North's Last Boys in Blue*. Vol. 2. Salem, MA: Higginson, 2007.

_____. *The South's Last Boys in Gray*. Bowling Green, OH: Bowling Green State University Press, 1986.

_____. *The South's Last Boys in Gray*. Vol. 3. Salem, MA: Higginson, 2010.

Holzman, Robert S. *Adapt or Perish: The Life of General Roger A. Pryor, C.S.A.* Hamden, CT: Archon, 1976.

Horwitz, Tony. *Midnight Rising: John Brown and the Raid That Sparked the Civil War*. New York: Henry Holt, 2011.

Lake Region Chautauqua Corporation. *Ramsey County Centennial Book*, Vol. 3. Dallas: Taylor, 1982.

McLaughlin, Jack. *Gettysburg: The Long Encampment*. New York: Bonanza, 1963.

McPherson, James M. *The Negro's Civil War*. New York: Pantheon, 1965.

_____. *Ordeal by Fire: The Civil War and Reconstruction*. New York: McGraw-Hill, 1991.

Miller, William J., and Brian C. Pohanka. *An Illustrated History of the Civil War*. Alexandria, VA: Time-Life, 2000.

Morgan, Michael. *Ocean City: Going Down the Ocean*. Charleston, SC: History Press, 2011.

Murphy, Richard W., and the Editors of Time-Life Books. *The Civil War: The Nation Reunited*. Alexandria, VA: Time-Life, 1993.

Naval History Division, Navy Department. *Civil War Naval Chronology, 1861–1865*. Washington, D.C.: U.S. Government Printing Office, 1971.

Peck, Theodore S., Adj. Gen. *Revised Roster of Vermont Volunteers*. Montpelier: Watchman, 1892.

Peterson, C. Stewart, Ex-Lieut., MA. *Last Civil War Veteran in Each State*. Baltimore: Self-published, 1951.

Potter, Jerry O. *The* Sultana *Tragedy: America's Greatest Maritime Disaster*. Gretna, LA: Pelican, 1992.

Price, William H. *Civil War Handbook*. Fairfax, VA: Literary Licensing, 2013.

Quarstein, John V. *The CSS* Virginia: *Sink Before Surrender*. Jefferson, SC: History Press, 2012.

Robertson, James. *The Untold Civil War:* *Exploring the Human Side of War*. Washington, D.C.: National Geographic Society, 2013.

Schouler, William. *Annual Report of the Adjutant-General of the Commonwealth of Massachusetts, for the Year Ending December 31, 1865*. Boston: Wright & Potter, 1866.

Seigler, Robert S. *South Carolina's Military Organizations During the War Between the States*. Charleston, SC: History Press, 2008.

Serrano, Richard A. *Last of the Blue and Gray*. Washington, D.C.: Smithsonian, 2013.

Simmons, Donald C. *Confederate Settlements in British Honduras*. Jefferson, NC: McFarland, 2001.

Sketches of Representative Citizens of the State of Maine. Boston, MA: New England Historical, 1903.

Stewart, James, Jr., et al. *The Union Army: A History of Military Affairs in the Loyal States, 1861–65* Vol. 3, *New Jersey, Indiana, Illinois and Michigan*. Madison, WI: Federal, 1908.

Stokes, Karen. *The Immortal 600: Surviving Civil War Charleston and Savannah*. Charleston, SC: History Press, 2013.

Sutherland, Daniel E. *The Confederate Carpetbaggers*. Baton Rouge: Louisiana State University Press, 1988.

Toomey, Daniel Carroll. *The Civil War in Maryland*. Baltimore: Toomey, 1983.

Ward, Geoffrey C., et al. *The Civil War: An Illustrated History*. New York: Alfred A. Knopf, 1990.

Warren, Robert Penn. *The Legacy of the Civil War*. New York: Random House, 1961.

Waugh, John C. *Surviving the Confederacy: Rebellion, Ruin, and Recovery; Roger and Sara Pryor During the Civil War*. New York: Harcourt, 2002.

Wheeler, Joseph. *Libby Prison Breakout: The Daring Escape from the Notorious Civil War Prison*. New York: Public Affairs, 2011.

Electronic Media

Author's Note: The reader is advised that Internet addresses change frequently as well as being modified or deleted at the discretion of the contributor. Those listed below were current at the time of publication. Whenever and wherever possible, attribution is given to the author or contributor of the source document.

Alaskaweb.org. "CSS *Shenandoah*: Civil War's Last Shots were Fired in the Bering Sea." http://alaskaweb.org/maritime/shenadoah.htm.

Ancestry.com. Message Boards. "Need Gaston's Help." http://boards.ancestry.com/thread.aspx?mv=flat&m=224&p=surnames.dupuis.

_____. Rootsweb. "John Frederick Asbury Hutchison." http://worldconnect.rootsweb.ancestry.com/cgi-bin/igm.cgi?op=GET&db=seeeye&id=17433.

_____. Rootsweb. "Michael Bon Doll Last Living Civil War Veteran in Nebraska." http://www.rootsweb.ancestry.com/~nesuvcw/MBONDOLL.htm.

_____. Rootsweb. "[OBITS] Pleasant Riggs Crump (December 23, 1847–December 31, 1951)." http://archiver.rootsweb.ancestry.com/th/read/OBITUARIES/2009-06/1245924826.

_____. Rootsweb. "Search Historical Newspapers: Union Civil War Veterans and Widows, Washington State, Part 1." http://wc.rootsweb.ancestry.com/cgi-bin/igm.cgi?op=GET&db=miscsea&id=1775.

Barnett, Douglas Q. An Online Reference Guide to African American History. "Conna, John N. (1836–1921): The Black Past: Remembered and Reclaimed." http://www.blackpast.org/aaw/conna-john-n-1836–1921.

_____. The Free Online Encyclopedia of Washington State History. "Conna, John N. (1836–1921)." http://www.historylink.org/index.cfm?DisplayPage=output.cfm&file_id=7111.

Calvin B. Taylor House Museum/Historical Landmark Berlin, Maryland Isaiah Fassett. "Isaiah Fassett." http://taylorhousemuseum.org/history/isaiah-fassett/.

The Civil War Archives. "Union Regiment Histories: United States Colored Troops Infantry, 66th U.S. Colored Troops."

https://www.google.com/?gws_rd=ssl#q=66th+regiment%2C+u.+s.+colored+troops.

Civil War on the Western Border. "Price's Missouri Expedition (or Price's Raid)." Extracted by the Kansas City Public Library from an encyclopedia entry written by Christopher Phillips and posted on the Internet. http://www.civilwaronthewesternborder.org/content/price%E2%80%99s-missouri-expedition-or-price%E2%80%99s-raid.

Civil War Voices. "What Happened to Civil War Soldiers after the War?" http://www.soldierstudies.org/blog/2011/06/what-happened-to-civil-war-soldiers-after-the-war/.

Cole, William. Honoluluadvertiser.com. "Native Hawaiians served on both sides during Civil War." http://the.honoluluadverstiser.com/article/2010/May/31/ln/hawaii5310346.html.

The Daily Hatch. "Ronald Wilson Reagan (Part 80) (Who was Last Civil War Veteran?)" http://thedailyhatch.org/2011/05/02/ronald-wilson-reagan-part-80who-was-last-civil-war-veteran/.

Department of New York: The Grand Army of the Republic. "The James A. Hard Story." http://www.suvcw.org/ny/gar/commanders/GARhard2.htm.

Dunham, Mike. *Alaska Dispatch News.* "Civil War's Last Shots Were Fired in the Bering Sea." http://www.adn.com/article/20110416/civil-wars-last-shots-were-fired-bering-sea.

Dwyer, Mimi. *Vice.* "The Brazilian Town Where the American Confederacy Lives On." http://www.vice.com/read/welcome-to-americana-brazil-0000580-v22n2.

ElderWeb. "Census: Civil War Veterans Pensions." http://www.elderweb.com/book/export/html/2823.

Fablinger, Glenice A. "History of the Fablinger Family, 1813–1997," posted on Ancestry.com, rootsweb. http://www.findagrave.com/cgi-bin/fg.cgi?page=gr&GRid=42199287.

Facts. The Civil War (U.S. National Park Service). *Facts.* "Civil War Facts: 1861–1865." http://www.nps.gov/civilwar/facts.htm.

Family Search. *4th Regiment, South Carolina State Troop Junior Reserves.* https://familysearch.org/learn/wiki/en/4th_Regiment,_South_Carolina_State_Troop_Junior_Reserves.

_____. *Wauchilla* [*sic*] [*Wauchula*] *Militia, Florida.* https://familysearch.org/learn/wiki/en/Wauchilla_Militia,_Florida_%28Confederate%29.

FindAGrave.com (aka Find A Grave, Inc.). In compliance with the corporation's privacy policy, names of Web site creators and contributors are respectfully withheld.

G.A.R. Indiana Department Commander, John C. Adams. "Grand Army of the Republic, John C. Adams, Department Commander 1946–1948: Indiana's Last Union Civil War Veteran." http://suvcw.org/in/JCAdams.html.

Gettysburg Sculptures. "Gettysburg Sculptures: Featured Monument Albert Woolson Statue, Last Survivor of the Grand Army of the Republic (G.A.R.) ..." http://gettysburgsculptures.com/albert_woolson_monument.

Gilder Lehrman Institute of American History. "Horace Greeley: 'Go West,' 1871." http://www.gilderlehrman.org/history-by-era/development-west/resources/horace-greeley-%E2%80%9Cgo-west%E2%80%9D-1871.

Graff, Nancy Price. VTdigger.org. "In this State: Veteran Gilbert Lucier Embodied Vermont's Deep Passion for the Civil War." http://vtdigger.org/2014/03/30/state-veteran-gilbert-lucier-embodied-vermonts-deep-passion-civil-war/.

Graves Registration/Picacho Peak Camp #1. "Graves Registration." http://www.suvcwaz-camptl.org/graves-registration/.

Gwinn, Chris. From the Fields of Gettysburg: The Blog of Gettysburg National Military Park. "The Last Veteran/The Blog of Gettysburg National Military Park." https://npsgnmp.wordpress.com/tag/last-gettysburg-veteran/.

History.com. "Louisiana Purchase: Facts & Summary." http://www.history.com/topics /louisiana-purchase.

History of the Colonel Sherod Hunter

Camp 1525, 2005–2006. Camp History. "Ceremony for Arizona's Last Union Veteran, November 2005, Greenwood Memory Lawn Cemetery, Phoenix, Arizona." http://azrebel.tripod.com/2005-2006.html.

Huff Post Green. "Thurman, Iowa 75 Percent Destroyed by Possible Tornado, Official Says." http://www.huffingtonpost.com/2012/04/14/thurman-iowa-75-percent-destroyed-tornado_n_1426261.html.

Jackson, Joelle. "1st Louisiana Native Guard, USA/Corps d'Afrique (1862–1863): The Black Past: Remembered and Reclaimed." http://www.blackpast.org/aah/1st-louisiana-native-guard-usa-corps-d-afrique-1862-1863.

Kennemore, Keuttah (Goswick), and Henry H. "Goswick Genealogies." http://freepages.genealogy.rootsweb.ancestry.com/~keuttaqhg/kssarahegc.htm.

Kuchera, Roger W. The Civil War. "The Last Naval Veterans of the War of the Rebellion." http://www.navyandmarine.org/ondeck/1862lastnavalvets.htm.

Larson, Cedric A. "Death on the Dark River: The Story of the *Sultana* Disaster in 1865." http://www.rootsweb.ancestry.com/~genepool/sultana.htm (first published in *American Heritage*, October 1955).

Maryland Civil War Trails (Worcester County Tourism). "Corp. Isaiah Fassett: 'Uncle Zear.'" http://visitworcester.org/printables/Fassett.pdf.

McMillon, Inell. Watersheds.org. "John Hutchison: Missouri's Last Civil War Veteran." http://www.watersheds.org/history/hutchinson.htm.

Memorial Day Greetings; Remembering Joseph Clovese of the USCT and the GAR. "Jubilo! The Emancipation Century." https://jubiloemancipationcentury.wordpress.com/2013/05/27/memorial-day-greetings-remembering-joseph-clovese-of-the-usct-and-the-gar/.

National Archives. "Confederate Pension Records." http://www.archives.gov/research/military/civil-war/confederate/penstion.html.

_____. "Teaching with Documents: The

Homestead Act of 1862." http://www. archives.gov/education/lessons/home stead-act/.

National Archives and Records Administration. "Records of the *Sultana* Disaster, April 27, 1865." N.A. Identifier 615651; HMS Entry No. NM 68 98; Record Group 249; Micro-Film Publication: M1878; Roll: 0003. http://rese arch.archives.gov/description/615651.

North Dakota Studies: Official Portal for North Dakota State Government. "Judge Dallas Duell and the Grand Army of the Republic." http://ndstudies.gov/ content/civil-war-era-north-dakota-8.

NPS.gov. The American Civil War. "State by State—Hawaii." http://www.nps.gov/ cwwindepth/StateByState/Hawaii.html.

Offbeat Oregon History. "Black Sheep of the Union Army Was Oregon's Last Civil War Vet." http://offbeatoregon. com/o1111c-black-sheep-of-union-army-last-oregon-vet.html.

Out of the Box: Notes from the Archives @ the Library of Virginia. "'General' John Salling: Virginia's Last Confederate Veteran?" http://www.virginiamem ory.com/blogs/out_of_the_box/2010/ 10/06/generaljohn-salling-virginias-last-confederate-veteran/.

Pettem, Silvia. "Robert T. Bryan, Boulder's Last Civil War Veteran, Memorial Day Activities." Daily Camera. http:// www.dailycamera.com/ci_15136424.

Prechtel-Kluskens, Claire. "'A Reasonable Degree of Promptitude': Civil War Pension Application Processing, 1861–1885." http:/www.archives.gov/publica tions/prologue/2010/spring/civilwarp ension.html.

Remember Jamaica Plain? "Tiger Cat Killed at Glen Road." http://rememberja maicaplain.blogspot.comsearch?q=riley.

Smith, Jeffrey Allen. *New York Times*: Opinion Pages. "The Civil War and Hawaii." http://opinionator.blogs.nyti mes.com/2013/08/13/the-civil-war-and-hawaii/?_r=0.

Sons of Union Veterans of the Civil War. "Photos from the Past: James P. Martin (from his Obituary 1949)." http://suv cw.org/past/jpmartin.htm.

South Carolina Division Sons of Confederate Veterans. "The Last Confederate Soldier of South Carolina: Pvt. Arnold D. Murray." http://scscv.com/the-last-confederate-soldier-of-south-caro lina/.

Strongsville Post. "Witness at Appomattox: Pleasant Riggs Crump, Last Surviving Confederate Soldier, Great-Great-Uncle of Strongsville Resident." http://www.thepostnewspapers.com/ strongsville/local_news/witness-at-appomattox/article_dceaabb6-ab2f-59b2-b295–4dfaa9a6f25e.html.

SUVCW Dept. of Wisconsin. Last Soldier Project: Chippewa County. "The Last Soldier Project: Chippewa County and Wisconsin's Last Civil War Veteran, Lansing A. Wilcox." http://www.suvcw-wi.org/last_soldier/chippewa.shtml.

Taylor, Amy Murrell. "The Border States." http://www.nps.gov/resources/story. htm?id=205.

Taylor, Jim. "Captain Barnes Co., Home Guards." Jim Taylor Home Page. http:// www.datasync.com/~jtaylor/msbarhg. htm.

U.S. Biographies Project. "Barrett, Robert Turner" (posted by Carol Eddleman). http://www.usbiographies.org/bio graphies/read.php?377,6245.

Vermont in the Civil War. "Virtual Cemetery: Gale, Hiram Randall" (created by Tom Ledoux). http://vermontcivilwar. org/get.php?input=81865.

Wikipedia, the Free Encyclopedia. "Alfred 'Teen' Blackburn." http://en.wiki pedia.org/wiki/Alfred_%22Teen%22_ Blackburn.

_____. "Border States (American Civil War). https://en.wikipedia.org/wiki/Bo rder_states_(American_Civil_War).

_____. "Land Grant." http:en.wikipedia. org/wiki/Land_grant.

_____. "Land Rush of 1889." http://en.wiki pedia.org/wiki/Land_Rush_of_1889.

_____. Wikiquote. "The Civil War (documentary)." http://en.wikiquote.org/ wiki/The_Civil_War_%28documen tary%29.

Wisconsin State Historical Society. "Wilcox, Lansing A. (1846–1951)." Microfilm file 1950–1951: P46228. http://www.usgennet.org/usa/wi/county/clark/5data/104/110.htm.

Electronic Media for Regimental Histories

Note: The regimental histories below are extracted from The Civil War *(U.S. National Park Service) under "Battle Unit Details."*

_____. *1st Minnesota Heavy Artillery.* http://www.nps.gov/civilwar/search-battle-units-detail.htm?battleUnitCode=UMN0001RAH.

_____. *1st Vermont Heavy Artillery.* http://www.nps.gov/civilwar/search-battle-units-detail.htm?battleUnitCode=UVT0001RAH.

_____. *1st Wisconsin Heavy Artillery.* http://www.nps.gov/civilwar/search-battle-units-detail.htm?battleUnitCode=UWI0001RAH.

_____. *2nd Rhode Island Infantry.* http://www.nps.gov/civilwar/search-battle-units-detail.htm?battleUnitCode=URI0002RI.

_____. *2nd Wisconsin Cavalry.* http://www.nps.gov/civilwar/search-battle-units-detail.htm?battleUnitCode=UWI0002RC.

_____. *4th Massachusetts Heavy Artillery.* http://www.nps.gov/civilwar/search-battle-units-detail.htm?battleUnitCode=UMA0004RAH.

_____. *4th Wisconsin Cavalry.* http://www.nps.gov/civilwar/search-battle-units-detail.htm?battleUnitCode=UWI0004RC.

_____. *5th Wisconsin Infantry.* http://www.nps.gov/civilwar/search-battle-units-detail.htm?battleUnitCode=UWI0005RI.

_____. *6th Louisiana Cavalry.* http://www.nps.gov/civilwar/search-battle-units-detail.htm?battleUnitCode=CLA0006RC.

_____. *6th West Virginia Infantry.* http://www.nps.gov/civilwar/search-battle-units-detail.htm?battleUnitCode=UWV0006RI.

_____. *7th Iowa Infantry.* http://www.nps.gov/civilwar/search-battle-units-detail.htm?battleUnitCode=UIA0007RI.

_____. *7th Virginia Cavalry.* http://www.nps.gov/civilwar/search-battle-units-detail.htm?battleUnitCode=CVA0007RC.

_____. *8th Pennsylvania Infantry.* http://www.nps.gov/civilwar/search-battle-units-detail.htm?battleUnitCode=UPA0008RI.

_____. *9th U.S. Colored Troops (USCT).* http://www.nps.gov/rich/historyculture/9thusct.htm.

_____. *10th Alabama Infantry.* http://www.nps.gov/civilwar/search-battle-units-detail.htm?battleUnitCode=CAL0010RI.

_____. *10th Tennessee Cavalry (USA).* http://www.nps.gov/civilwar/search-battle-units-detail.htm?battleUnitCode=UTN0010RC.

_____. *12th Maine Infantry.* http://www.nps.gov/civilwar/search-battle-units-detail.htm?battleUnitCode=UME0012RI.

_____. *12th Missouri Cavalry* (Shelby's Escort Company). http://www.nps.gov/civilwar/search-battle-units-detail.htm?battleUnitCode=CMO0012RC.

_____. *12th Ohio Cavalry.* http://www.nps.gov/civilwar/search-battle-units-detail.htm?battleUnitCode=UOH0012RC.

_____. *14th Georgia Infantry.* http://www.nps.gov/civilwar/search-battle-units-detail.htm?battleUnitCode=CGA0014RI.

_____. *15th Connecticut Infantry.* http://www.nps.gov/civilwar/search-battle-units-detail.htm?battleUnitCode=UCT0015RI.

_____. *17th Indiana Infantry.* http://www.nps.gov/civilwar/search-battle-units-detail.htm?battleUnitCode=UIN0017RI.

_____. *17th Kentucky Cavalry (USA).* http://www.nps.gov/civilwar/search-battle-units-detail.htm?battleUnitCode=UKY0017RC.

_____. *17th West Virginia Infantry.* http://www.nps.gov/civilwar/search-battle-units-detail.htm?battleUnitCode=UWV0017RI.

_____. *18th Pennsylvania Cavalry (163rd Volunteers)*. http://www.nps.gov/civilwar/search-battle-units-detail.htm?battleUnitCode=UPA0018RC.

_____. *21st Illinois Infantry*. http//www.nps.gov/civilwar/search-battle-units-detail.htm?battleUnitCode=UIL0021RI.

_____. *21st North Carolina Infantry*. http://www.nps.gov/civilwar/search-battle-units-detail.htm?battleUnitCode=CNC0021RI.

_____. *22nd U.S. Colored Troops (USCT)*. http://www.nps.gov/rich/historyculture/22nndusct.htm.

_____. *23rd Illinois Infantry*. http://www.nps.gov/civilwar/search-battle-units-detail.htm?battleUnitCode=UIL0023RI.

_____. *26th Battalion, Virginia Infantry (Edgar's)*. http://www.nps.gov/civilwar/search-battle-units-detail.htm?battleUnitCode=CVA0026BI.

_____. *32nd New York Infantry*. http://www.nps.gov/civilwar/search-battle-units-detail.htm?battleUnitCode=UNY0032RI.

_____. *40th Massachusetts Infantry*. http://www.nps.gov/civilwar/search-battle-units-detail.htm?battleUnitCode=UMA0040RI.

_____. *45th Arkansas Infantry (Mounted)*. http://www.civilwaronthewesternborder.org/content/price%E2%80%99s-missouri-expedition-or-price%E2%80%99s-raid.

_____. 46th *Missouri Infantry*. http://www.nps.gov/civilwar/search-battle-units-detail.htm?battleUnitCode=UMO0046RI.

_____. *46th Wisconsin Infantry*. http://www.nps.gov/civilwar/search-battle-units-detail.htm?battleUnitCode=UWI0046RI.

_____. *47th Wisconsin Infantry*. http://www.nps.gov/civilwar/search-battle-units-detail.htm?battleUnitCode=UWI0047RI.

_____. *48th Wisconsin Volunteer Infantry*. http://www.wisconsinhistory.org/Content.aspx?dsNav=N:4294963828-4294963805&dsRecordDetailS=R:CS2082.

_____. *49th Pennsylvania Infantry*. http://www.nps.gov/civilwar/search-battle-units-detail.htm?battleUnitCode=UPA0049RI.

_____. *51st Missouri Infantry*. http://www.nps.gov/civilwar/search-battle-units-detail.htm?battleUnitCode=UMO0051RI.

_____. *63rd U.S. Colored Troops (USCT)*. http://lestweforget.hamptonu.edu/page.cfm?uuid=9FEC38F1-0E31-6A6F-9C4758132E191A92.

_____. *66th U.S. Colored Troops (USCT)*. https://www.google.com/?gws_rd=ssl#q=66th+regiment%2C+u.+s.+colored+troops.

_____. *72nd Illinois Infantry*. http://www.nps.gov/civilwar/search-battle-units-detail.htm?battleUnitCode=UIL0072RI.

_____. *96th Illinois Infantry*. http://www.nps.gov/civilwar/search-battle-units-detail.htm?battleUnitCode=UIL0096RI.

_____. *132nd Pennsylvania Infantry*. http://www.nps.gov/civilwar/search-battle-units-detail.htm?battleUnitCode=UPA0132RI.

_____. *140th Illinois Infantry*. http://www.nps.gov/civilwar/search-battle-units-detail.htm?battleUnitCode=UIL0140RI.

_____. *144th Ohio Infantry (National Guard)*. http://www.nps.gov/civilwar/search-battle-units-detail.htm?battleUnitCode=UOH0144RIN.

_____. *145th Illinois Infantry*. http://www.nps.gov/civilwar/search-battle-units-detail.htm?battleUnitCode=UIL0145RI.

_____. *154th Illinois Infantry*. http://www.nps.gov/civilwar/search-battle-units-detail.htm?battleUnitCode=UIL0154RI.

_____. *155th Illinois Infantry*. http://www.nps.gov/civilwar/search-battle-units-detail.htm?battleUnitCode=UIL0155RI.

_____. *191st Pennsylvania Infantry*. http://www.nps.gov/civilwar/search-battle-units-detail.htm?battleUnitCode=UPA0191RI.

_____. *195th Ohio Infantry*. http://www.nps.gov/civilwar/search-battle-units-detail.htm?battleUnitCode=UOH0195RI.

Libraries, Historical Societies and Other Organizations

Carnegie Branch Library for Local History, Boulder, CO
Department of Nebraska, Sons of Union Veterans of the Civil War, Omaha
Grand Army of the Republic Civil War Museum and Library, Philadelphia
Hawaii State Public Library System, Honolulu
Iredell County Public Library, Statesville, NC
Lake Region Heritage Center, Devils Lake, ND
Londonderry Historical Society, Londonderry, NH
Montana Historical Society, Helena
Newport Public Library, Rhode Island
Oregon Historical Society, Portland
Phillips Historical Society, Phillips, ME
Tacoma Public Library
Western Maryland Historical Library, Hagerstown
Whitman College and Northwest Archives, Penrose Library, Walla Walla
Wisconsin State Historical Society, Madison
Worcester County Tourism, Snow Hill, MD

Newsletters

Swanson, David (Camp Commander). "Last Civil War Soldier Project ... We Need Your Assistance." Sons of Union Veterans of the Civil War, Picacho Peak Camp #1, Arizona Camp-at-Large, *Camp Newsletter*, October 2004.
Walker, Frank S. Jr. "James Albert Spicer and His Mill by the Rapidan." *Orange County Historical Society Newsletter* 37, no. 2 (December 2006).

Newspapers

Albany (OR) Democrat-Herald
Anchorage Daily News
Anchorage Dispatch News
Beatrice (NE) Daily Sun
Binghamton (NY) Press

Boston Daily Globe
Butte Montana Standard
Cameron (WV) News
Champaign (IL) Daily Illini
Chicago Daily Tribune
Dallas Morning News
Dansville (NY) Breeze
Duluth News-Tribune
Eugene Register-Guard
Everett (MI) Daily Herald
Hattiesburg American
Honolulu Republican
Honolulu Star-Bulletin
Lansdale (PA) Advance of Bucks County
Laurel (NE) Advocate
Lebanon (OR) Express
Manchester (NH) Union
Montgomery (AL) Advertiser
Moundsville (WV) Weekly Echo
Mount Vernon (GA) Montgomery Monitor
O'Brien County (IA) Bell, Primghar
Omaha World-Herald
Philadelphia Inquirer
Phoenix Arizona Republic
Pittsburg Post-Gazette
Portland Oregonian
Portsmouth (NH) Herald
Princeton (KY) Leader
Providence (RI) Journal
Rapid City (SD) Journal
Richmond Virginia Times-Dispatch
Salt Lake Tribune
Somerset (PA) Daily American
Spokane Spokesman-Review
Statesboro (GA) Herald
Thorp (WI) Courier
Topeka Daily Capital
Tulsa Tribune
Wall Street Journal
Washington (DC) Times-Herald
Washington Post
Wheeling (WV) Daily Intelligencer
Zanesville (OH) Sunday Times Signal

Pamplets and Periodicals

Greene (AG), Diane E. *Nevada's and Clark County's Last Civil War Veterans*. Boulder City, NV: Self-published, 2006.
Hunt, Gaillard. "The United States Pension Office." *Atlantic Monthly* 65, no. 387 (January 1890).

Kam, Ralph Thomas. "Commemorating the Grand Army of the Republic in Hawaii, 1882–1930." *Hawaiian Journal of History* 44 (2009).

Life. Speaking of Pictures. "These are the last five veterans of the Civil War." June 1, 1953.

Marvel, William. "The Great Imposters." *Blue and Gray* 8 (February 1991).

Osborne, John. Speaking of Pictures. "These 68 Veterans are all that survive of the 3,000,000 young soldiers who wore the blue or the gay in the Great War that ended 84 years ago." *Life*, May 30, 1949, pp. 8–9.

Reeves, Mary E. "Idaho's Last Civil War Vet." *Scenic Idaho* 5, no. 1 (1950).

Record Document

U.S. Federal Census (1860 through 1930)

Index

Adams, John Christian 22–23
addiction: alcohol and drugs, 16
African Americans 24, 39, 50, 126, 143, 158–59, 164, 166
Afro-American League 126
Alabama, last veteran 64, 133–35
Alaska 123–27; last veteran 124–27; territory 123–32
Alexandria, LA 73–74, 116
Alexandria, VA 26, 40, 135
Alley, Uriah Talmage 95–96
Anderson, Richard H. 155
Andersonville Prison 96, 161, 169
Antietam, Battle of 26, 69, 103, 133, 135–36, 155, 168
Appomattox Campaign 26, 47, 57, 62, 77, 90, 92–93, 113–114, 123, 133–34
Arizona, last veteran 98–100
Arkansas, last veteran 64–67
Armstead, Thomas Steward 159–61
Arthur, Chester A. 168
Ashby, George 37–39
Atlanta Campaign and siege of 20–21, 65, 105, 160, 168
Augusta, ME 28
Australia 152

Bailey, Charles W. 25–27
Baker University 27
Baltimore, MD 53, 93, 106, 166
Baltimore & Ohio Railroad 95
Baltimore & Potomac Railroad 168
Barrett, Robert T. 6, 90–91
Baton Rouge, Battle of 53–54, 155
Beauregard, Pierre Gustave Toutant (P.G.T.) 159
Bentonville, Battle of 105
Biddle, Eli George 157–59
Biloxi, MS 33
Blackburn, Alfred 76–78
Blackburn, John Augustus 77–78
Blue and Gray magazine 7–8
Bon Doll, Michael 105–06
Booth, John Wilkes 164–65

border states 87–88
Boston, MA 158; police department 30–31
Brattleboro, VT 51
Brazil *see* Confederados
Bridwell, Lowell 7
British Honduras 151
Broadsword, Israel Adam 101–02
USS *Brooklyn* 170
Brooklyn Navy Yard 157
Brown, Owen 153–54
Brown, William Jasper 70–73
Bryan, Robert T. 100–01
Buck, William Mercer 112–14
The Buffalo Harvest (Mayer) 10
Burnside, Ambrose E. 19
Bush, James 127
Bush, William Joshua (aka Jordan) 6, 70–71
Butler, Benjamin F. 38, 155

California, last veteran 17–18
Camp Butler 20, 99–100, 108
Camp Chase 40, 107
Camp Fry 20
Camp Parole 108, 127
Camp Sprague 45
Camp Washburn 120
Campaign of the Carolinas 72, 105
Cantrell, William L. 166
Castle, Thomas Arthur 103–04
Cedar Creek, Battle of 26, 28, 44, 51–52, 114
Chaffin's Farm, Battle of 38, 88
Chamberlain, Joshua Lawrence 171
Chambersburg, PA 92
Champion's Hill, Battle of 110
Chancellorsville, Battle of 26, 46, 77, 103, 136, 155
Chappel, Charles L. 6
Chattanooga, Siege of 20, 138, 140
Chesapeake and Ohio Canal 93
Chicago, IL 20, 109–10, 114
Chickahominy, VA 19
Chickamauga, Battle of and Siege 20–21, 161, 173–74
Chisum, John Greene 64–67

193